VICTORIAN PUBS

MARK GIROUARD

Yale University Press
New Haven and London 1984

TO P.F.
FELLOW DRINKER

First published 1975 by Studio Vista Ltd

Designed by Dorothy Girouard
Calligraphy by Anne Moring
Filmset in Monophoto Bembo and printed in Spain by
Artes Graficas Toledo s.a.
D. L. TO:285-1984

Library of Congress Cataloging in Publication Data

Girouard, Mark, 1931-
Victorian pubs.

Includes bibliographical references and index.
1. London (England)—Bars, saloons, etc.—History.
2. Architecture, Victorian—England—London. 3. London (England)—History—1800–1950. I. Title
TX950.59.G7G57 1984 725′.72′09421 83-51291
ISBN 0-300-03199-8
ISBN 0-300-03201-3 (pbk.)

PREFACE

VICTORIAN public houses have been much and rightly admired, but even the most perceptive writers about them have tended to treat them as folk-art and taken it for granted that exact dates, names or architects and craftsmen, or particulars of what they cost or who commissioned them cannot be hoped for. This book is an attempt to treat Victorian pubs as buildings built or altered at identifiable dates by identifiable architects and craftsmen for identifiable clients, in order to deal with identifiable social, political and economic situations.

The possible existence of large untapped sources of information was first suggested to me when I noticed that the weekly lists of buildings put out to tender, which were published on the last pages of the Victorian building magazines, included many hundreds of pubs together with particulars of work done, architects, clients, builders and (sometimes) craftsmen. Further research revealed a mass of sometimes unexpected material including collections of original architects' drawings and plans, descriptions of pubs in the trade press, and material in brewery archives, and parliamentary Blue Books; but delighted as I was at how much proved easily accessible, I am only too aware of how much more remains to be discovered.

The book is mainly concerned with Victorian pubs in London, but for purposes of comparison I have a much less deeply researched epilogue on city pubs in the rest of England and in Ireland. Regretfully, I have not been able to extend the coverage to Wales and Scotland. Although I have included a large selection of surviving Victorian pubs, the book is essentially a study of the Victorian pub in its prime, not as it is today, and I have not hesitated to describe and illustrate pubs that have been demolished or mutilated. What survives is only a tiny fragment of the splendours that have gone and even this is fast being depleted; it is, alas, all too probable that work still in existence at the time of writing will have been destroyed or radically altered by the time of publication. The breweries are, it is true, less prone to destruction than they were ten years ago but they are continually altering, 'improving', rearranging, renaming and touching up their Victorian pubs, sometimes with skill and tact but all too often with neither.

I have had much help from many public libraries and record offices, especially from Mr Neate and his staff at the GLC Record Office; from the Clerk of the Court and Mr P. Leonard, Clerk to the Licensing Magistrates, at Camberwell Magistrates Court; from many breweries, especially from Mr Ben Davis, Mr Ralph Humphries and Mr P. J. Brown of Ind Coope, Lord Moyne and Mr T. Sheppard of Guinness's and Mr D. Scott of Watney Mann; from Mr I. C. Robey of Cakebread, Robey and Co. Ltd, Mr P. V. Flowers of Goddard and Gibbs Studios, Mr D. C. Chalk of James Clark and Eaton Ltd, Miss P. A. Pemberton and Mr John Mochrie of Pilkinton Brothers Ltd, Mr S. M. Scott of Reed, Millican and Co. Ltd and Monsieur A. Sellin of the Institut du Verre, Paris; from Mr James P. Bristow, late of the London Brick Company, and Lt-Commander J. S. Williams of the Kennel Club. Tanys Hinchcliffe helped with the preliminary research. Robert Thurlow kindly let me use some of the photographs taken for his projected book on Liverpool pubs. Among the many others who have helped me are Elizabeth Aslin, David Cheshire, Howard Colvin, Alan Crawford, Aileen Ferriday, Roderick Gradidge, Remo Gramelli, H. Gray, Brian Harrison, R. J. Hetherington, Hermione Hobhouse, Edward Hubbard, Barbara Jones, Derek Linstrum, Christopher Monkhouse, Barbara Morris, John Nicoll, Michael Port, Peter Savigear, Jeanne Sheehy, Francis Shepherd, Brian Spiller, Alex Starkey, Ann Tilley, J. N. Wallace and Richard Wollheim.

I owe an especial debt to Robert Thorne for reading and commenting on my manuscript and for information, discussion and suggestions at all stages of the book.

CONTENTS

1. Detail of the former Noah's Ark, Oxford Street, now a shoe shop (J. T. Alexander, 1890)

Introduction

A Pub Crawl in the 1890s

London is full of dead pubs. In Oxford Street between St Giles Circus and Marble Arch there were nineteen pubs in 1890; today there is only one. In the same year there were thirty pubs in the Strand, exclusive of bars in restaurants and hotels; today there are six. Some of the buildings which they occupied have been demolished, but many are still there, with shops on the ground floor and offices up above, monuments to changing commercial values and the policies of the licensing authorities. All over London, once one starts to look for them, dead pubs start up at every corner, converted into modish dress shops, architects' offices, private houses, Wimpy bars, antique shops, employment exchanges or travel agencies, or just standing empty, waiting for the demolition contractor (Plate 1).

Yet London, apart from the occasional stretch which for reasons of history is dry or nearly dry, does not strike one as short of pubs. In the centre, in particular, they still exist in abundant numbers, from big brassy pubs at main street intersections to dim forgotten little bars down side alleys. In Victorian days their abundance was reckless and, in the eyes of Temperance reformers, scandalous. It is true that London as a whole did not have so many pubs in proportion to the population as the industrial towns in the north. In 1896 it had 345 persons per pub as opposed to Sheffield's 176 and Manchester's 168. But in central areas, like St James's with 116 per pub, it could rival anything that Manchester or Sheffield had to offer; and its vast and rapidly increasing size, and the size and splendour of its pubs made it the biggest congregation of drinking places in the world.[1]

There were proportionately even more pubs in London in 1870 than in 1890, but the 1890s was their golden age. The pubs then were bigger and brighter, their lamps more enormous, their glass more elaborate, their fittings more sumptuous than they had ever been before or were to be again. What survives of them today is rich enough but only a shadow of what they were in their prime. A pub walk along the main thoroughfares of London in, say, 1898 must have been a curious experience for a stranger—a walk starting on a dark autumn evening about seven o'clock, when the western sky was still red, the roads jammed with horse-buses, carts, traps and cabs, the horses' breath smoking on the frosty air, and the sidewalks equally jammed with a silent moving throng of people. A great proportion of London's working population still walked to and from work, often several miles a day. To solace them on their long and cold journey home, main thoroughfares like Bishopsgate, Shoreditch and the Mile End, Bethnal Green, Tottenham Court and Old Kent roads were studded and in places crowded with pubs. As the street lights dimly lit up in the twilight the pubs lit up far more brightly; long rows of monstrous lanterns stretched out into the street on curling and caparisoned tentacles of wrought iron and underneath them walls of sinuously bending and elaborately engraved glass were lit from the inside by an inner row of blazing globes. Innumerable glass-paned doors swung open and shut to reveal the warmth and glitter inside: little secret sparkling private bars, big public bars with deal-lined walls and sawdust on the floors, or saloon bars rich with ferns, carpets, mirrors, a glowing fire and a view through to the billiard room and to distant figures leaning out of the dark over the brilliantly lit tables.

2. The Old King's Head, Euston Road

Pubs were still closely connected with transport, though the pattern was changing. As the railways spread, the great stage-coach depots of Southwark, Holborn and St Martin's fell into neglect and were gradually demolished, but new or enlarged pubs sprang up beside the stations. The numerous different lines of horse-buses all had their depots at outer London pubs, which served as combined waiting and refreshment rooms for passengers and drivers, to the great gain of the publican. These forgotten termini often explain the richness of particular pubs. The Elgin in Ladbroke Grove, with its saloon bar walls lined with ornamental tiles, gold-engraved glass and multi-coloured crystal (Colour Plates X, XIII), the Half Moon on Herne Hill, with its little wine bar glittering with painted mirror storks and bullrushes, the World's End with its turret and extravagant Flemish gables at the kink of the King's Road, Chelsea, were all horse-bus termini, as was the demolished but once famous Yorkshire Stingo in Marylebone, the Angel, Islington, and the Elephant and Castle, Newington Butts. Even with the coming of the underground the habit of connecting transport with pubs lingered on, and underground stations were named after the Royal Oak, Elephant and Castle, Angel and Swiss Cottage.

The Customers and What They Drank

But London pubs, of course, did not cater only for travellers. The pubs on the main thoroughfares usually had a residential hinterland behind them which they served as well; residential areas had their quieter and smaller neighbourhood pubs, unless a Temperance ground landlord had made the neighbourhood a dry one. Markets, barracks, the docks, business and commercial areas, and the conglomeration of theatres and music-halls around the Strand and Charing Cross Road in central London produced their own drinking pattern in the surrounding areas.

Similar patterns are still in existence, but the people who pushed their way in and out of the swinging glass doors in the 1890s were markedly different from the people who frequent pubs today. Many more of them were demonstrably very poor or very drunk, even if the particular combination of toughness, squalor, drunkenness and glitter that had made the early Victorian gin palace so attractive a subject to moralists had been noticeably softened. Huge, gaudy undivided bars without seats, jammed with singing, swearing or shouting people, had largely disappeared. There were now seats and tables in all bars, and partitions and screens segregated the different types and classes. Manual workers and omnibus drivers congregated in the public bars; bargains were struck or women gossiped and drank in little one-sex groups in the private bars, shopkeepers, bookies and clerks, often with their wives, were to be found in the saloon bars, variegated by butlers and valets in Mayfair and St James's, or music-hall artists around Kensington Road or along the Strand. Children were legally allowed in any bar, but publicans had not been allowed to sell spirits to children under sixteen since 1839 or beer to children under thirteen since 1886. Children of any age could come into a pub to fetch drink for home consumption, but by the 1890s many and perhaps most publicans confined this traffic to a jug-and-bottle department with its own entrance.

The various bars had their characteristic drinks. Mild ale had replaced porter (a milder form of stout, known as 'entire') as the favourite drink in the public bars; it was known as four-ale because, like porter, it sold at 4*d.* a quart and public bars were often called four-ale bars as a result. The saloon and private bars preferred bitter, selling at 3*d.* or 4*d.* a pint. Although those who disliked the more exuberant pubs of the 1890s continued to call them gin palaces, gin had long ago lost the pre-eminence it had enjoyed in the days of the genuine gin palaces of the 1830s. Gin in those days, at 3*d.* a quartern (or quarter-pint), was competitive with beer, but while the price of beer scarcely changed between 1830 and 1900, successive rises in spirit duty pushed gin up to 6*d.* a quartern. Moreover, the greater part of the spirit market had been captured by whisky, even though it was more expensive than gin. Little whisky had been drunk in London before the 1860s, when a vigorous selling campaign put Irish whiskey on the map; Scotch followed in the 1870s, and in the 1880s handsomely overtook Irish.[2]

Gin (along with port and lemon) continued to be a favourite drink among women, who were now frequenting pubs in increasing numbers. Few respectable women had gone into pubs in the mid-nineteenth century; it was the private and saloon bars and higher standards of comfort and finish which brought them into the pubs of the eighties and nineties. The same higher standard may have pushed up the social range of drinkers, but, except possibly in some West End pubs, it still scarcely reached above the lower middle classes.

The situation had been quite different well into Victoria's reign, when members of all classes were to be found in pubs. In the case of the upper classes an element of deliberate slumming was probably never absent. Young bloods went ratting and dancing in the pubs along the docks, or frequented the bar parlours of pugilist publicans like the ex-world champion Tom Cribb at the Napier in High Holborn. The pathetically dissolute Marquess of Hastings, roistering in the docks at the Jolly Sailors in Ship Alley and elsewhere in the 1860s to cries of 'The Markis will take the chair', 'The Markis, Gawd bless him', was probably the last of these pub-crawling grandees. By the 1880s fast young lords had other places to go; as the Hon. Algy Bourke, secretary of White's Club, crushingly put it in 1896: 'The West Enders (I am speaking of my own class) are not attracted to the public house . . . The class I deal with and the class I associate with and the class I know do not go into public houses.'[3]

The same remark could have been made at the time about the professional and business classes and even about most artists and writers. But in the eighteenth and early nineteenth centuries lawyers, doctors, artists, writers, clergymen, merchants and shopkeepers had frequented inns and taverns throughout London without second thoughts. They went there for purely social reasons, or for meals, or to discuss business, or to attend political meetings or debating and discussion societies like the famous Old Codgers society which met in the Old Barley Mow in Salisbury Court. *Punch* started up in the parlour of the Edinburgh Castle in the Strand in 1841, and its staff later frequented the Crown and Sugar Loaf in Fleet Street in such numbers that its name was changed to Punch's Tavern. *Punch* was only the best known of early Victorian periodicals associated with taverns. Apart from respectable middle-class activities, for those who wanted a more raffish evening there were central London pubs like the Cyder Cellars in Maiden Lane, in the basement of which 'Judge Nicholson' parodied contemporary events with notable obscenity in his 'Judge and Jury' series.

The Victorian middle classes abandoned pubs partly because the efforts of the Temperance Movement gave them an increasingly bad name, most of all, probably, because the clubs that began to proliferate from the 1830s, the big new hotels of the mid-century and the cafés and restaurants of the seventies, eighties and nineties gave them somewhere else to go. In the 1890s the *Licensed Victuallers' Gazette* was lamenting that 'the children of Bohemia had taken to clubs', that 'the better class' of the audiences of the Haymarket Theatre had deserted the Waterloo in the Haymarket for the Café de l'Europe in Leicester Square and that 'Mr Beerbohm Tree does *not* frequent its snuggery after the manner of his predecessors'. In 1888 the same paper commented, 'In these days when taverns are voted vulgar, it would be almost the ruin of a barrister's reputation to be seen entering a public house unless it were called a restaurant.'[4] Most London taverns in the eighteenth and early nineteenth centuries had combined the dual function of eating and drinking places, and in central London it was only those which concentrated on their eating side that kept up the social level of their clientele. These City restaurant-pubs included the Rainbow in Fleet Street, the Daniel Lambert and the Blue Last on Ludgate Hill and, most famous of all, the Ship and Turtle in Leadenhall Street (bought by Pimms in 1899). Here one wall of the restaurant consisted of a glass tank in which turtles glided up and down, blandly surveying the clientele who were to eat them.[5]

Once the reputation of pubs began to go down, the growing Victorian urge for respectability rapidly cleaned even the more easy-going members of the middle classes out of them. On the other hand the fact that they had ceased to be socially respectable gave them a new cachet in the eyes of those members of the middle classes who reacted against their background and set out to *épater la bourgeoisie*. In spite of what the *Licensed Victuallers' Gazette* had to say, there was at least one section of the children of Bohemia who frequented a particular group of bars and pubs in the 1890s. Their drinking places were in and around the Strand, Fleet Street and Charing Cross, bars like the Bodega in Bedford Street or Henekey's and the Bun Shop (later Yates's Wine Lodge) in the Strand or bars attached to restaurants like Romano's and Gatti's. Here were to be found a gang of writers, artists, actors and journalists who did their best to copy the Bohemianism of Paris; they drank absinthe, ate in Soho, went with music-hall girls, found drink glamorous and not infrequently died of it. Lionel Johnson and Ernest Dowson both died of drink in their middle thirties. Dowson died in 1900, a pathetic drunk haunting the Strand bars in search of acquaintances from earlier and happier days when he had scribbled 'I too have been faithful to you, Cynara, in my fashion' and other poems on the backs of envelopes on the marble-topped tables of the Cock in Shaftesbury Avenue (Plate 3).[6] Johnson fell off a bar stool and cracked his skull on the floor of the Green Dragon in Fleet Street in 1902.

The centre of this Bohemian nineties life was the saloon bar of the Crown in Charing Cross Road, before it was rebuilt in about 1897. Here, after the show had ended and while 'prosperous cab-proprietors and bookmakers' runners and the male assistants at the neighbouring music-halls and theatres' drank up at the bar, the benches along the walls were crowded with an animated group that might include Johnson, Dowson, Arthur Symons, Selwyn Image, Charles Conder, William Rothenstein and, more rarely, Oscar Wilde, Robert Ross, George Moore and Aubrey Beardsley. Here Verlaine was brought after lecturing on his London visit in November 1893, along with Edmund Gosse, pillar of the literary establishment,

3. The Cock, Shaftesbury Avenue

looking 'extremely unhappy at finding himself at such an hour in the bar-parlour of a London public-house'.[7]

The recognized time for gathering at the Crown was between 11 o'clock at night and closing time at 12.30. Although Sunday morning closing had been introduced in 1839, and opening hours further curtailed in 1864, 1872 and 1874, London pubs were still open from 5 a.m. till 12.30 a.m. on weekdays, and from 1 p.m. till 3 p.m. and 6 p.m. till 11 p.m. on Sundays. These long opening hours were one reason for their being used much more intensively than they are today; in addition, many alternative attractions and meeting places now taken for granted were not then in existence. Pubs were local centres for sport and entertainment and for dissemination of information, as well as meeting places for innumerable local groups and societies. Inquests and auctions were held in them. In spite of bitter opposition from Lord Shaftesbury and others, wages were still often paid out in pubs; workmen went there to pick up jobs or read the newspapers and tradesmen to change banknotes. Most pubs let rooms or took lodgers, often on a sufficient scale to justify their calling themselves hotels.

Sport, Pleasure and Entertainment

Boxing and racing were intimately tied up with the world of pubs and publicans and were given space in proportion in the pages of the *Licensed Victuallers' Gazette*, the *Licensing World* and other public house newspapers. Although illegal, bets continued to be passed in pubs, but since the publicans were liable to be fined and quite possibly to lose their licences if they were successfully prosecuted, it tended to be only the less successful or more disreputable pubs that allowed it. George Moore was probably close enough to reality in *Esther Waters* (1894) when he made William Latch encourage the passing of bets to bring in custom to his pub, 'a humble place in the old fashioned style' which attracted little business in the face of competition from new pubs with 'painted tiles and brass lamps'. But many publicans were bookies as well (like William Latch) and drove out to the racecourses with their gear at weekends. Others were retired jockeys.

Similarly, many publicans were ex-prize fighters, like Tom Cribb at the Napier, and often had a boxing school and ring attached to their pubs. Boxing had been at a low ebb in the sixties and seventies, when it had ceased to be disreputable and fashionable and had become merely disreputable. It was kept going by publicans with boxing pubs, like Jack Harper at the Market House, Islington, Bill Richardson at the Blue Anchor, Shoreditch, and Nat Langham (the only boxer who ever beat Tom Sayers) at the Mitre, St Martin's Lane. A boxing match was still treated as a breach of the peace, and was therefore illegal, until the replacement of bare-fisted by gloved fights and the use of the Queensberry rules gradually made it legally acceptable in the 1890s. In 1891 John Fleming, a publican turned boxing manager and promoter, founded the National Sporting Club and equipped it with a permanent boxing hall, a large middle- and upper-class membership and Lord Lonsdale as the chairman. A new era of clubs and big fights was beginning which would gradually put the boxing pubs out of business, but there were still plenty of them in the eighties and nineties. A quick dip into the *Licensed Victuallers' Gazette* for September 1888 reveals Sergeant W. Green opening his season at the Red Lion, Red Lion Court, with the 'usual exhibition match'; a smoking concert at the Corn Exchange Tavern, Mark Lane, with a 'three-round spar' as the principal event; and, at the Wheatsheaf, Holborn, a match between thirteen-year-olds with ladies present—considered by the *Gazette* to be in bad taste.[8]

In the same month are notices of running matches from the Golden Anchor, St John Street, Clerkenwell, to New Cross and back, and from the Queen's Head, West Smithfield (known as 'Posh Price's' from the name of its pugilist publican), to the Elephant and Castle and back. Boat races on the river also tended to run from pub to pub. Many pigeon-fancying clubs still met in pubs, but ratting, cock-fighting and finch-singing contests were probably on the way out and to be found only in old-fashioned beerhouses in very poor neighbourhoods. Many pubs had skittle alleys and bagatelle tables; by the late nineties many more had billiard tables, often with an elaborately decorated new billiard room built on to contain them, for billiards, skilfully promoted by Messrs Thurston the billiard table manufacturers, was the great public house craze of the 1890s.

By then the outdoor activities of London pubs were on the wane. Pleasure gardens attached to pubs were vanishing fast, partly because space became increasingly valuable as London expanded, partly because they were under pressure from

the non-conformist lobby. Of the two most famous the Highbury Barn Tavern (Plate 4), with its 'great room', Leviathan outdoor dancing platform lit by gaslight, theatre, and orchestra playing from a cast-iron kiosk in the Chinese style, had been closed down after being refused a dancing licence in 1870 and 1871, and the gardens were built over by 1883.[9] The Eagle in the City Road, similarly equipped and with even more exotic architecture, had been bought up by the Salvation Army in 1882; although the lease of the actual pub had to be allowed to run out, the gardens were closed immediately and the pleasure kiosks replaced by the huts of a Salvation Army barracks. The gardens of the Monster Tavern, Pimlico, where artificial animals and monsters were devised so as to spring out at customers from behind the bushes, closed to make way for the railway in 1865. The grounds of the Rosemary Branch, Peckham, used for horse-racing, quoits, cricket and pigeon-shooting, were built over in 1874.[10]

A number of pubs had dance halls, but these had to be licensed. The Metropolitan Board of Works and its successor the London County Council, which from 1878 increasingly took over this aspect of licensing, deliberately controlled and reduced their numbers. By 1888, for instance, all the once-notorious dancing pubs along Ratcliff Highway in the docks had been closed by the LCC under pressure from a local lobby led by the vicar of St Georges-in-the-East and the local Wesleyan minister; this resourceful and indefatigable couple actually purchased the two most notorious, Paddy's Goon and the Mahogany Bar, and converted them for missionary purposes.[11]

Almost all pubs had one or more public rooms, often of very large size, up on the first floor or tacked on to one side. These were the venue for a vast and complicated network of local societies and activities which spread all over London. The local lodges of the trades unions often had their meetings in pubs, and though by the late nineteenth century the Temperance element in the trade union movement was pressing for them to meet elsewhere, often there was no other large room available. Local political meetings were held in pubs, which in the mid-century

4. The Leviathan Dancing Platform, Highbury Barn Tavern

had been considered centres of radical intrigue but by the 1890s were more likely to be made use of by the Conservatives, who by then were unequivocally identified with the drink interest. Many lodges of Freemasons had their meetings in pubs, and some of the bigger pubs like the Cock at Highbury, the Horns at Kennington and the Crown in St John's Wood had upstairs rooms used only as Masonic temples; at the Albion, Aldersgate, no fewer than thirty Masonic chapters and lodges were meeting in 1899.[12] Even more pubs were patronized by the less secretive and socially less ambitious (beer rather than whisky) Royal and Antediluvian Order of Buffaloes and the Ancient Noble Order of United Oddfellows. These wore their regalia, held their initiation ceremonies, paid in their subscriptions, sang, drank and made merry in upstairs rooms of pubs all over London; unlike the Masons, they still do so today.[13]

The secret societies (there were others, like the Foresters and the Druids) were all, to a certain extent, benefit societies. Many other more straightforward and often very humble benefit societies were attached to pubs, usually with the publican as chairman or treasurer and an annual handout at Christmas. But the range of pub societies was enormous. For instance, in 1899 the Salisbury Hotel, Green Lanes, was the meeting place of the Harringay Lodge of Freemasons, the Harringay Cycling Club, and the Bohemians Society, who held a grand concert there every month. The South of London Angling Society met weekly at the George and Dragon, Camberwell Road, where the landlord was an ardent angler. The Kilburn Busmen's Philharmonic Society met at the Cock in Kilburn High Street. In February 1898 the local branch of the Postmen's Federation had their annual dinner at the Junction, Westbourne Park; they started late, with an extension, 'having to complete their night deliveries before sitting down'. In 1896 the Baxendale Arms, Columbia Road, Hackney, was the headquarters of the London Society of Sawyers, Clickers and Rough Stuff Cutters; the Society of Cigar Box Makers and Paperers; the French Huguenots No. 1 Dockers' Branch; the Friends Benevolent Society; the Loan and Benevolent Society; the Nelson Military Band; and the Bethnal Green Branch of the Social Democratic Federation.[14]

While the societies were meeting upstairs in the club room, patrons in the bars were likely to be offered a number of facilities and entertainments in addition to the billiards, bagatelle or skittles already referred to. The criticism that pubs offered alcohol and nothing else, as opposed to the food and good cheer nostalgically ascribed to the old English inn, had been a favourite weapon of the Temperance lobby, and one that had had considerable justification in the mid-nineteenth century; but by the 1890s it was much less true. Pubs had been providing food in increasing quantities for some decades: in the 1840s Captain's biscuits and sponge-cakes were the most customers could usually hope for; in the mid-nineteenth century 'a glass of ale and a sandwich for fourpence' had become a popular advertisement in beerhouses, and the fully licensed houses had retaliated by introducing the Melton Mowbray pork pie; by the nineties most pubs offered pork pies or sandwiches, and many had luncheon counters and grill rooms and were offering Bovril, tea, coffee and ginger beer as well as alcoholic drinks.[15]

Even so, food seldom provided more than a small percentage of the total sales and tended to be aimed at better-off customers. As pubs grew smarter and more sophisticated, publicans were less prepared to heat up chops brought in by workmen for their midday dinner. This had been a widely provided service in the mid-century. A pamphlet of 1878 tells how 'the skilled artisan . . . having secured a good cut and wrapped it in a cabbage leaf or a bit of newspaper . . . has long been accustomed to make tracks for the tap room of his favourite "pub" where he enjoys the prospect of his steak being boiled for him, and is accommodated with plate, knife, and fork, and condiments, for a half penny, on condition that he buys a pint of porter'. By 1898 the *Licensing World* was recording the complaints of local working men who would lose this facility as a result of the rebuilding of the old-fashioned Greyhound in Kensington Square; and there must have been many similar examples.[16]

The fittings in these rebuilt pubs were much more splendid than anything that had preceded them but they all had a strong family resemblance; they reflected the taste of the time and the capabilities of a comparatively small group of architects, craftsmen and decorators. Acknowledgement of the publican seldom went further than incorporating his initials into the decorations.[17] The contents gave more scope for him to express his personal tastes, though this was limited by the fact that the majority of late Victorian publicans were restless men, moving on every few years from pub to pub. But at least collections of engravings or photographs of racing scenes, boxing matches or music-hall stars in the saloon bar or bar parlour would give some indication of their particular enthusiasms. A few had something more unusual to offer. Frank Crocker, who moved from the Volunteer, Kilburn, to the lavishly appointed and marble-lined Crown, Aberdeen Place, St John's Wood, in 1898, proudly displayed at both pubs the three-foot-high Fullerton Cup, bought from Colonel J. T. North the 'Nitrate King' and surmounted by a silver effigy of Fullerton, a greyhound who won the Waterloo cup four years running. The Bell and Mackerel, Mile End Road, was exhibiting 20,000 stuffed creatures in cases in the 1890s. The Duke of Kent in the Old Kent Road had a renowned collection of stuffed fish. The Hole in the Wall, Borough High Street, had an equally renowned collection of skulls, and a stuffed Borneo monkey 'who used, when alive, to be a great favourite with the customers'. The collection at the Vale of Health, Hampstead, included one of Dick Turpin's pistols, a stuffed porpoise, a donkey once ridden by Nell Gwynne, and a two-headed calf. This was rivalled by the pig with one head but two bodies, an ivory model of a Chinese pagoda, at the Edinburgh Castle, Mornington Crescent, where the publican, T. G. Middlebrook, formed the best known of Victorian pub collections. When it was sold on his death in 1908 the vast miscellany of junk, dubious relics and real rarities included a Benin bronze, a marble head of Justinian, a collection of 80,000 butterflies and moths, the spear which killed General Gordon, the bugle which sounded the Charge of the Light Brigade, two pictures by Ruskin and three great auk's eggs.[18]

On the whole the clientele did not go to London pubs to pick up prostitutes. This was against the law, and, in London at any rate, the law was fairly strictly enforced and prostitutes were not encouraged by the publicans. The place to find them was on the streets or, most likely, in the music-halls, where their presence was equally illegal but was connived at by the police because it was easy to supervise. In pubs one was more likely to be approached by people selling less personal goods, matches or street ballads or flowers, and even their presence depended on the goodwill of the publican. Charlie Chaplin described how as a boy, when his father died, he cased the pubs along the Kennington Road on a Saturday afternoon, with a black crepe band on his arm and bundles of daffodils: 'I would go into the saloons, looking wistful, and whisper: "Narcissus, miss. Narcissus, madame." The women always responded "Who is it, son?" And I would lower my voice to a whisper: "My father" and they would give me tips.'[19]

On another occasion he was locked out from home one night and consoled in his misery by the sudden irruption, 'brilliant in the empty square', of 'The Honeysuckle and the Bee', played in the vestibule of the White Hart, Kennington Road, by a blind harmonium-player and a drunken clarinettist.[20] There must have been a good deal of this itinerant music in Victorian pubs, apart from the more elaborate musical entertainments that developed into the music-halls. From the mid-1890s there were musical automatons, Monopol musical boxes ('repay their outlay in a few weeks, beside the pleasure and attraction to Saloon bars, billiard rooms, etc., during the winter evenings'), Polyphons and other mechanical music machines, grinding out their metallic music on the receipt of a penny. But it was not till 1901 that the Automatic Machine Company began to advertise its 'Automatic Games Machines' (and cigarette machines) in the pub journals.[21]

Publicans and Barmaids

Presiding over all these attractions were the publican, his family, and attendant waiters, pot-boys and barmaids. The bars with 'sawdust on the floor and a spittoon in the corner' were usually served by men; the barmaids were in the private and saloon bars. Among them were no doubt many smart, jolly, warmhearted girls, who were just what barmaids are expected to be; but their life was not an easy one, as is testified by the late nineteenth-century campaigns for their protection and by the advertisements in the pub journals of cures for bunions, flat feet and varicose veins. At the end of 1898 the *Licensed Victuallers' Gazette* ran a competition for 'your favourite barmaid'; photographs were sent in in large numbers and batches of them published over several weeks, and the photographs of the winner and runners-up came out on 13 January 1899 (Plate 5). Even allowing for poor quality reproduction, it is unlikely that they would have won a competition today; but beauty queens today do not have to stand at a counter twelve to fifteen hours a day, for six and a half days a week.[22]

In the same decade both the *Licensed Victuallers' Gazette* and the *Licensing World* published numerous short biographies, together with photographs, of publicans in the news or 'popular publicans'. Combined with other sources these help to

give some sort of picture of the kind of people who took on Victorian pubs. They varied, of course, in status, from the successful publican with a big pub or a string of pubs who was a Mason and a member of the local vestry or the LCC, to the small man who invested his savings in a quiet local pub and stayed there. They varied, perhaps, less in type, or at least there was a race-course, big-cigar, loud-checks type which was especially associated with publicans, of whom the beau-ideal was someone like Bob Prudhoe of the Norfolk Arms, a flash little house in Norfolk Street off the Strand, with his 'showy dog-cart, with high-stepper, silver-mounted harness and crest and motto', his pretty barmaids, keen business sense and glamorous reputation of being an illegitimate son of the Duke of Norfolk.[23]

The London breweries started to buy up pubs in large numbers in the 1880s and, even more, in the 1890s, but until then most publicans held their pubs on long leases from non-brewing ground landlords and quite a few were freeholders. Brewery-owned pubs were usually leased to tenants on twenty- or thirty-year leases; the system of installing managers rather than tenants was still rarely used by the brewers, but common enough with the numerous publicans who owned more than one pub. Many publicans moved on from pub to pub every two or three years; in 1889 the *Licensed Victuallers' Gazette* considered a five-year stretch 'a long term for this ever shifting age'.[24] Publicans were often the children or relatives of other publicans, but a good few of these knocked around for a few years before going into their father's business and others came in from a different walk of life altogether. The previous occupations of publicans featured in the *Gazette* and *Licensing World* include working as chemist, tobacconist, boxer, Trinity Pilot, sailor, corporal in the Horse Guards, police inspector, courier, commercial traveller in mineral waters, tea merchant, manager in a timber firm, speculative builder, comic dancer, and steward and confidential man to a race-horse owner.

Alf Standbrook, of the Dover Castle, Greenwich Church Street, had been a page-boy, yacht steward, hotel porter and teacher of boxing. Sydney Pease, of the Grey-hound Hotel, Croydon, alternated between being an actor and a sailor; he had

5. Prizewinners in the 'Your Favourite Barmaid' competition, 1899

sailed round the world before he was sixteen and travelled round America with a menagerie before coming home to manage his father's pub on Stamford Hill, after which he moved on to Croydon and composed music-hall sketches in his spare time. William Bennett had travelled as a courier in the 1860s 'conducting the grand tour for families of distinction', spent the Siege of Paris living on horse-meat in a cellar, came home to run a cigar divan in Beak Street for eighteen years and ended up in the 1890s in the Old Cock off the Haymarket. Mark Wheeler, of the Joiner's Arms, Denmark Hill, had travelled all over the world showing his 'Fairy Fountains', dissolving views and optical illusions in circuses and variety shows. In 1869 he went out to Egypt with Rencey's Circus for the opening of the Suez Canal; in 1884 he took on his nine-year-old nephew Teddy Haynes as an apprentice acrobat and wire-walker. The couple retired to the Joiner's Arms in 1887, when Wheeler was in his early forties, and in 1897 he retired altogether and set up his nephew in the Horn of Plenty, Poplar, where Haynes would show to favoured customers the gold medal on his watch-chain inscribed 'Presented to Master T. E. Haynes by his uncle, Mark Wheeler, for his first appearance on the wires, Teatro Valencia, Venezuela, April 26, 1885'.[25]

The career of Alfred Savigear (Plate 6) of the, in its day, renowned Savigear's Riding School was equally varied in a different way, for like many of the more active publicans his activities were not confined to pubs. After ten years as riding instructor at Sandhurst and the Staff College, he retired from the army as a sergeant-major in 1877 at the age of thirty-nine and became a publican. At one time or another he ran at least half a dozen houses, including the Swiss Cottage, the Mitre in Chancery Lane and the Railway Hotel at Acton, which he rebuilt in 1899. But his main base was in and around the Prince Teck in Earl's Court Road, where he acquired the whole block and developed the centre of the site first as a factory for manufacturing Royal Amaranth Bitters and then, about 1894, as a riding school. The bitters were a flop, but Savigear's Riding School flourished to such an extent that he devoted more and more time to it, and his pubs were leased, sold off or handed over to his son. This many-sided man also helped initiate the Royal Tournament, invented a patent stirrup and a patent wheel, owned one of the first fleets of taxis, indulged in property development in the Barkston Gardens area and for a time mysteriously described himself as Count Savigear.[26]

Pubs and the Music-Halls

In January 1896 Florrie Smith, daughter of Duck Smith of the Seven Stars, Brick Lane, Spitalfields, gave her annual party for her friends. 'Some 300 children resident in the neighbourhood assembled . . . After the usual distribution of toys, sweetmeats and fruits to the children, the following artistes appeared during the evening: Miss Daisy Wood, the Sisters Lena, and Miss Gracie Lloyd . . . Mr Henry Keys was very funny in his sketch "Gentleman, a good finish". Dancing was kept up till midnight when the function was brought to a close by the National Anthem.'[27]

Apart from giving a brief insight into the social life of publicans, this newspaper report nicely illustrates the connection between the pub and music-hall worlds. The music-halls had developed out of the musical entertainments given in the upper or back rooms of pubs in the 1850s. This type of entertainment caught on and the music rooms developed into more ambitious music-halls attached to pubs, and ultimately into music-halls built on their own. Even these showed their origin in the prominence given to the drinking side of the entertainment: up till the end of the century much of the seating was arranged in the form of benches and tables so that the audience could drink as they watched, and there was almost always one or more long bars off the auditorium with a glass screen giving a view of the stage.

In the 1890s the music-halls were in an intermediate stage of their journey towards the completely independent variety theatres of the early 1900s. There were still a good many pub music rooms in existence, and there was a great flourishing of music-halls unattached to pubs; but there were also a few examples of an in-between arrangement, sizable music-halls with complete pubs slotted into them at ground floor level, in addition to the auditorium bar. The Oxford Music Hall, for instance, had the midget Boar and Castle tucked in between its two entrances; the Hammersmith Theatre of Varieties had the larger Hammersmith Tavern; the Rosemary Branch Music Hall in Peckham incorporated two pubs. The Washington Music Hall in Battersea also had two pubs, the Washington and the Royal Standard, with a box-office in the bar of the Royal Standard.[28]

Several pub architects, like Finch Hill and Paraire, Wylson and Long, and W. M. Brutton, were music-hall architects. The best known of music-hall and variety theatre architects, Frank Matcham, designed a few pubs as a young man.[29] Music-hall artists retired to pubs, or ran a pub as a side line. William Bishop, 'the marvellously comic eccentric dancer whose appearance in the Empire Ballet has always

6. Alfred Savigear and his family in about 1903

been hailed with delight', was also the publican of the Apple Tree, Cursitor Street, which had a small concert room attached to it; Marie Lloyd set her mother up at the Princes Tavern in Wardour Street. Conversely, successful publicans financed new musical halls, or hoped to finance them, like the previously mentioned Sydney Pease of the Croydon Greyhound, who was described in 1898 as playing the piano, composing and writing music-hall sketches and hoping to buy a theatre.[30]

Music-hall artists, unlike most late Victorian painters, writers and actors, were great frequenters of pubs. Their main drinking ground was in Kennington and Lambeth, where they lived along Kennington Road and attended the agents' offices around Waterloo. All along the Kennington Road after eleven o'clock at night broughams were to be seen clustered outside the pubs, with wicker trunks on the dicky containing the costumes of the music-hall artists who owned them and were drinking inside after finishing at, perhaps, the Empire or Alhambra in Leicester Square, or the South London or Canterbury south of the river. The pubs included the Horns, with its enormous concert room and row of antlered deerheads protruding from the facade, the White Hart, the Tankard, the Three Stags, and the Hercules, where the landlord Douglas White, who had been a sailor in the Japanese War of 1864, lined the saloon bar with framed portraits of music-hall stars.[31] On Sunday morning the same broughams or a smart pony trap could be seen standing outside their lodgings, waiting to take them on a spin to Norwood or Merton ending with a tour of the Kennington Road pubs. Charlie Chaplin, as a twelve-year-old, used to stand outside the Tankard 'watching these illustrious gentlemen alight from their equestrian outfits to enter the lounge bar, where the elite of vaudeville met . . . How glamorous they were, dressed in chequered suits and grey bowlers, flashing their diamond rings and tie pins! At two o'clock on Sunday afternoon the pub closed and its occupants filed outside and dallied awhile before bidding each other adieu; and I would gaze fascinated and amused for some of them swaggered with a ridiculous air.'[32]

The Anti-Drinkers

Chaplin's father, Charles Chaplin the elder, was a minor music-hall star; his uncle was a publican who owned pubs in and around Lambeth. He saw his father sitting in the bar of the Three Stags in Kennington Road: 'I opened the saloon door, just a few inches, and there he was . . . He looked very ill; his eyes were sunken, and his body had swollen to an enormous size . . . Three weeks later he was taken to St Thomas's Hospital . . . He was dying of dropsy. They trapped sixteen quarts of liquid from his knee . . . He died of alcoholic excess at the age of thirty-seven.'[33]

After doing their act music-hall artists were expected to go to the bar and drink with customers; according to Chaplin some were paid large salaries as much in anticipation that these would return to the management by way of the bar as because of their talents. Death by drinking was one of the hazards of a music-hall career and also, for that matter, of a publican's. In the 1890–2 period the death rate from

drink among London publicans was more than nine times the average for employed males. Even this average was far above what it is today; the national average was ·019 per cent in 1895, rose to a peak of ·026 per cent in 1900 and should be compared to the ·0041 per cent in 1935.[34] The average yearly consumption of beer per head in 1895–1900 was 31·2 gallons, and of spirits 1·03 gallons; in 1930–5 the figures were 13·3 gallons and ·22 gallons and although they have risen appreciably since the Second World War are still nowhere near Victorian levels.[35] Drink, in short, was being knocked back in the 1890s in far greater quantities than it is today, and that drink was stronger drink. The gaiety and glitter of Victorian pubs and music-halls had its seamy side. The Temperance Movement in Victorian England had more than just puritan disapproval behind it, however mistaken its analysis of the causes of drunkenness and however unattractive or even ridiculous many of its methods may seem today.

Temperance in nineteenth-century England started in the 1830s with an agitation against spirits, as opposed to healthy British beer. It quickly developed into a movement for promoting complete abstinence and then into one for prohibition—or at least 'local option', the option of local government to make its particular neighbourhood a dry one. The United Kingdom Alliance, the prohibition movement founded in 1853, was a formidable pressure group by the 1870s, and only slightly less so in the 1890s.

The clientele of public houses were likely to be stopped on their way in by earnest, soberly dressed women who pressed leaflets luridly painting the evils of drink into their hands; or to find that the building adjacent to their local pub or even the pub itself had been converted into a 'coffee public house', a means of weaning the lower classes from drink into which much upper- and middle-class money was poured in the seventies and eighties, often with pathetically little result. But as a whole the Temperance Movement was far from pathetic; even if its achievements in getting anti-drink legislation passed were less than it had hoped for, as a pressure

7. Publican, wife and barmaid in the Napier, High Holborn, 1899

group it helped to push through laws which closed pubs for a substantial time on Sundays, replaced all-night weekday drinking by a closing time of 12.30 a.m. in London and earlier elsewhere, kept children from being served with drink, imposed stricter regulations on publicans and made it easier for the licensing authorities to regulate and reduce the number of pubs.

Above all, Temperance agitation helped to produce a climate of opinion in which most of what one might call the well-informed classes regarded pubs at least with very mixed feelings, if not with suspicion and dislike, while the working and lower middle classes tended to separate into two distinct cultures: on the one hand the majority, who drank, gambled, followed the dogs and horses, attended the music-halls and voted Tory; on the other hand the 'self-improvers' who attended chapel, took the pledge, saved money, thought that music-halls, racecourses and boxing rings were the haunts of the devil and voted Liberal.

The pubs and the music-halls were a perfect reflection of the life-style of the former group. They exuded a kind of easy-going derision of the puritan virtues. But publicans still had to accommodate themselves to stricter laws and stricter administration of the laws; the pubs of the 1890s were on the whole better conducted, as well as better built and better furnished, than the pubs of the fifties, and their plans were carefully devised to make supervision easier. They were also worth a great deal more money. One of the ironies of the Temperance Movement was that by successfully reducing the number of pubs and scaring the brewers into buying them up in order to secure their markets, it helped to inflate the price of public house property. The buying, doing up or rebuilding, and selling of pubs became tempting speculations. A stranger in London in 1898 would have been amazed not only at the multitude and splendour of pubs but at the number of them under scaffolding. Even today it is remarkable how often, once one starts to look, one sees pubs inscribed with the dates of the boom years 1896, 1897, 1898 and 1899.

The economic and financial background of pubs is described in some detail in chapters IV and X. These may help to dissipate any over-romanticized view of Victorian, especially late Victorian, pubs. Genial 'Mine hosts', well loved and long established on the local scene, were seldom to be found in them; they were largely the creation of tough, flashy men who were out to make money quick and had a sharp eye for new gimmicks to keep their customers from succumbing to Temperance propaganda or counter-attractions, who exploited and overworked their staff and sold their pubs as soon as they could make a good profit on them. For a few years they flourished triumphantly; these were the years in which what is today thought of as the typical Victorian pub was created. In the end (in London, at any rate) they were overtaken by financial disaster, or as the Temperance Movement could call it, nemesis. The history of the Victorian pub falls into three phases: a slow rise, much publicized in its early stages in the 1830s by the over-exposure of the gin palaces; a brief but glittering culmination in the late eighties and the nineties; and a fall.

8. Gin-temple turn-out at church time, by George Cruikshank

Beer and Porter are the natural *beverage of the Englishman . . . the increase of Gin-drinking and that of suicides, murders, and all kinds of violence, are contemporaneous.*

'The Times', October and December 1829

Gin is become a great demi-god, a mighty spirit dwelling in gaudy, gold-beplastered temples.

George Cruickshank, 'Sunday in London', 1833

The gas was bright, the night was dim!
In the noisy hour when I went in.
The wind it whistled, the air was cold,
And I welcomed so gladly the gin he sold.

From a broadsheet put out by Burgess's Wine and Spirit Stores, Great Saffron Hill, *c.* 1835

1

The Rise of the Gin Palace

IN THE years around 1830 educated people in England became violently and angrily gin-conscious. The lower orders, it was widely announced, were destroying themselves with gin. Beer was still commonly believed not only not to injure but actually to improve the human body. Gin was different. The gin scare started in the middle 1820s, when, as a result of Free Trade agitation and in order to reduce smuggling, the duty on spirits (together with that on tea and coffee) was drastically reduced: from *6s. 2d.* a gallon in Scotland and *5s. 7¼d.* in Ireland to *2s. 3¼d.* in both countries in 1823, and from *11s. 8¼d.* to *7s.* a gallon in England in 1825. The consumption of spirits (or rather of spirits which had paid duty) immediately doubled. Meanwhile, criminal convictions in the London area had quadrupled between 1811 and 1827, and gin was blamed for it.[1]

At the end of November 1829 the Middlesex Quarter Sessions, representing the justices who were responsible for licensing pubs in all London north of the river except the City, issued a much-publicised broadside: 'The attention of the Middlesex magistrates has been called to the demoralising consequences likely to ensue in the middling and lower classes from the alarming increase of gin-shops in every direction, in and around the metropolis, by the conversion of what used to be quiet respectable public-houses, where the labouring population could find the accommodation of a tap-room or parlour in which to take the meals or refreshment they might require, into flaming dram shops, having no accommodation for persons to sit down, and where the only allurement held out was the promise of "Cheap Gin". This court do most earnestly recommend to the Justices . . . not to license any publican who shall be found to have obtained a beer-licence, as a mere covert or pretext for obtaining a spirit-licence.'[2]

On 14 December *The Times* followed this up with a report that 'a correspondent states, that he watched one shop in Holborn, of great business, and saw, on an average, six individuals enter per minute, being equal to 360 in an hour'. The 'shop in Holborn' was immediately identified as the well-known establishment of Thompson and Fearon on Holborn Hill, commonly known as a gin shop, although, like all the gin shops, strictly speaking 'a wholesale and retail spirit and wine stores'. Here, according to a description of 1833, 'gin is served by young women dressed up like the "belles Limonadières" of a Paris Coffee House, and the establishment in all the parts is nearly as fine as Verey's or the Café de Paris'. A contemporary engraving (Plate 10) shows these same 'belles Limonadières' surveying a scene of riot and debauchery beneath huge spirit barrels, and Cruikshank caricatured it and a neighbouring gin shop with the caption 'The bell chimes to church and out stagger the queer 'uns, from Wellers in Old Street and Thompson and Fearons' (Plate 8).[3]

Anti-spirit societies were founded in Belfast and New Ross in the summer of 1829. They required total abstinence from spirits and moderation in other drinks from their members. Doctor John Edgar, the Belfast founder, celebrated his conversion by hurling the family whisky out of the parlour window. English societies followed in Bradford and Leeds in 1830, and the London Temperance Society, later to become the British and Foreign Temperance Society, had its first public meeting in June 1831. Meanwhile a separate campaign, inspired by the Free Traders, had been launched to abolish duty on beer and alter the licensing system. Spirit, beer and wine licences, for sale both on and off the premises, were all under the control of the local magistrates, who issued, renewed or refused them at annual 'Brewster' sessions. The magistrates' restriction of beer licences was said to encourage illegal beershops, and the glamour of illegal drinking to encourage drunkenness. The system was also criticized for increasing the monopoly of the big brewers and enabling them to keep up prices: they already owned around an eighth of London public houses, had lent money to many more publicans who were tied to buy their beer in return, and were accused of getting the lion's share of new licences because they came from the same class as the magistrates (and were often magistrates themselves). Cheap beer legally available everywhere would, it was hoped, be drunk in moderate quantities and keep people from gin.

Both anti-spirits and Free Trade movements were catered for by Wellington's Beer Act, which took effect from October 1830. All duty on beer was abolished and beer licences were taken out of the control of the licensing justices and made available to any householder who paid a two guinea fee. Within a year 31,000 new beer licences were issued and the total number of licensed houses in England and Wales increased from around 50,000 to 80,000 as a result.[4]

In spite of, or according to some critics because of, the Beer Act, gin shops continued to flourish. There are many highly coloured references to them in the literature of the 1830s, and by 1834 the alternative and much more picturesque term 'gin palace' had been coined for gin shops in the new flamboyant style.[5] Cruikshank weighed in with increasingly savage drawings and satire, and quoted as substantiation of his 'gaudy, gold-beplastered temples' a passage from Loudon's *Encyclopaedia of Cottage, Farm, and Villa Architecture and Furniture* of 1833: 'We may observe here that the fitting up of public house bars in London forms almost a distinct trade; and that the expense incurred in this way by the owners of public houses is almost incredible, everyone vying with his neighbour in convenient arrangement, general display, rich carving, brass-work, finely-veined mahogany, and ornamental painting. The carving of one ornament alone, in that of Mr. Weller, the Grapes, in Old Street Road, cost £100; the workmanship was by one of the finest carvers in wood in London. Three public houses, or rather gin-shops, have lately been fitted up in Lamb's Conduit Street, at an expense, for the bar alone, of upwards of £2000 each.'[6]

Gin shops and gin palaces figure prominently, and never favourably, in the evidence given before a Select Committee of the House of Commons 'on the Prevailing Vice of Drunkenness' held in 1834 under the chairmanship of James Silk-Buckingham, MP, an ardent Temperance advocate. The most vivid evidence was that of Mr George Wilson, a grocer of Tothill Street, Westminster: 'A public-house nearly opposite to my residence, where the consumption of spirits was very trifling, was taken for a gin-palace, it was converted into the very opposite of what it had been, a low dirty public-house, with only one doorway, into a splendid edifice, the front ornamented with pilasters, supporting a handsome cornice and entablature, and balustrades, and the whole elevation remarkably striking and hand-

9. Holborn Hill in about 1860, showing Fearon's (formerly Thompson and Fearon's) gin shop on left, with iron-work balcony

some; the doorways were increased in number from one, and that a small one only three or four feet wide, to three, and each of those three eight to 10 feet wide; the floor was sunk so as to be level with the street; and the doors and windows glazed with very large single squares of plate glass, and the gas fittings of the most costly description . . . When this edifice was completed, notice was given by placards taken round the parish by a number of men, that it would be opened on Saturday evening at six o'clock; a band of music was stationed in front of the house; the street became almost impassable from the number of people collected; and when the doors opened, the rush was tremendous; it was instantly filled with customers, and continued so till midnight.'[7]

Looking back today the whole 1830s gin scare appears exaggerated, the product not so much of an increase in drunkenness as an increasing middle-class awareness and disapproval of drunkenness, combined with a misreading of statistics and a conservative dislike of change in the traditional image of the public house. The dramatic increase in official spirit consumption was probably largely due to the shift from smuggled to legal spirits. Consumption had anyway reached its peak in 1828 and was slightly on the decline in 1829–32. The equally dramatic increase in criminal convictions can probably be explained as a result of more efficient police, and it is impossible to relate crime and drunkenness convincingly to one another.

The gin shops were crowded because they sold drink to take away as well as to consume on the premises; they were as much busy shops as busy bars. The drink which they sold was by no means only gin or spirits; most of them had beer licences, and the retail wine and spirit dealers claimed to be 'even in the absence of tap room accommodation . . . in many instances the largest vendors of malt liquors in the metropolis'.[8]

Even the 'flaming dram shops' now seem to have flamed mildly when compared to the pubs that were to be built later on in the century and even later on in the 1830s. There are two rival claimants for the distinction of being the first gin palace—an unidentified one designed by Stephen Geary, the architect who laid out Highgate Cemetery,[9] and Thompson and Fearon's, the wine and spirit stores already referred to, near the junction of Holborn Hill and Field Lane and opposite Wren's St Andrew's Church. A correspondent made the claim for Thompson and Fearon's in *Notes and Queries* in 1890 and appears to be backed up by Henry Vizetelly in his *Glances Back through Seventy Years*: 'It was near Field Lane that the first London Gin Palace was built. The polished mahogany counters, the garish bar fittings, the smartly painted vats, inscribed 'Old Tom' and 'Cream of the Valley', the rows of showy bottles of noyau and other cordials, and above all the immense blaze of gas light within and without these buildings as soon as dusk set in, were all so many novelties and came as a vision of splendour to the besotted denizens of the neighbouring slums. I remember that one of these so-called palaces had a second and lower counter for the accommodation of the children and juvenile thieves it counted among its patrons.'[10]

The shop front of Thompson and Fearon's is clearly shown in a very detailed drawing of Holborn Hill made in about 1860, just before the houses were demolished to make way for Holborn Viaduct (Plate 9). It comes as something of a shock to see that this infamous gin palace consisted of a very modest and even elegant little shop under a plain facade with an ornamental cornice. The design is, in fact, exactly what one would expect from the architect, who is known from another source to have been J. B. Papworth, the creator of Regency Cheltenham.[11] Inside, according to Henry Bradshaw Fearon's own account (in an indignant pamphlet published in 1830 in response to the *Times* article), the public part of the establishment consisted of only one room, 15 feet wide by 11 feet 8 inches deep; certainly the drawing bears this out.[12] The engraving said to be of the interior (Plate 10), once the drunken clientele are removed and the spirit barrels reduced from their obviously exaggerated size, also subsides to something which, if not exactly self-effacing, is modest compared to the pub interiors of the 1890s.

Cruikshank's engraving 'Gin-temple turn-out at church time' (Plate 8) bears no resemblance to Thompson and Fearon's, and so can be surmised to be 'Wellers in Old Street', the 'Mr. Weller, the Grapes, in Old Street Road' where, according to Loudon, one ornament cost £100. If so, it was clearly not a large establishment, though a little gaudier than Thompson and Fearon's. Cruikshank's drawing shows only the ground floor and has an obvious element of caricature in it. The engravings on surviving trade circulars of the period provide more complete and reliable

10. Engraving said to show the interior of Thompson and Fearon's gin shop, Holborn Hill

evidence of what the early gin palaces actually looked like (Plate 11). They show what was to become the standard London pub formula, but it is still very much in the bud: continuous shop-type windows punctuated by columns or pilasters, external lighting bracketed out between the ground and first floors, stucco enrichments to the windows, and the name of the establishment inscribed on the parapet and fascia. In the course of the next thirty years the enrichments were to become lusher, the lights to multiply and swell, single sheets of plate glass to replace the smaller panes, the name-tablet to be made more elaborate and the inscriptions to sprawl over more and more of the facades. The beginnings were modest enough, and one can take with a grain of salt the sums of thousands of pounds mentioned by Loudon and others.

But if the relative modesty of the first gin palaces seems to bear little relationship to the fuss they caused and the lurid descriptions they evoked, one must remember that people in the 1830s did not have the benefit of our knowledge of the future. They judged gin shops by what they were beginning to replace.

This was the traditional public house, which had been evolving over many centuries and which (though the term was very loosely used at the time) can conveniently be referred to as the tavern.[13] A standard early nineteenth-century tavern was scarcely distinguishable from the houses which surrounded it. Its ground floor accommodation usually consisted of five separate rooms: a public parlour, tap room, bar, kitchen and publican's private parlour. The last two of these were not accessible to the public, except, perhaps, in a few village taverns where the old

DREWRY'S

WINE AND SPIRIT ESTABLISHMENT,

SHIP AND SUN, 33, CROSBY ROW, WALWORTH ROAD.

arrangement of serving working men in the kitchen still survived. Elsewhere they went to the tap room. This was usually sturdily and simply furnished with wooden tables, fixed wooden benches round the walls, and a large open fireplace. In contrast the public parlour was for the more genteel customers and had pictures, higher quality furnishings, chairs rather than benches, and perhaps a marble chimney-piece with a mirror over it. Food was usually served up in the tap room or the parlour. Superior taverns had a coffee room for their middle-class customers; this, confusingly, was not a room for coffee but what today would be called a restaurant, usually divided up by low partitions into separate stalls for each table. Drinks in all parts were brought to the customer by waiters, barmaids, or pot-boys, for there was no bar in our current sense of a counter over which drinks could be purchased.

The bar in most early nineteenth-century taverns was a separate, self-contained room into which the public could not enter. Loudon, who has a large section on country inns and public houses in his *Encyclopaedia*, defines it as 'the bar or office, to which all enquiries are addressed, and from which all orders are issued. This is always placed in a conspicuous part of the interior, so as to be seen on entering, and so as the bar mistress may observe all comers and goers as they pass.'[14] It approximated, in fact, to the reception desk and office in a modern hotel. It was often surrounded by glazed partitions to give it a good view and could be furnished with 'an iron-safe or chest' and 'pigeonholes, marked with the letters of the alphabet'. 'Adjoining the bar there is usually the private room of the master and mistress of the house; and the larder, and general store room are commonly near,

11. Trade circular for Drewry's (the Ship and Sun), Walworth

and within sight of it.' Glasses, tankards and any drink that was not in the cellar were in the store; in the smaller public houses the bar and the store were often the same room.

Of much more recent origin than the tavern, and with a different *raison d'être*, was the spirit store or dram shop. This was a city phenomenon dating from the eighteenth century when cheap gin was first sold in large quantities in London. It was, as its name suggested, a shop, known by the name of the proprietor, with no parlour, no tap room, no seats and no food: wine, spirits and sometimes, to a lesser extent, beer were sold across the counter either to take away or to drink standing on the premises.

At some time, probably in the early years of the nineteenth century, a dram shop element began to appear in some public houses. The practice came in of opening up one side of the bar with a counter, behind which were kept glasses, tankards and the drink that was not in the cellar; from it not only all orders but also all drink was issued. In addition to a number of traditional plans, Loudon in his *Encyclopaedia* also published a 'Suburban Public House in the Old English Style' in order 'to show the arrangement of the bar and counter in those public houses which are supported chiefly by the sale of liquors in small quantities, either drunk in the shop, standing at the counter, or carried home in brought vessels by the purchasers'[15] (Fig. 1). It still has the conventional tap room and public parlour, but a third room is divided across the middle by a counter. To one side of this is the 'shop, or place for standing customers', a very much smaller space than the tap room or parlour; the other is the 'bar'. Two drawings show how this is fitted out (Plates 12, 13). It is in effect a little room open to one side with casks and vats for spirits, shelves for glasses and pewter, a fireplace and a counter fitted with a sink, drawers, shelves, twelve cocks connected by tubes to spirit casks on the top shelves, and 'a six-motion beer machine to draw the beer and ale from the butts in the cellar'. A door at the back of the bar leads into the private parlour.

However modestly the counter was first introduced, it was a revolutionary innovation. It immediately began to erode the whole traditional image of the tavern as a house: a house that was (to a certain extent) public instead of private, but still a house. The owner of the house made some of his rooms available to the public, but his relation to them was that of a host ('mine host') to his guests; the rooms were furnished like rooms in a private house; visitors were looked after according to their status as they would be in a private house, the upper ranks by waiters instead of footmen in the parlour, the lower by pot-boys in the tap room instead of the servants' hall; the bar, in Loudon's words, was 'the housekeeper's room placed in a conspicuous situation instead of in a private one'. Above all, a public house from the outside looked exactly like a private house, except for the signboard hanging over the door.

Introducing a counter immediately introduced the image of a shop where goods were sold over the counter to customers—instead of guests—by shopkeepers who advertised their goods. The change is gently underlined in the exterior of Loudon's 'suburban public house'. This is indistinguishable from a Gothic villa except in one

12, 13. Details of the bar and beer-engine for a 'suburban public house' in J. C. Loudon's *Encyclopaedia of Cottage, Farm and Villa Architecture and Furniture*, 1833

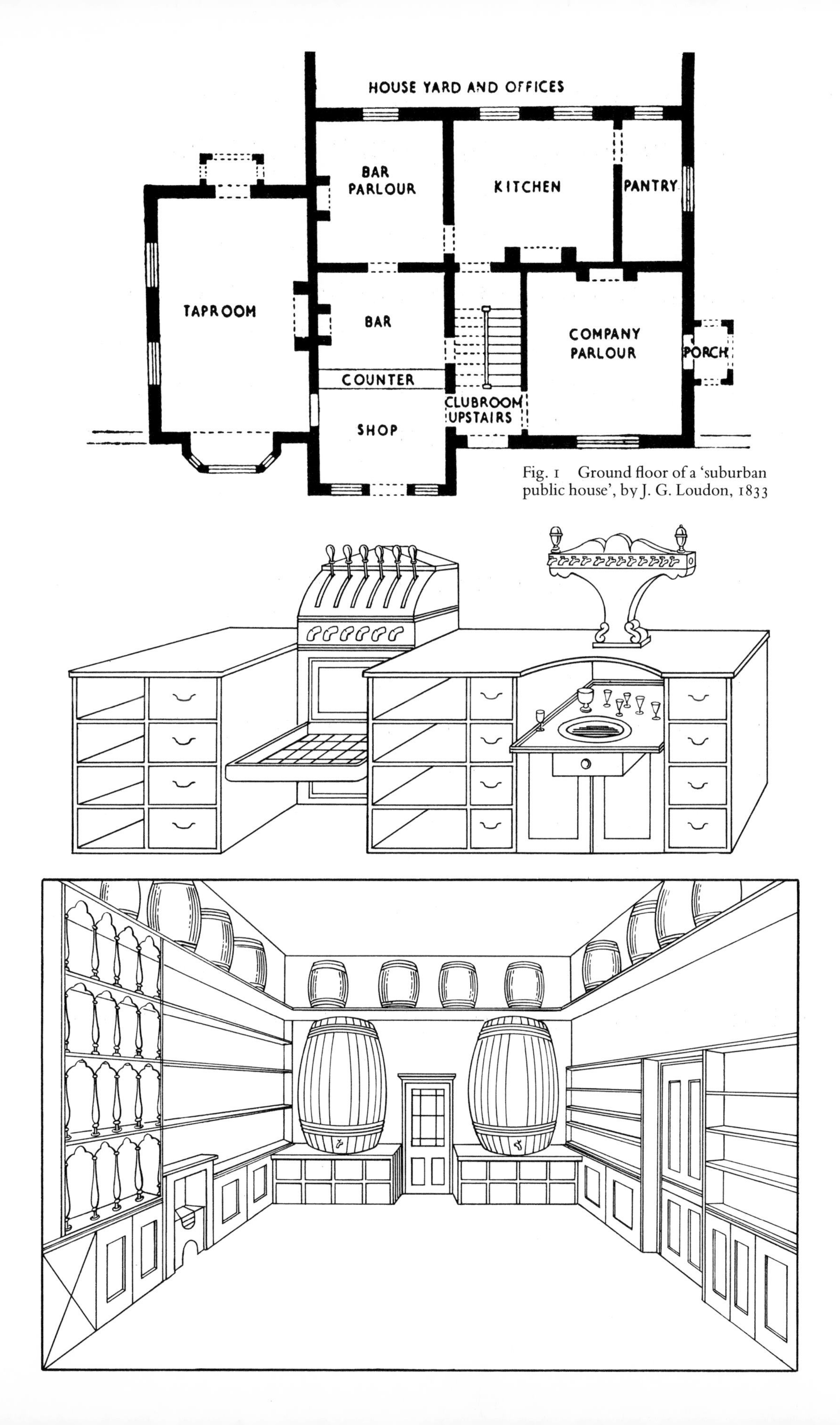

Fig. 1 Ground floor of a 'suburban public house', by J. G. Loudon, 1833

particular: the front of the 'shop or place for standing customers' is, however inconspicuously, a shop front.

The shop fronts of its equivalents were rather more conspicuous, and had been so for some years. Loudon's suburban public house was designed for him by William Robert Laxton, whom Loudon describes as having 'had great experience in fitting up public houses'. Laxton had been connected with the drink trade since at least 1804, when he designed a new brewery for Meux and Company: two more breweries followed in 1810.[16] It may be surmised that he helped to introduce the shop front and bar with counter service to the city pub. Both features were established at least by 1820. In that year one of George Cruikshank's *Tom and Jerry* cartoons (drawn before his teetotal days) shows a sizable counter fitted into what is clearly a tavern rather than a dram shop, for it has a parlour upstairs. A design by Thomas Cubitt, also made in 1820, for the Albion in Bloomsbury shows a shop front extended along both exposed sides of what is otherwise a standard brick corner house with no frills. Inside, the plan was very similar to that of Loudon's suburban public house, with a parlour, a tap room and a small bar.[17]

The Albion's shop front filled the entire available length of facade, but it was not at all eye-catching. In this it followed the style of shops of the time (Plate 14). But during the 1820s London shops underwent what amounted to a revolution. A new feeling for salesmanship combined with two new inventions, gas lighting and plate glass, to produce shop fronts that acted as advertisements of the goods sold in the shops. Gas was an especially effective form of advertising in the twenties and thirties because public gas lighting was only just beginning to be introduced into the streets, so that any gas-lit shop front was immediately conspicuous. Salesmanship continued inside, with elegant fittings, well-displayed goods, and well-turned-out shop girls. The innovation naturally spread to the gin shops; the significance of Papworth's employment by Thompson and Fearon was that he was one of the pioneers of the improved shop front and designed at least twelve in London between 1814 and 1834. The process of change was vividly described by Dickens, who compared it to an epidemic working its way through drapers, haberdashers, chemists and hosiers until 'it burst forth with tenfold violence among the publicans and keepers of "wine-vaults" . . . onward it has rushed to every part of the town, knocking down all the old public houses, and depositing splendid mansions, stone balustrades, rosewood fittings, immense lamps, and illuminated clocks at the corner of every street'.[18]

Even without the advertising trimmings, the spread of the dram shop formula would probably have been assured, because it served the needs of a rapidly expanding city. The bar with counter service and taps and cocks connected to the alcohol supply made possible an infinitely quicker turnover than the traditional service by waiters scuffling in and out of storerooms and cellars. Quick turnover and quick service were an obvious advantage in public houses for which either casual passers-by or off-sales made up an important part of their custom. Many of the people pouring in and out of the gin palaces (including the children, who so shocked contemporaries) were in fact collecting drink for home consumption; Thompson and

Fearon reckoned that about a third of their customers and a good deal more than a third of their takings came from this side of their trade.[19] Moreover, as London rapidly expanded and before any form of public transport was introduced, more and more working people were walking farther and farther along the great thoroughfares that led into the centre of the city, and a place where they could stop in for a quick drink was both convenient and attractive to them.

Quick turnover also had obvious advantages when the customers had little money to spend. Gin palaces in the neighbourhood of the now rapidly increasing slum quarters could quickly divest customers of their money and, with no seats or other attractions to keep them, encourage them to leave as quickly as possible to make room for fresh customers. Although gin shops spread over the whole of London, it was those in the slum neighbourhoods, the gin shops in Old Street, Lamb's Conduit Street and Holborn to the north, Tothill Street in Westminster, and the New Cut south of the river, which attracted unfavourable publicity, because they drew out the inhabitants of the neighbouring rookeries and tenements with the blandishments of bright light and cheap gin. Their customers tended to get drunk because semi-starving people get drunk very easily. It was not a pretty system, but it was as much due to the society that had notoriously failed to house or feed

14. Shop-type front of *c.* 1820–30 in the Grenadier, Old Barrack Yard, Belgravia

Public Office,

No. 12,

Walworth Road.

Redford & Robins, Printers, London Road.

£200. REWARD. *MISSING, from VICKRESS's White Hart, No. 12, Walworth Road, between the 1st of October and the 1st of November, Ten Thousand Gallons of Gin, also an immense quantity of Rum, Brandy, Wines, &c.; and these being of the very best quality, there seems no doubt but the parties who have been partakers of them are well satisfied, or some of them before this time would have been returned to their original owner, or at least complained of; but as no such occurrence has taken place, and the parties persist in their privilege of taking it for the benefit of their health, the £200. will be awarded to those who can contradict the right of His Majesty's Subjects buying where they find the first-rate articles at the following extraordinary low prices*

	PINT.	QTS.		PINT.	QTS.
Strong Cordial Gin for	1s. 0d.	3d.	Fine Old Cognac Brandy	3s. 4d.	10d.
Walworth Cream	1 2	3½	Fine old Port or Sherry Wine	1 8	5
Jamaica Rum	1 6	4½	Very fine Cape	1 0	3

Which for quality are not to be surpassed by any House in the Trade. A private Bar, for Jugs and Bottles.

a vast new immigrant population as to the publicans, who at least gave their customers warmth and some form of glamour as an escape from the squalor in which they lived. But the middle classes were shocked to see the face of poverty exposed and dramatized, especially when it was dramatized in what Cruikshank called 'gold-beplastered temples'. The 1830s saw the first beginnings of one of the major nineteenth-century marketing discoveries, that if the turnover is big enough there is money to be made out of the poor and they can be given something approaching the amenities of the rich. The rich found this very upsetting.

As far as can be judged from rather inadequate evidence, the dram shop formula spread to the taverns less because tavern keepers imitated the dram shops than because a new type of publican was buying up taverns and converting them. Conversion, wherever it can be checked up on, was always preceded by a change in management. One can suspect that these new-style publicans had had previous experience as wine and spirit retailers in the dram shop trade, which was undeniably their model. The change invariably followed a similar pattern: not only was the building altered or rebuilt on the lines already described, but it proclaimed itself a 'wine and spirit' stores; its new licensee suppressed or played down its tavern name (in small letters) in favour of his own (in very large ones) and inaugurated a lively campaign of advertising. A band played on the opening day, sandwich-board men paraded, almanacs were presented free to customers, from time to time drink was sold at a loss to bring in trade, and a barrage of eye-catching broadsheets and circulars plugged the charms of the establishment and the cheapness of its drink in doggerel verse, riddles or acrostics (Plates 15, 16, 17).

Conversion could produce establishments varying from those which had a large bar but kept a tap room and parlour to those (usually on the main thoroughfares) that had a large bar and nothing else. Most of the wine and spirit stores also sold beer, and even advertised it, although spirits got the lion's share. Among the spate of broadsheets put out by W. Vickress's Wine and Spirit Mart (the White Hart), Walworth Road, between 1835 and 1839, one is entirely devoted to a series of verses extolling the establishment's stout:

> Whose is the Cheapest STOUT in Town,
> Real malty, smooth, imperial brown,
> And brewed by brewers or renown?
> 'TIS VICKRESS.[20]

15, 16, 17. Gin shop broadsheets of the 1830s

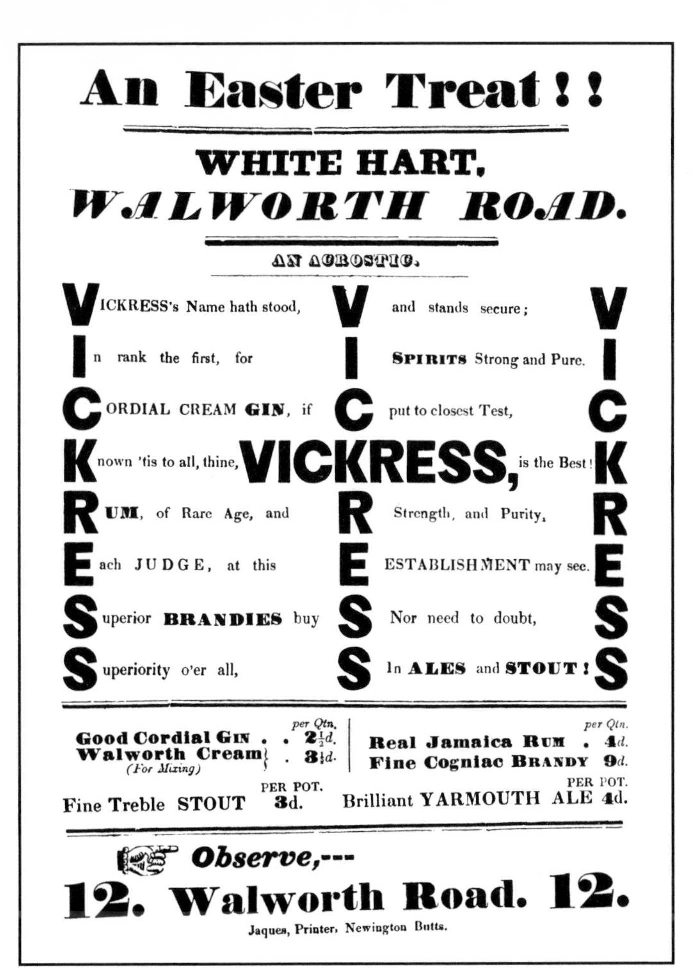

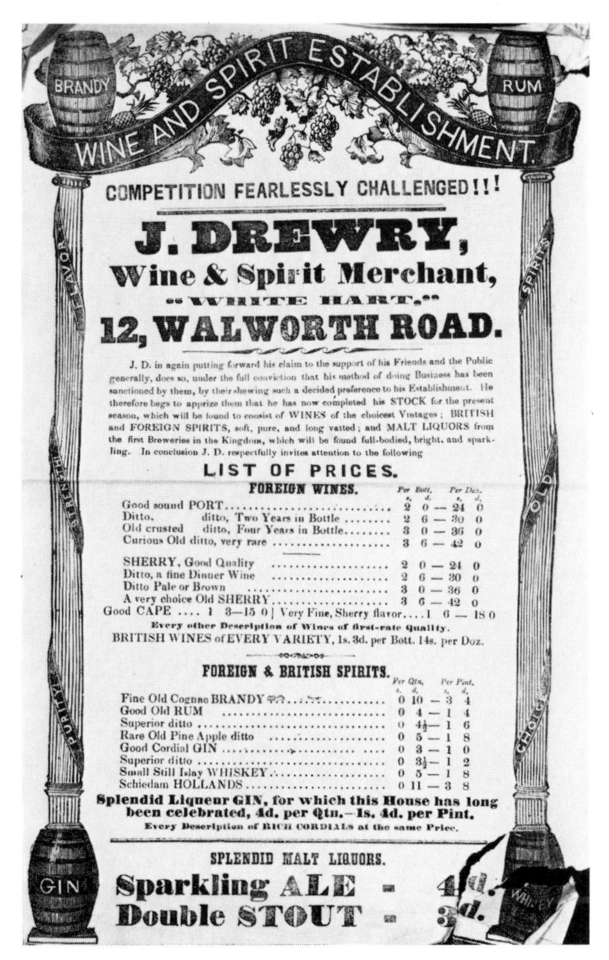

Burgess's Wine and Spirit Stores on Great Saffron Hill (round the corner from Thompson and Fearon's) posed the riddle, 'Why is Burgess like an undertaker?' Answer: 'Because he does great business in the bier (beer) way'.[21] Beer varied from 3*d.* to 4*d.* a pint, gin from 3*d.* to 4½*d.* a quartern (quarter of a pint) depending on the quality. Rum cost 4*d.* to 4½*d.* a quartern, brandy 9*d.* to 10*d.* and port 5*d.* Beer was normally bought by the pint, gin by the glass containing a gill (eighth of a pint). In 1830 Thompson and Fearon, who sold no beer, reckoned that their orders worked out on the proportion of nine of gin (in glasses) to nine of rum (chiefly in half glasses), one of brandy (in one-third glasses), and four of port. Whisky was on sale, but little drunk except by the Irish; it was not till after the mid-century that it overtook gin in popularity.[22]

There is no doubt that, as the Middlesex justices and others complained, many of these converted taverns ceased to provide food. But this did not necessarily mean that working men were left with nowhere to go. The period that saw the spread of gin shops also saw the spread of coffee shops. Both were stimulated by the excise reductions of 1825, which applied to coffee as well as spirits. The coffee shops of the 1820s and 1830s differed from the coffee houses of the eighteenth century in that they were aimed at working men. They provided coffee, cheap meals and newspapers. It seems likely that by 1830 they were a serious competitor to the taverns; their success may have been one reason why tavern keepers were ready to sell up to spirit dealers. For these the existence of the coffee shops provided an excellent excuse for giving up what was probably the least paying branch of their trade in favour of more room at the bar.[23]

By 1837, too, there were 40,000 beerhouses in England and Wales as a competing attraction to the fully licensed houses. At the time and since, the gin palace has often been explained as the publican's answer to the beerhouse; as R. E. Broughton, a City police magistrate, put it to the Buckingham Committee in 1834: 'They [the beerhouses] very much interfered with the business of the regular publicans . . . and this is the cause of a great number of what are called in the newspapers gin palaces. The old public houses, where a man could have his steak dressed, and sit down and take his ale, are extinct; they are obliged to convert them into splendid houses, and sell gin at the bar.'[24] No doubt the existence of the beerhouses did put pressure on publicans to provide an alternative attraction and encouraged the spread of the gin palace formula. But they certainly did not create the gin palace, for it existed before the Beer Act of 1830. It was the result of a more complex series of pressures, as the fully licensed houses attempted to adapt themselves to a changing sales market as well as to keep their end up against competition.

There is little evidence that they did more than keep their end up. The furore about gin palaces might lead one to think that the consumption of spirits was soaring upwards in the 1830s; in fact only in 1836 did it overtop the consumption of 1828 (when the gin palace movement was scarcely under way), and in the ten years after 1836 consumption was, with variations, in general on the decline. Similarly, the creation of the beerhouse led only to a temporary and not very large increase in beer consumption. In the immediate euphoria of the Beer Act, as Sydney Smith put it, 'everybody is drunk. Those who are not singing are sprawling. The sovereign people are in a beastly state.'[25] But from 1836 beer consumption, like that of spirits, was generally on the decline. The blandishments of advertising and numbers were less powerful than an economic stagnation that by and large continued until the end of the 1840s.

But the Beer Act had one important and unexpected consequence. Before it was passed, licensing magistrates had had complete control over the numbers of public houses, and they had kept a tight hold on their increase as a result. They now saw little point in limiting the number of fully licensed houses which at least were under their control, when beerhouses could increase *ad infinitum* without their having the power to stop them. Until 1869, when the beerhouse licensing system was returned to the control of the magistrates, the number of fully licensed houses steadily increased; after 1899 the number levelled out, and from 1880 it steadily decreased, although the population was getting larger. This decline was to have an enormous effect on the architectural development of the public house.

18. Three stages in the life of the Black Prince, Walworth Road, in 1830, in the late 1830s, and in 1840

All parts of the metropolis discover, at every turn, large buildings of splendid elevation fitted up in a style of grandeur, not to say elegance, quite unsuited to the rational demands of the humbler classes that throng them daily . . . the corner public is radiant of gas, redolent of mahogany, and glittering in mirrors! There are no settles, no stools . . . the old and dun colored taps and parlors are all transformed into gorgeous saloons or refulgent halls; or else the drawing-room is arranged as a theatre for music, song, and scenic performances.

'Building News', 15 May 1857

2 The Development of the Pub 1840–80

MOVING from the London pub of the middle 1830s to the London pub of the middle fifties is curiously like returning to the same conversation after twenty years. The plan types appear to have changed remarkably little. Cruikshank is still rolling out his anti-gin cartoons, which grow increasingly savage after he takes the pledge in 1848. The educated classes are still complaining about the growing numbers and excessive splendours of the gin palaces, and the foolish desire of the lower orders to live above their stations.

There are changes, however. In the first place these same educated classes are rapidly abandoning public houses for clubs, magnificent Italian palazzi which allow them, too, to live above their station. Secondly, publicans have discovered a new attraction to boost their sales; the music, song and scenic performances referred to by the *Building News* are the lively embryos which are about to develop into the music-halls. Finally, pubs are coming rather closer to the splendours luridly described by their critics than they ever did in the gin scare of the early 1830s.

The process can be nicely followed even in the course of the 1830s by looking at three circulars (Plate 18) put out for the same house in Walworth Road by three successive proprietors.[1] As run in 1831 by George Edwards, 'importer of foreign wines and spirits', its shop front and stucco facade were of a comparatively modest nature. By the late thirties, under George, Charles and William Parker, Wine and Brandy Merchants, it has sprouted an elaborate pedimented tablet at parapet level, containing the licensee's name and a clock; and Edwards's modest single lamp over the entrance has been replaced by three very large ones spread round the two street

19. The Adam and Eve, Petty France, SW1 (*c.* 1840), photographed before rebuilding in 1881

facades. By 1840 W. Jones (late of the Alfred's Head) has turned it into the Black Prince Wine and Spirit Establishment, enlarged it at the back, extended the length of the shop front and replaced its original design by an arcade of ten arches, glazed with much bigger sheets of glass and lit up by eight lamps bracketed out above the Corinthian pilasters.

The Black Prince (which was to be completely rebuilt in 1876) or even the decorative little Adam and Eve in Petty France (Plate 19) pales beside its contemporary, the Eagle in Shepherdess Walk off the City Road, rebuilt in 1839–40 (Plate 20). The Eagle set a new standard of splendour for public houses which was not to be equalled for many years.[2] But then, the Eagle was unlike any other pub. The original tavern, with a garden at the back, was acquired in the 1820s by Thomas Rouse. He developed it into one of the main pleasure resorts in early Victorian London. Its amenities can be gathered from an advertisement of 1838, listing 'the pleasure grounds, the collection of statuary, the garden orchestra, the fountains, the gas devices, the brilliant illuminations of variegated lamps, in stars, wreaths, and mottos; the beautifully painted cosmoramas, the set scenes in the grounds, the magic mirrors, the Olympic Temple, the Saloon, the double band, the great French rope-dancers, with the infant prodigies, the Grotesque brothers, standard and select vaudevilles, laughable ballets, and the peculiar extravaganza, the *pas de coco*, together with a first rate concert of vocal and instrumental music'.

The 'Saloon' was the famous Grecian Saloon, built to put on the entertainments which Rouse has originally started in the upper room of the tavern. A separate

20. The Eagle Tavern, City Road (1839-40)

building in the pleasure-gardens, it was first opened in 1831 and remodelled in 1837–8. By then the grounds were filled with different buildings of exotic and elaborate design, containing caves, grottoes, alcoves and little refreshment rooms for patrons to retire to; was claimed that 10,000 people could be accommodated. The original tavern was now dwarfed by its offspring and was rebuilt in 1839–40. One would dearly like to know the name of the architect, for it was a magnificently robust classical design, towering above the surrounding houses, with four eagles perched on the parapet above tablets containing the name of the proprietor. Inside, a hall painted in imitation of marble, with coffee rooms to one side and bars and bar parlour to the other, ended in a spacious stone staircase, which led up to 'a magnificent lofty and well-proportioned ballroom, with orchestra, capable of holding several hundred persons'. Marble chimney-pieces abounded, and 'the walls throughout are stuccoed and painted and the whole of the woodwork is grained'.

Thomas Rouse, the creator of the Eagle, was a unique figure in many ways, but he had one feature in common with many of his contemporary publicans: he was a speculative builder by origin. Wine and spirit merchants converting old pubs dominate the pub world of the 1830s, builders building new ones that of the forties and fifties. In London in the late twenties and the thirties there had been a depression which extended to the building trade; but the forties and fifties were more prosperous, and the frontiers of London once more began to advance over the countryside. The process was vividly described in the *Builder* of 25 February 1854: 'On the pastures lately set out for building you may see a double line of trenches with excavation either side . . . and a tavern of imposing elevation standing alone and quite complete, waiting the approaching rows of houses. The propinquity of these palaces to each other in Camden and Kentish New Towns is quite ridiculous. At a distant of 200 paces in every direction they glitter in sham splendour . . . the object of erecting them is to obtain a larger sum than the builder can acquire for any other species of property, and this will continue to be the case so long as the present *licensing system* is maintained. In some instances one speculative builder, reserving all the angle plots, runs up half-a-dozen public houses; he obtains licences for all that he can, and lets or sells such at incredible prices or enormous rentals—: others he sells to adventuring publicans who try for the privilege, or, in case of failure, open as beer shops at war with the Bench . . . from £2000 to £3000 is an ordinary price, and for good standings £5000 to £8000 is not infrequent.'

Recent research into the development of Pimlico and North Kensington in the 1840s and 1850s has confirmed the accuracy of the *Builder*'s picture.[3] The pattern of landownership and development in early and mid-Victorian London varied enormously. Major landowners, like the Marquess of Westminster, handed over their property to be developed by major speculative builders, like Thomas Cubitt. Others, like Felix Ladbroke on Notting Hill and Lord Holland around Holland Park, parcelled out their property among numerous different speculators or speculative builders. At the other end of the scale were the small landowners developing a few acres. But whatever the variations in landownership, the patterns when it finally came to putting up the houses remained much the same: a patchwork of builders putting up a row of houses or a street or a block but not much more. Even the great Cubitt developed only selected portions of the Grosvenor estate with his own work force, and subcontracted out the rest to smaller builders.

Many of these individual building blocks included a pub. In Notting Hill, for instance, the Prince of Wales, Princedale Road, was built by James Emmins in about 1845 along with seven adjoining houses. The Pembridge Castle and six houses in Ledbury Road were put up after 1846 by William Cullingford, a builder who afterward erected large numbers of houses in the district. The Campden Arms (now the Winston Churchill), Campden Street, was built about 1849 by Henry Gilbert, 'builder and victualler', along with seven adjoining houses.[4] The pub was often the first part of a speculation to be built, with the builder as the first licensee. This had two advantages for the builder. It gave him a base in which his workmen could drink, eat and be paid, in effect a combined site office and canteen; and the lease could be sold off at a good price (for licensed premises always fetched more than unlicensed ones) to raise capital to finance the rest of the development. The Prince Albert in Kensington Park Road, Notting Hill, to take one example, was the first building put up by William Chadwick, a builder who leased land from the Ladbroke estate and afterwards covered it with what are now the villas and terraces of Ladbroke Road, Kensington Park Road, and Pembridge Road; in about 1850, when development was almost completed, he built a second pub, the Sun in Splendour, in Pembridge Road.[5]

Sometimes a pub could stand a long time waiting the approaching rows of houses. Victorian property development in the forties and fifties tended to outrun demand, especially in the mid-forties, when there was a recession and bankruptcies were frequent. The most notorious disaster in North Kensington was that of Dr Samuel Walker, a property-speculating clergyman who bought up land at inflated prices around Talbot Road and the northern stretches of Ladbroke Grove, and managed to lose £180,000 between inheriting a fortune in 1851 and collapsing financially in 1855. One of his few buildings which got off the ground was the Elgin at the corner of Ladbroke Grove and Westbourne Park Road, which stood alone in 1860 except for a Poor Clares convent and the melancholy shell of the uncompleted All Saints, Talbot Road, several hundred yards away. It was described as the only building 'in a dreary waste of mud and stunted trees . . . with the wind howling and vagrants prowling in the speculative warnings around them'.[6]

The distance of 200 paces between pubs described by the *Builder* is no exaggeration; indeed the intervals could be even smaller. Thomas Cubitt sometimes covenanted with the builder to whom he was sub-contracting a pub that no others would be allowed within a certain distance; on a busy road it was considered a good concession to have a monopoly of 300 feet either way. Cubitt prided himself that 'my plan has been to allow fewer public houses than is generally done by other builders'. In 1847 he wrote to the Commission of Woods and Forests pointing out that a proportion of one pub to 160 houses and wharves as well was 'considerably less than the usual average. I am always particular on this point so that the Publicans may have sufficient trade to keep their houses in respectable order.'[7] One pub to 160 houses, at an average density for middle-class housing, works out at a pub about every 200 yards. Chadwick's two pubs at Notting Hill were part of a development of 114 houses (but with a larger catchment area) and stood about 500 feet apart.

If their plot included a corner site, builders almost invariably put the pub on it; failing that they made it close a vista down a street. They seldom seem to have had difficulty in getting licences; the fact that if they were refused one they could not be stopped from opening the house as a beerhouse, 'at war with the bench' as the *Builder* put it, weighed the scales heavily in their favour. Numbers were more likely to be kept down by the developers than the licensing magistrates: the social status of early Victorian pubs is nicely demonstrated by Cubitt's exclusion of them in aristocratic Belgravia from everywhere except the mews; in middle-class Pimlico, on the other hand, he allowed them into the main residential streets, but kept them out of the squares.

A builder who built a pub and installed himself as the licensee usually sold it after a year or two, or even sooner, either to another publican or, less often, to a brewery. Paul Felthouse, builder, for instance, who built and obtained a licence for the Warwick Castle in Portobello Road, sold it for £3,000 in 1853, on a ninety-nine-year lease to Sir Harry Meux, the brewer.[8] Felthouse built nothing else in the area, and seems to have been one of the occasional examples of builders who specialized largely or entirely in pubs, instead of putting them up as part of a larger development. Another example was Robert Clements, builder, of Kingston, whose only contribution to the Norland Estate off Holland Park Road was the handsome Norland Arms (Plate 23) in Addison Avenue.[9] Paul Dangerfield was involved in a number of pubs in the Cubitt developments, starting with the Lowndes Arms in Belgravia as early as 1829. In Pimlico he built the Perseverance, Lupus Street, in 1840–3, the Morpeth Arms, Millbank (in partnership with Richard Lacy, who was building houses in the area), in 1845 and the Kenilworth (now the Greyhound), Cambridge Street, in 1847. In or off the Caledonian Road he built the City of Rome and the Offord Arms with three adjoining houses in 1847. He moved in as the licensee of the Offord Arms, while the Morpeth Arms was initially kept by William Dangerfield, perhaps his brother; one or the other of them must have briefly kept the Perseverance, for a skittish piece written about Cubitt's foremen about 1840 advises one of them 'not to pay so much attention to Miss Dangerfield at the Perseverance'.[10]

In addition to builders who were also publicans there were publicans who became builders and builders who retired into pubs. George Ingersent, for instance, who was erecting houses in large numbers on the Archer estate in Westbourne Grove around 1850, was in financial trouble in 1854; he built the Mall Tavern and three adjacent houses in Kensington Mall in 1855 and went into the tavern as licensee, having, as the *Survey of London* puts it, 'evidently exchanged building for the less frenetic trade of licensed victualler'.[11] The reverse procedure took place in the case of Charles Chambers of St Marylebone, who abandoned his pub in the 1860s and covered the western edge of the Holland estate with mean but profitable houses.[12]

A good many builders probably acted as their own designers of both their pubs and their houses, but occasionally the name of a separate architect is preserved. Stephen Phillips, for instance, who was a speculator rather than a builder, employed an architect, William King, on his projects in Islington, Westbourne Park and Brompton. These included the Walmer Castle (1852–3) in Ledbury Road, a robust and capable design which handsomely closes the vista down Lonsdale Road (Plate 21). Its greater height, row of pedimented windows and boldly scrolled name-tablet, clearly mark it out as a pub from the four adjoining shops and houses, which were part of the same speculation. Generally speaking, although a few extra trimmings, a foot or two of extra height, perhaps even an extra storey or a row of pilasters, and of course the big plate glass windows along the ground floor, distinguished pubs in residential districts from the adjoining houses, they were recognizably of a piece with them. This was scarcely surprising, as they were usually put up by the same builder. Some pubs were grander than others but few approached the splendour of the Eagle and some, especially in the 1840s, were scarcely distinguishable from ordinary terrace houses. Pubs serving an estate of detached or semi-detached villas sometimes assumed a villa character themselves, like the old Swiss Cottage in St John's Wood, or the Bath Tavern in Asylum Road, Peckham. The latter was at the end of a row of villas, all of which have been destroyed; its two Italianate towers unmistakeably related it to them, but its

21. The Walmer Castle, Ledbury Road, Notting Hill (William King, 1852-3)

elongated pilasters and elongated window-strips gave it a curious hallucinatory effect, as though it had been stretched like a piece of chewing gum (Plate 22).

The ground floor fronts of the pubs of this period have usually been completely remodelled, or at least reglazed; the Doric columns and ironwork railings of the Norland Arms, Addison Avenue, give some idea of how handsome they could be (Plate 23). The ground floor bars have also almost invariably been very much changed; it is sometimes possible to work out the main lines of the original layout from the surviving fabric, but the few surviving contemporary plans are more reliable evidence. In spite of the fuss made at the time, the gin palace plan with its one big bar was still very far from universal. In residential areas, in particular, where there was a regular local clientele, the traditional tavern plan survived with only minor modifications.

Designs for a pub of this type, by E. L. Tarbuck, are given in the *Builders' Practical Directory*, a fat and copiously illustrated copybook for London builders published

22. (left) The Bath Tavern, Asylum Road, Peckham

23. The Norland Arms, Addison Avenue, Holland Park (Robert Clements, 1850)

about 1855 (Plate 24 and Fig. 4). They are for a 'first class tavern', and the exterior seems just what a gin palace should be, with lush Italianate detailing and big double plate glass windows all the way around the two exposed facades on the ground floor. One would have expected the windows to be lighting a single large bar, but in fact the interior is very close to Loudon's suburban public house; the bar is the pivot of the plan but it takes up comparatively little of the ground floor, the lion's share of which is given to the kitchen, tap room, public parlour and bar parlour. The tap room has shrunk to a small room and is described as 'by no means a necessary adjunct to a Tavern'. The customers' part of the bar (what Loudon called the 'shop') is divided into a very small 'private bar' and a larger 'public bar'; the description 'bar' has, in fact, been extended to the space on either side of the counter, and from the 1850s onwards this was the normal usage. The public bar is for 'casual customers' and the private for 'orders'; neither has seats. A hatch from the serving bar allows convenient waiter service to the parlour and tap room. On the first floor there is a very large club room, also usable for public meetings, a small billiard room, and a very small coffee room 'for the better class of customers'. The second floor contains bedrooms and a private sitting room.

The 'bar parlour' had developed since the 1830s. In Loudon's suburban public house it was basically the private family parlour of the traditional tavern, but placed behind the bar. In the course of the 1840s it assumed a semi-private, semi-public character; it became the sanctum of the publican, into which favoured customers came by invitation only, but in which they continued to pay for their drinks. As a result of this dilution of privacy, pubs started to have a separate private sitting room for the publican, often on the top floor as in Tarbuck's plan.

In non-residential areas, where pubs were largely dependent on casual traffic, the bar was likely to be much more prominent. In the Lamb, Caledonian Market (Fig. 3), for instance, although there was still a bar parlour, tap room, parlour and (probably) coffee room on the ground floor, the bar was the largest and most important room.[13] The Lamb was one of four identical pubs and two hotels built in 1855 by the City of London to cater for the needs of its new cattle market; James Bunning, the City architect, provided them with classical facades of considerable splendour. If the pubs had been commissioned by the publicans rather than the City Corporation, the bars would probably have taken up even more space, but there was still a considerable prejudice among those in authority against the one-bar pub. The plan of the Fountain and Grapes, Southwark (Fig. 2), is a good example of what they disliked.[14] It was a busy pub on the corner of Mint Street and Blackman Street at the junction of three main roads. The plan is given in a survey made in June 1857, before the pub was demolished for road widening and rebuilt on a smaller site. It was a pure gin palace, with a type of plan that was to be constantly repeated on corner sites until the early 1880s. It was organized like an open fan: at the base were the stairs and bar parlour; the inner ring consisted of the serving-bar and the bar counter; between that and the outer ring of the street facades was all bar space. Except for the stairs and bar parlour the pub was one large open area; and the facade was more glass than wall, with the corner curved and pierced by the main entrance, making a prominent central feature.

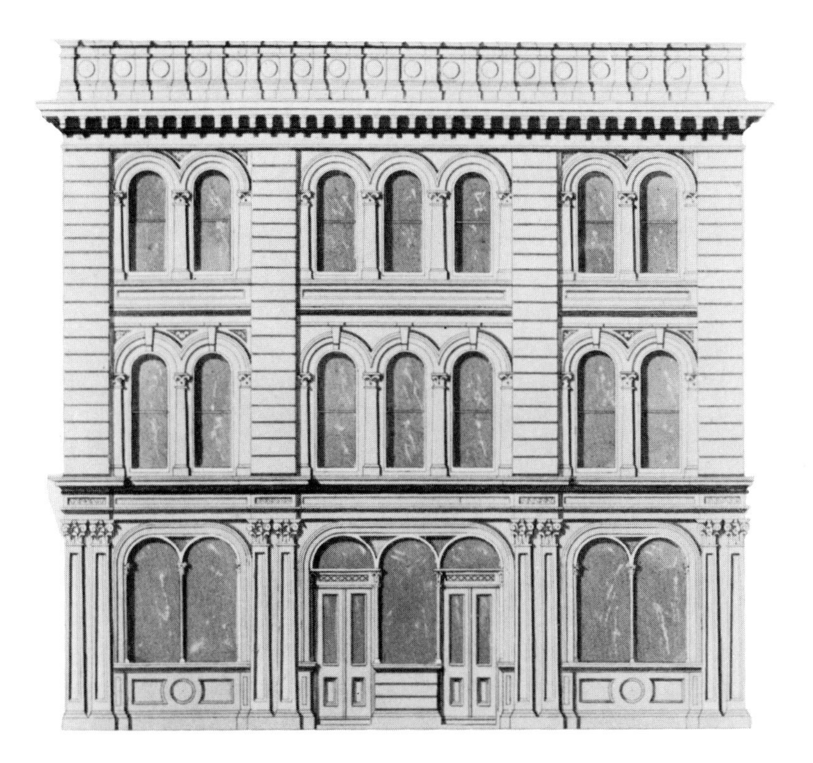

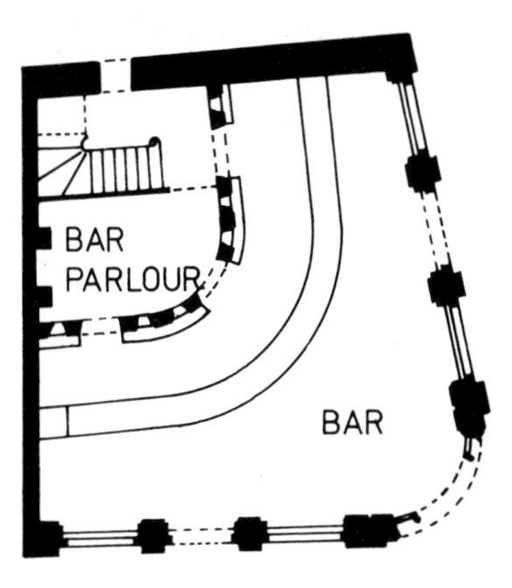

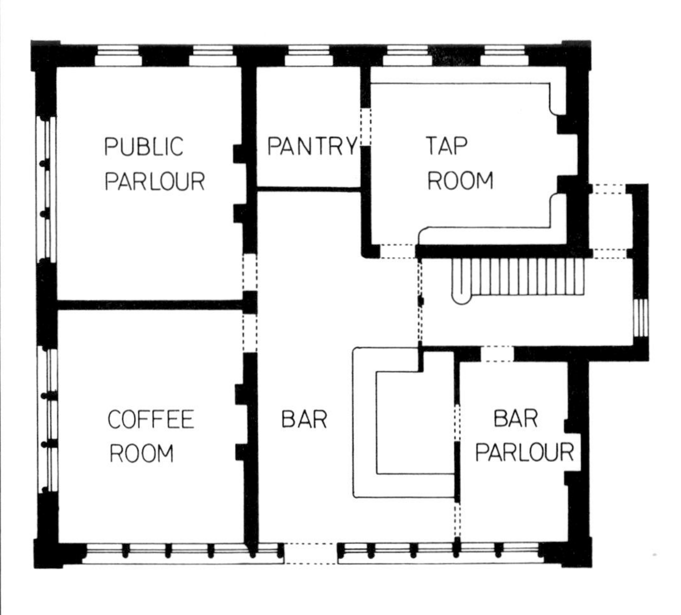

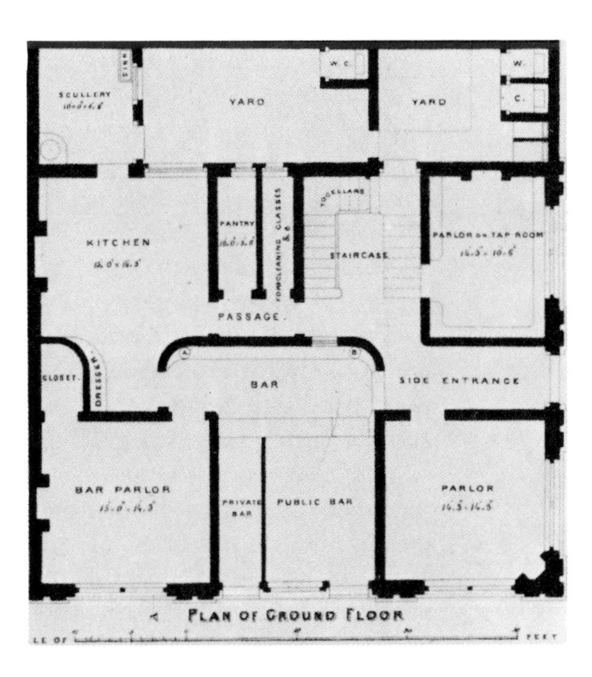

24. (top left) Design for a 'first class tavern', by E. L. Tarbuck, *c.* 1855
Fig. 2. (top right) Ground floor of the Fountain and Grapes, Mint Street, Southwark
Fig. 3. (bottom left) Ground floor of the Lamb, Caledonian Market
Fig. 4. (bottom right) Ground floor of a 'first class tavern', by E. L. Tarbuck, *c.* 1855

Inventories and pictures help to put flesh and blood to plans of this type. The Clarendon Hotel, in Clarendon Road on the Ladbroke estate, is vividly recreated by a minutely detailed inventory made in 1847, the year after it was built by William Reynolds.[15] Reynolds was a builder who had already erected numerous houses on the estate, and he established himself in the Clarendon as the licensee. It was emphatically a 'first class tavern', like Tarbuck's design, and its layout and accommodation were similar, except that the private sitting room was on the ground floor and the kitchen in the basement. There were a parlour, private parlour, bar parlour, tap room and bar on the ground floor, and a large club room on the first floor. The tap room was sturdily furnished with deal tables, wooden forms and painted wooden settles all round the wall, The parlour also had settles and a 'capital strong well made . . . drinking table', but they were of mahogany, not deal, and the seats had horse hair stuffing. In addition there were four Windsor chairs, four iron spittoons, thirty-five feet of mahogany bar rail fixed round the room and a large chimney-glass in a gilt frame. The bar parlour was snugly furnished with caneseat chairs, scarlet silk curtains hanging from brass rods and a mahogany Pembroke table. The bar was fitted up with some splendour. It had a 'capital painted and panelled front return counter with stout metal top and gate fitted with twelve brass spirits taps, rincing [*sic*] basin, five drawers, cupboard shelves, etc., metal top to same, double metal door and receiver, a handsome seven motion Beer engine with ivory pulls, six metal taps, and one brass stop cock, metal drainer, length of waste pipe in carved Spanish mahogany case (by Angliss)'. Below the bar in the cellar were three large butts, the largest with a capacity of 148 gallons, connected to the beer engines. On shelves above the bar were, not the gigantic casks of the Cruikshank cartoons, but fourteen small painted and grained iron-bound gift casks, for spirits and cordials, linked by pipes to the taps on the counter. A 'return Cabinet' contained mugs, bottles, dice and snuff-boxes, the whole 'finished with a noble cornice, carved pilasters, etc.' The 'fine plate chimney-glass' in a mahogany frame was matched by the plate glass lining of the Spanish mahogany door leading from the bar to the bar parlour. All this was behind the bar counter; the 'front of the bar', unlike the parlour and tap room, was largely intended for standing customers, and its only furnishing was one deal form. 'Eleven spring bells on carriages with brass pendulums, cranks and wires' kept the bar in touch with the parlour, tap room and club room.

The club room was a large room heated with two register stoves with 'Elizabethan bars' each surmounted by a large pier-glass and furnished with two six-foot mahogany drinking tables, five mahogany matchpots, two evergreens in pots, twenty-one Windsor chairs, and twenty-nine iron spittoons. There were two handsomely furnished bedrooms on this floor, and five more on the floor above; in the 1851 census three of these were occupied by lodgers, and the resident staff consisted of the publican, his wife, his twelve-year-old daughter, one waiter, one servant and a pot-boy. None of the public rooms had floor coverings, but there was a plaid drugget in the bar parlour and a carpet behind the bar. The ground floor and club room were lit by gas. The supply of glass and pewter suggests the

amount of custom that the Clarendon attracted, or perhaps epitomizes the reckless lavishness which bankrupted the publican within a year; it included 272 pewter pintpots, 864 pewter half-pint pots and 1,172 pint glasses. Out at the back were a skittle ground, a bowling green and a movable urinal.

Four contemporary pictures can be selected to show a parlour, two bars and a club room of the 1850s. A lively oil painting[16] shows the parlour at the Queen's Head, Haymarket, as it was in 1855 (Colour Plate 1). There, as in the Clarendon inventory, are the mahogany tables, gas lighting, matchpots, and uncarpeted floors; but the walls are encrusted with prints of rat matches and boxers, and a dog show is in progress, with the top-hatted and white-shirt-fronted dog owners sucking at their long pipes and holding their glasses or pewter tankards while dogs of every shape and size cover the floor and spill up on to the tables. Jemmy Shaw, the publican, who was an ex-prize fighter and one of the originators of dog shows, stands in his shirt-sleeves in one corner by a hospitably glowing fire.

A bar in a public house opposite the Royal Victoria Theatre is shown in an illustration by William McConnell from Sala's *Twice Round the Clock* (1859). The Royal Victoria (now the Old Vic) was at the time an extremely popular theatre, with an exclusively working- and lower middle-class clientele; the engraving (Plate 25) shows it during the interval, filled with 'honest, hard-working mechanics, their wives and families', sailors, a Life Guardsman, and an 'Ethiopian Seranader'. McConnell had no axe to grind, and the scene is a lively and far from disagreeable one. The little girl carrying a bottle or a jug is an inevitable prop in almost every contemporary illustration of a bar—usually shown pushing the bottle up on the

25. A bar opposite the Royal Victoria Theatre, Waterloo Road, in 1859

counter, which she can scarcely see over. She is, of course, not coming there to drink herself but to collect the drink for the family dinner; but Temperance advocates claimed that, apart from mixing in unsuitable company, children were inclined to take a sip of drink on the way home, and so get into bad habits.

The bar in McConnell's drawing is a big, undivided one, but in the 1850s partitions five or six feet high dividing the bar into two or three parts were beginning to appear and are shown in a pub depicted in the *Working Man's Friend* of 1852 (Plate 27). The pub is of the same radiating type as the Fountain and Grapes; the smaller subdivision looks like an early example of a private bar in which patrons, by paying a little extra for their drinks, could drink in slightly superior company. Neither here nor in the Royal Victoria pub is there any sign of seating in the bars.

Another illustration from *Twice Round the Clock* shows a superior scene, a middle-class discussion group in session in the club room of the Belvedere, Pentonville (Plate 26). The long tables are crowded, a waiter is handing round hot punch, smoke is rising in clouds, top hats are waving, and a gentleman in check trousers is declaiming. The gaslights and cornices are of excellent quality; the wooden chairs are the equivalent of the Windsor chairs of the Clarendon; the iron spittoons are not in evidence.

In fact the days of discussion groups like that in the Belvedere were numbered. The passage from the *Builder* quoted at the head of this chapter goes on to refer to the 'mutations of habit in the higher and middle classes' which were removing them from the taverns to the clubs. As early as 1852 the statistician G. R. Porter had declared that 'no person above the rank of a labouring man or artisan, would venture to go into a public house to purchase anything to drink'.[17] Anyone touring the club rooms of public houses in the 1850s would have been likely to run into a meeting of a local trade union or to find a far from select audience listening with enthusiasm to the 'sentimental vocalist, the male impersonator, the comic singer, the Ethiopian minstrel, the ventriloquist, and the step-dancer'. Out of the womb of their upstairs rooms, public houses were in the course of giving birth to the music-halls.[18]

If the entertainments held in them were successful, the upper room soon proved too small and a new hall had to be built on at the side or back. The process was already at work in the thirties and forties. Some of these new rooms were called 'saloons' and featured a curious mixture of variety turns, songs, stage plays and excerpts from opera; the famous Grecian Saloon at the Eagle, City Road, was the best known of them. Others featured songs and turns only and began to be called music-halls. A socially slightly superior variant was the song and supper rooms, in which it was possible to watch and listen to the same kind of show while eating a meal.

At all three types of entertainment the audience could drink as they watched. But in 1843 the saloons were knocked on the head by the authorities, who required them either to register as theatres, in which case they lost the right to provide drinks in the auditorium, or to stop putting on anything which could be described as a theatrical entertainment. Most of them then developed into popular theatres.

26. A club meeting at the Belvedere, Pentonville, in 1859

27. A gin shop interior of 1852

OLD TOM
ARMS

In the 1850s, pubs, music-halls and popular theatres were a closely interconnected world and one particular firm of architects, Hill and Paraire, specialized in all three. It is worth looking at their work in some detail; they are the first of the architects who specialized in pubs to have a distinctive architectural personality, and besides being a link between pubs and music-halls they are also a link between the architecture of the 1850s and the very different architecture of the 1870s.[19]

William Finch Hill first appears on his own. Nothing is known about his origins or about any aspect of his life except his architecture. He is probably the 'Mr Hill' who was the architect of 'Assembly Rooms and 4th rate house adjoining Green Dragon', whereabouts unspecified, in 1852. In 1854 he rebuilt the Earl of Effingham Theatre (formerly the Effingham Saloon) and the adjoining Effingham Tavern in Whitechapel Road. In 1855 he established his reputation with a new hall (Plate 28) for Evans's Song and Supper Rooms in Covent Garden Piazza.[20]

Evans's was a famous early Victorian institution. It had been started by W. C. Evans, a chorister from Covent Garden theatre, who regaled his clientele with songs of an 'erotic and bacchanalian order'. It reached its greatest fame and prosperity under his successor, John Greenmore, better known as Paddy Green. He took over in 1844, 'elevated the moral tone of the amusements' and attracted a clientele that ranged from bank clerks on the spree to Thackeray and the Prince of Wales. At its round marble-topped tables, the audience could consume an excellent steak or chop, drink wine or stout, and smoke cigars while being entertained with glees, ballads, madrigals, comic songs and selections from the opera, sung by a first-rate choir of men and boys or by individual singers of the highest quality—not to mention oddities, like a man who played tunes on a coffee-pot or another who whistled and imitated bird songs. The entertainment started at eight and went on till the early hours of the morning. Ladies were allowed to watch only from behind screens in the gallery.

Finch Hill (who was joined by E. L. Paraire in 1857) went on to design Weston's Music Hall (later the Royal Holborn), Holborn (1857), the Britannia Theatre, Hoxton (1858), the Oxford Music Hall, Oxford Street (1861), the Royal Cambridge Music Hall (1864), and the Philharmonic Hall (later the Islington Empire), Islington (1866).[21] The architecture of all these halls was considerably chaster than the entertainments which took place in them. Finch Hill was a master of the opulent but never licentious classicism of the 1850s. Audiences knocked back their beer in sumptuous settings designed by an architect who knew the churches of Gibbs, Archer and Hawksmoor. With the exception of the Britannia none of them had proper auditoria; this, incidentally, was the main reason why none of them survived, for in the course of the century the form of the music-hall was to develop closer and closer to that of the theatre and they were rebuilt as a result. Finch Hill's inspiration was literally ecclesiastical; his halls had level floors and galleried aisles leading the eye to a ceremonial culmination above a raised platform at what one is tempted to call the ritual east end. The hall at Evans's had arched arcades reminiscent of Gibbs's St Martin-in-the-Fields, and the Oxford Music Hall (Plate 29) had more than a touch of Hawksmoor's St Anne's, Limehouse.

28. Evans's Song and Supper Rooms, Covent Garden (W. Finch Hill, 1855; demolished)

29. The Oxford Music Hall, Oxford Street, (Finch Hill and Paraire, 1857; demolished)

At the Britannia the theatre was attached to the rear of a tavern of the same name which was also rebuilt by Hill and Paraire.[22] Weston's grew out of the Seven Tankards and Punchbowl; the Oxford incorporated the rebuilt Boar and Castle. Hill and Paraire also designed or altered numerous pubs where no music-hall element was involved, though some of them were built for publicans who ran music-halls elsewhere: the King's Arms, Titchfield Street (1859), for instance, and the Rising Sun, Euston Road (1861), were both built for the Turnham family, who ran Turnham's Music Hall (the forerunner of the Metropolitan) in Edgware Road, and who also employed Hill and Paraire for the Philharmonic Hall, Islington.[23] In all, the firm did documented work at twenty pubs, and in addition Paraire designed at least another half-dozen after Finch Hill died or retired in about 1867. It amounted to a sizable public house practice, even if still much smaller than the monster practices of the late nineteenth century.

The death rate of Hill and Paraire's pubs has been almost as high as that of their music-halls, and few, if any, of them were illustrated at the time. But the Museum Tavern (1855), opposite the British Museum, and the Hat and Feathers (1860) in Goswell Road survive.[24] The main elevations of the former had to follow those of the block as a whole, which was designed by another architect; but the ground floor front and lushly classical back fitting inside the bar (Plate 30) have the appearance of dating from Finch Hill's time, even though the glass is clearly later. At the Hat and Feathers, on the other hand, the bars have been completely remodelled, but the facade (plate 31) is Finch Hill's work, similar in treatment to the tavern front of the Britannia, designed two years previously. With its festive combination of two-storey Corinthian pilasters supporting statues and one-storey Ionic columns supporting urns, the whole rising up to a scrolled and framed tablet enclosing the name of the pub, it is up to the level of the firm's best music-halls; it is gay without being crude.

Crudity is rampant in the mangled remains of the Royal Oak, Bishops's Bridge Road (*c.* 1864), and in a block of offices and warehousing designed by the firm in 1866. Its appearance must be due to E. L. Paraire.[25] Paraire was a difficult character. He became a member of the Architectural Association in 1860, and in 1861 was elected to a new-broom committee which set about rescuing the Association from the disarray into which it had fallen in the late fifties. Paraire 'disagreed with every proposal, criticized the accounts, and the minutes, and finally wrote a letter of resignation "couched in such terms that the committee could not take any notice of it whatsoever".'[26]

Looking at Paraire's pubs one is not surprised; they are effective and even jovial, but certainly not gentle buildings. The Alfred's Head, Newington Causeway (*c.* 1870), the Admiral Keppel, Shoreditch High Street (1877), and the Duke of York, Clerkenwell Road (*c.* 1878), were all, like Hill and Paraire's Royal Oak, designed for the same publican, John Hancock;[27] the Horse Shoe, Tottenham Court Road (1875), was for another publican, Charles Best, for whom Hill and Paraire had designed the Old Crown, St Giles, in 1865.[28] The Alfred's Head was in a similar position to the Hat and Feathers, on a rounded corner at the Elephant and Castle

30. (top) Bar fitting in the Museum Tavern, Museum Street, Bloomsbury (perhaps by W. Finch Hill, 1855)
31. (bottom left) The Hat and Feathers, Goswell Road (Finch Hill and Paraire, 1860)
32. (bottom right) The Alfred's Head, Newington Causeway (E. L. Paraire, *c.* 1870; demolished)

MUSEUM TAVERN
MARTELL

THE
HAT AND
FEATHERS
DOUBLE DIAMOND
HAT & FEATHERS

Alfred's Head.
140
140
ON
DRAUGHT
FEB 14 1904

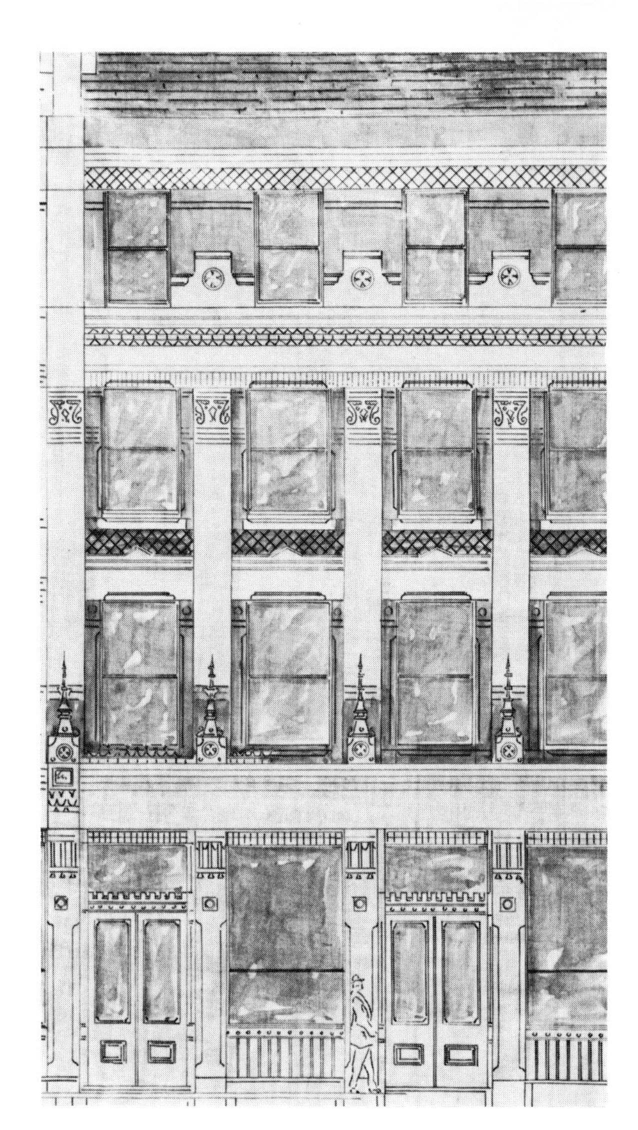

road junction (Plate 32). There is both a family likeness and a generation gap between the well-behaved gaiety of the one and the villainous gaiety of the other. The coarse jolly pilasters, inflated Greek ornament, bizarre pediments and curious notches and knobbles of the Alfred's Head reappear in the Duke of York, Admiral Keppel and Horse Shoe, with the addition of French mansard roofs, dormer windows, and spikes or palisades of cast iron (Plates 33, 34). The Horse Shoe was the most ambitious of all Paraire's pubs. When first acquired by Best it was the 'brewery tap' for Meux's Horse Shoe Brewery on the adjacent site. Best rebuilt it on the grand scale as something new in London, a combined pub, restaurant, grill and café, aiming to imitate a French *estaminet*, lavishly fitted up and serving, it was claimed, the best suppers and earliest breakfasts in the West End. The original front was extended by more than half in 1892 and the whole confection still survives, whitewashed and purged, above the new bar fronts inserted in the 1930s.

The transformation of Finch Hill into Paraire can be paralleled in pubs designed by other architects. It is similar to the development from lively classical pubs like

33. Design for the Admiral Keppel, Shoreditch High Street, by E. L. Paraire, *c.* 1875

34. The Horse Shoe, Tottenham Court Road (E. L. Paraire, 1877)

35. The Market House Tavern, Poplar

the Market House Tavern, Poplar, the former Mitre in Chancery Lane of about 1855, by George Legge, or R. W. Armstrong's Sun in Long Acre of 1856–7, to pubs like Lewis Isaac's King Lud at Ludgate Circus of 1871, which is equally lively but very much less classical (Plates 35, 36, 37, 38).[29] Indeed, there is no obvious stylistic tag to put to it, nor for that matter to Paraire's Horse Shoe. This was the result of deliberate effort. There was a good deal of discussion among architects of the 1860s and 1870s on the lines that a great age like their own (for they were not modest) deserved a style of its own. It encouraged an architecture that combined aggressive eclecticism with detail that had no stylistic precedence. The buildings

that resulted usually paid little attention to their neighbours, for architectural good manners were forgotten and even despised by a new generation of brash young commercial architects who subscribed to the *laissez-faire* ethics of the time.

Pubs were likely to be especially flamboyant when built or rebuilt by publicans rather than builders. There had always been a distinction between new pubs built as part of new housing developments and old pubs, usually along main roads, rebuilt by publicans to bring them up to date. Nearly all Hill and Paraire's pubs seem to have belonged to the latter type, which predominated after 1870 because, as will appear, builders found it increasingly hard to get licences for new pubs. One result of this predominance was to encourage the emergence of professional pub architects. Another was to make pubs more conspicuous, for rebuilt pubs were likely anyway to stand out from their neighbours and it was in the publicans' interest to make them as conspicuous as possible in order to bring in trade.

36. The former Mitre in Chancery Lane, now a restaurant (George Legge, *c.* 1855)

37. The Sun Tavern, Long Acre (R. W. Armstrong, 1856–7)

38. The King Lud, Ludgate Circus (Lewis Isaacs, 1871)

One way to be different was to build a Gothic pub. Ruskin's well-known complaint of 1872 has often been misquoted as evidence of the spread of these: 'I have had indirect influence on nearly every cheap villa-builder between Denmark Hill and Bromley; and there is scarcely a public house near the Crystal Palace but sells its gin and bitters under pseudo-Venetian capitals copied from the Church of the Madonna of Health or of Miracles.'[30] But the latter was an early Renaissance church, the former the Salute, about as un-Gothic a church as could be. Gothic pubs were never at any stage more than a small minority of the pubs being built. Gothic in the 1860s was in its most spiky, contrary and at times manic phase, and Gothic as interpreted by not over-literate pub architects can be very curious. Examples range from the gaily elephantine Percy in Ladbroke Grove to the Hollywood Arms in Hollywood Road, dated 1868, which has a certain inspired perversity (Plate 39).

WATNEY AN
CO'S ENTIRE
HOLLYWOOD
ARMS
1865
JOB MASTERS

I. A dog show at the Queen's Head Tavern, Haymarket, in 1855

39. (left) The Hollywood Arms, Hollywood Road, Fulham (1868)

40. Design for the Railway Hotel, Hackney, by Edward Brown, 1879 (demolished)

In the course of the 1870s pub Gothic tended to become less bizarre. Rowland Plumbe's Old Rodney's Head, Old Street (1879), and Edward Brown's Railway Hotel, Hackney (1879), were both handsome and competent designs, the first by an 'outsider' architect who later designed some of the first LCC housing and the YMCA building in Tottenham Court Road, the second (Plate 40) by one of the most prolific of pub professionals, whose earlier pubs had been rather staidly classical.[31] The Railway Hotel has gone but the Old Rodney's Head survives, though no longer a pub, complete with its admiral's head bizarrely skied on a Gothic column. Its modest machicolations were outdated by those of the near-circular City of Salisbury, Tooley Street (Colour Plate III), an enchanting *jeu d'esprit* (though more so in drawing than execution) designed in 1881 by the youthful Fitzroy Doll,[32] who was later to enrich Bloomsbury with what is now Dillon's University Bookshop and the Russell and Imperial Hotels in Russell Square.

The growing flamboyance of pubs in the 1850s and 1860s looked at from one point of view can be seen as a parallel development to the growing brio of the music-halls; it expressed the emergence of a new city brand of working-class culture. Looked at more generally, the growing richness of this architecture is paralleled by the growing richness of English architecture as a whole, and both are an expression of the fact that the rich were getting even richer and the poor a good

II. Looking across to the central bar of the Prince Alfred, Formosa Street, Maida Vale

deal less poor. Having weathered the 'hungry forties', the Corn Law agitation of 1840–6, the political troubles of 1848 and the Crimean War of 1854–5, England entered on a period of mounting prosperity which continued with only occasional checks for the next twenty years and more. And English people, having more to spend, spent more on drink. Drink consumption, after twenty years of fluctuation, began to rise in the middle 1850s and reached a peak for spirits in 1875 and for beer in 1876 (Figs. 5, 6). In 1876 the average Englishman, to judge from the available statistics, drank more beer than he had ever drunk before or was ever to drink again: 34·4 gallons in that year as opposed to the all-time low of 13·3 in 1935.

It was not surprising that Temperance advocates became steadily more extreme, moving from condemning spirits to condemning all alcohol in the 1840s, and from teetotalism to prohibition in the 1850s. Gin, the great bogey of the 1830s, lost its horrific image as people realized how easy it was to get equally drunk on beer. The beerhouses, welcomed as saviours of the people in the 1830s, had become universally discredited among the educated classes by the 1850s. Not only were people drinking more, but there were more places for them to drink in. The first plank of the Temperance programme became increasingly acceptable to many people who were far from prohibitionists: the number of licensed premises must be drastically reduced. The means of reducing fully licensed houses was available to the licensing justices; but what was the point of reducing these while the beerhouses were legally allowed to proliferate?[33]

It became evident that the days of the 1830 Beer Act were numbered. In 1869 a Tory private member put through a bill to place the beerhouses under the control of the magistrates, and it passed into law with the general agreement of both parties. But the Liberals, who were then in office, were prepared to go even further. Their 1871 licensing bill, although it did not go as far as the Temperance lobby would have liked, was the most drastic licensing proposal ever yet introduced in England. It involved a reduction in the number of licences, to be gained partly by imposing a rating qualification and partly by allowing local ratepayers to vote on the number of licensed houses their district should have; shorter opening hours; and inspection of public houses by a new branch of government inspectors.

The bill provoked a national uproar, fomented by the publicans, who for the first time began to organize themselves as an effective opposition to the Temperance lobby. Reduction of licences was attacked as an assault on property, government inspection as a system of spying, and the bill as a whole as an attack on the innocent enjoyment of the working man. There was so much fuss that the bill was quietly dropped and replaced by the much milder Aberdare Act of 1872, which reduced opening hours less drastically, increased fines for drunkenness and licensing offences and replaced the proposed system of government inspectors by inspectors appointed from, and responsible to, the local police.

The Beer Act of 1869, the Aberdare Act of 1872 and the political alignments which it produced were the soil out of which grew the distinctive Victorian pub as we know it today, for politics and architecture were inextricably meshed together.

41. Public-bar styling in the Royal George, Valence Road, Bethnal Green

Brewster Sessions. They are called Licensing Sessions, a meaning which is obvious, but they would now more often . . . be more accurately described as unlicensing sessions.

'Licensed Traders Dictionary'

3 The Plan

The combination of the Beer Act of 1869 and the Aberdare Act of 1872 left the licensing justices in a much stronger position. With beerhouses and fully licensed houses both now under their control, they were impregnably equipped to prevent the total number of licensed premises from increasing, if they felt like it. They appeared less well equipped to reduce the number of licences, because it was still widely accepted that a publican who applied for the yearly renewal of his licence could not be refused if he had behaved himself in the previous year. But some licences died a natural death; and in addition to refusing licences on the grounds of bad conduct, it was possible to reduce the total number by striking bargains with the brewers, such as agreeing to grant a licence to a new pub only if two or more old licences were surrendered. In 1891 the position of the justices was immensely strengthened when the ruling of Sharp v. Wakefield was confirmed by the House of Lords. This established that justices could refuse or grant licences at their own discretion, regardless of the previous record of the licensee.

How the justices administered their legal powers depended, of course, to a large extent on the sort of people they were. As a body of men they were far from extremist; but they did on the whole agree with what was by now the accepted opinion of the educated classes, that the ratio of pubs to people in England was far higher than it should be. From the 1870s onwards, although they made much less use than they might have of the powers given to them by Sharp v. Wakefield, they were grudging granters of new licences and moderate reducers of existing ones.

The result was an immediate end to the previous steady rise in the number of licensed premises. The number of beerhouses started to decline from 1869; some were granted full licences, more were closed down for one reason or another and today only a handful are left. The number of fully licensed houses increased very slightly until 1877 and then started to decline as well (Fig. 7). To take one local example, in the Kensington licensing division (Kensington, Chelsea, Fulham and Hammersmith) there were 172 beerhouses in 1886 and 148 in 1896; 393 fully licensed houses in 1886 and 392 in 1896.[1] Meanwhile the population of the borough had increased by something like 25 per cent, so that there were appreciably fewer licensed premises for appreciably more people. Similar statistics could be quoted for the rest of London and the rest of England.

This changing pattern of licensing probably had its biggest effect in the new residential districts. London was expanding as furiously as it had done in the 1850s, but gone were the days when the *Builder* could write of the new pubs that 'at a distance of 200 paces in every direction they glitter in sham splendour'. New licences were hard to come by; and existing old-fashioned country pubs, as the advancing tide of bricks amd mortar enveloped them, suddenly found themselves swamped with new business and were remodelled to deal with it. Both the public authorities and some private landlords supplemented the policy of the magistrates. From the 1870s onwards the Metropolitan Board of Works and its successor the London County Council were clearing slums and devising a network of new roads through London, armed with powers of compulsory purchase. Many pubs were

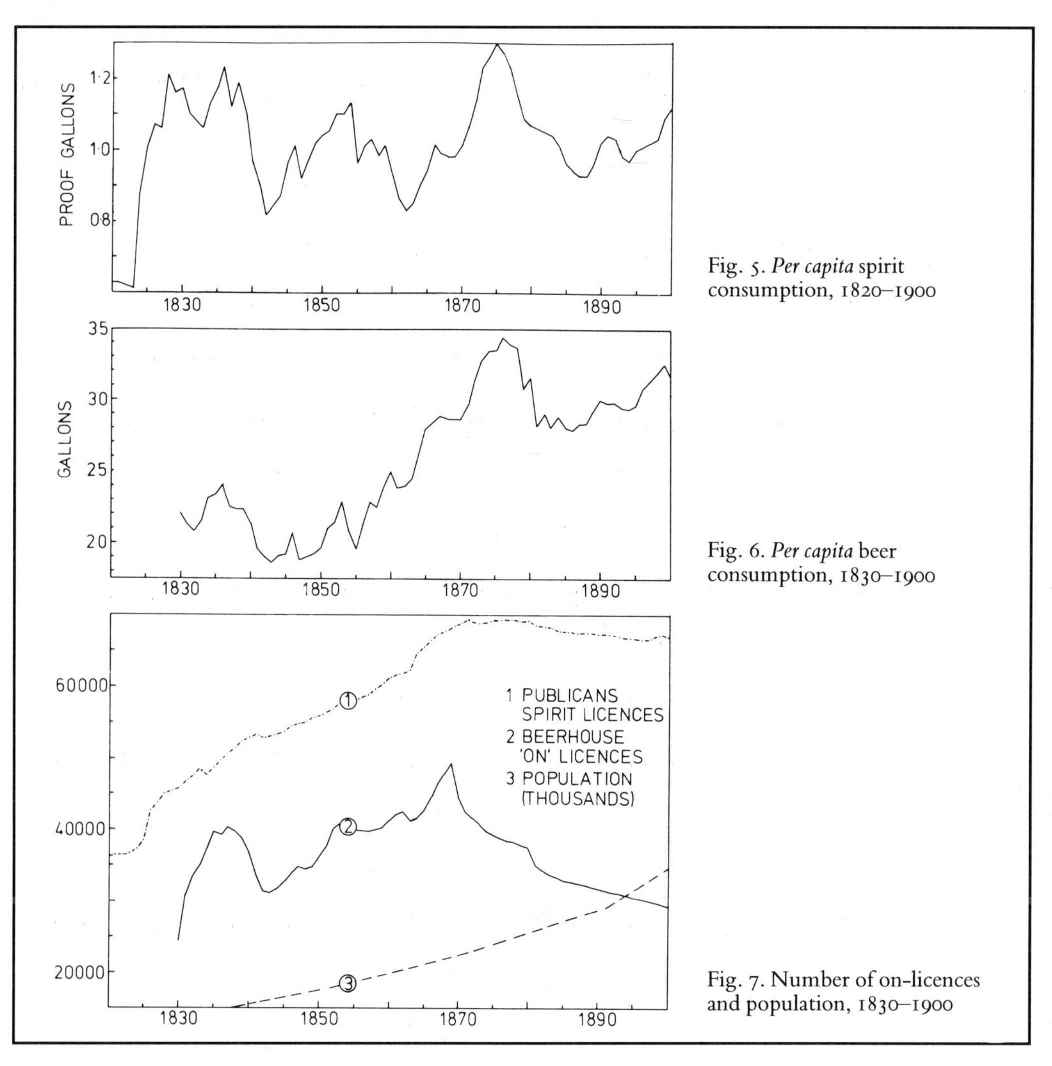

Fig. 5. *Per capita* spirit consumption, 1820–1900

Fig. 6. *Per capita* beer consumption, 1830–1900

Fig. 7. Number of on-licences and population, 1830–1900

bought up and demolished; new sites were available at the discretion of the public authority along the new roads, but in the 1880s it was Board of Works policy to permit only one new pub for every three demolished[2] and the LCC were to be even stricter. Moreover, increasing numbers of ground landlords were anti-drink. Some new housing estates were completely dry by policy, such as those built by the Artisans Dwelling Company, or on the Queen's Park estate near Kensal Green.[3] Ground landlords of existing property could refuse to renew leases when old ones fell in, but some were hamstrung by long leases granted by the previous less Temperance-minded generation. Two prominent anti-drink London landlords—the Duke of Westminster, the richest of them all, and the formidable Lady Henry Somerset—both found themselves in this position. The latter was an intelligent heiress who had accused her husband of being a homosexual and been cut by London society as a result. She devoted the rest of her life to teetotal agitation. It must have been a mortification to her that she was ground landlord by inheritance of nine public houses in Somers Town.[4] Similarly the Duke of Westminster, president of the Coffee Public House Association and the Committee for the Preventing of Demoralizing of Native Races by the Liquor Traffic, had to work

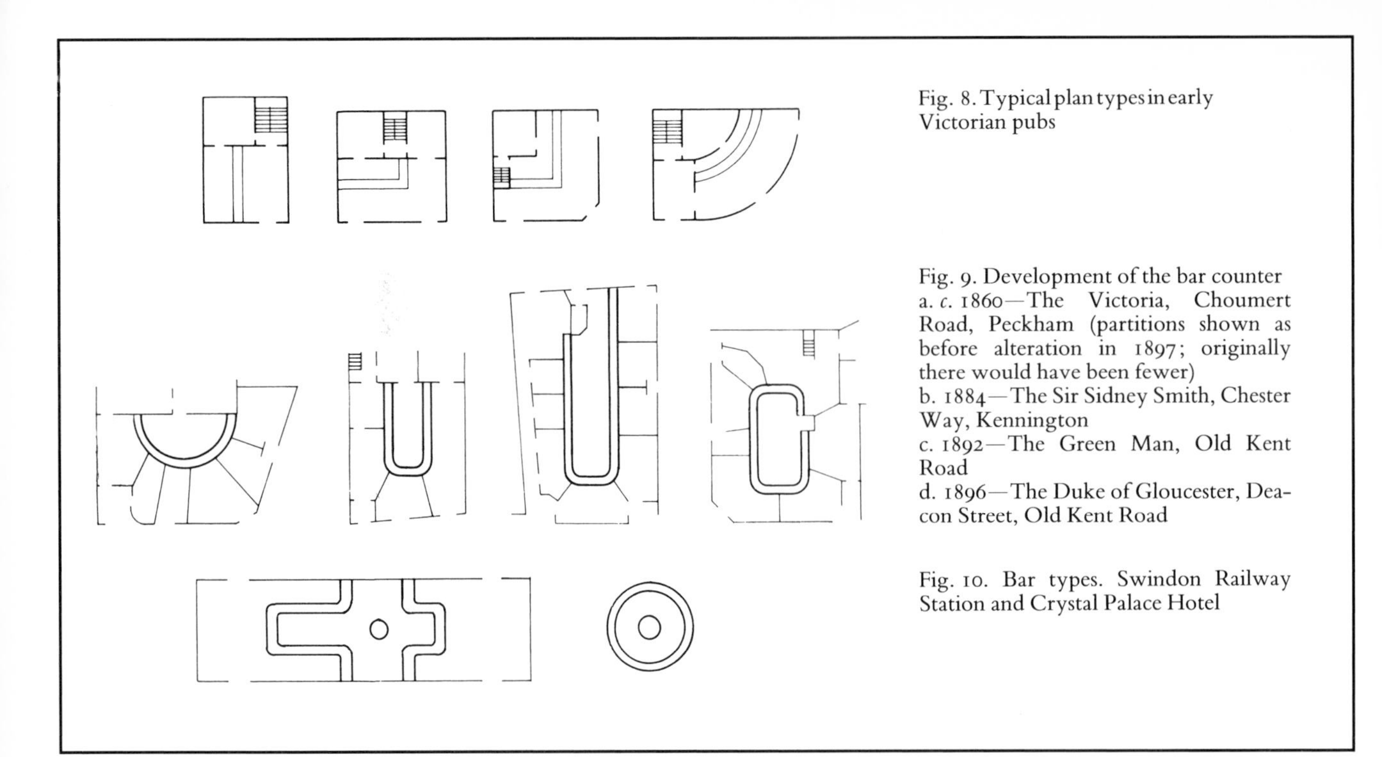

Fig. 8. Typical plan types in early Victorian pubs

Fig. 9. Development of the bar counter
a. *c.* 1860—The Victoria, Choumert Road, Peckham (partitions shown as before alteration in 1897; originally there would have been fewer)
b. 1884—The Sir Sidney Smith, Chester Way, Kennington
c. 1892—The Green Man, Old Kent Road
d. 1896—The Duke of Gloucester, Deacon Street, Old Kent Road

Fig. 10. Bar types. Swindon Railway Station and Crystal Palace Hotel

against the abundant quiverful of pubs erected in his father's and grandfather's time on the family's Pimlico and other properties.

The reduction in the number of pubs was encouraging for the Temperance lobby, but it was also profitable for the surviving publicans, who found themselves in a position of steadily increasing monopoly. To get the fullest benefit out of their expanding clientele, they had to adapt their pubs to deal with them. The plan of pubs changed between 1870 and 1900 largely to enable each individual pub to supply more drink faster to more people. There were two main ways of doing this: first to exploit the existing drinking area to the full by making it more efficient; and secondly, to expand the drinking area. To a certain extent the two processes went on at the same time, but by a logical development the emphasis up to about 1890 was on the first, and after 1890 on the second.[5]

The concept of counter as opposed to waiter service had been a great time-and-motion breakthrough when it hit the pub world in the 1830s, but between 1830 and 1870 publicans were not adventurous in developing it. By 1870 there were two common types of plan. Pubs with one front to the street usually had a straight bar counter, either at right angles or parallel to the frontage and in front of the bar parlour and stairs. Pubs on corner sites with two street facades usually had a radial plan: either fan-shaped, with a curved bar counter in front of a segmental bar-parlour-and-stairs area, or with the fan translated into right angles, so that the bar parlour and stairs formed a square in one corner, with an *L*-shaped bar counter wrapped round it (Fig. 8). The plan was further complicated when, as was still often the case, in addition to the space served directly by the bar counter, there were a tap room and parlour for the public, and a kitchen and possibly private sitting room for the publican.

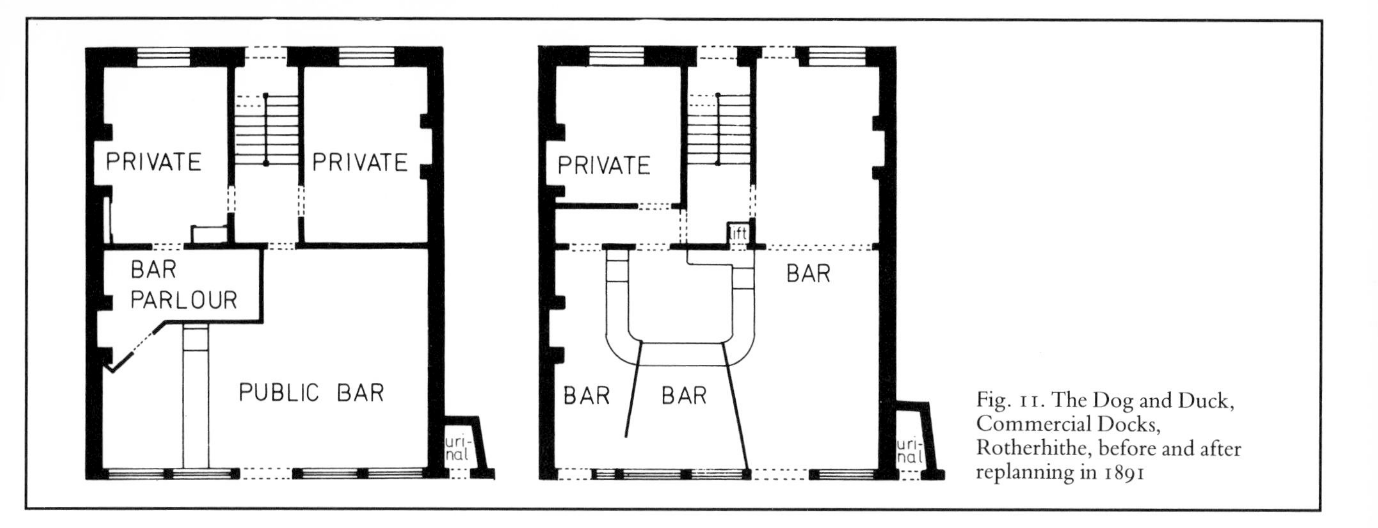

Fig. 11. The Dog and Duck, Commercial Docks, Rotherhithe, before and after replanning in 1891

Although the counter was in itself an efficient means of dispensing drink, the disadvantage of both these types was that if the public space was crowded there were more people in it than could conveniently get to the bar or be conveniently served when they got there. A solution was to make the bar counter a *U* instead of an *L* or an *I*, and the best solution was to make it an *O*. In the course of the seventies and eighties one can watch the bar counter pushing out like a gradually extruding tongue from the bar parlour. Finally the bar parlour itself disappears and only the thin link of a staircase or passage connecting the counter space to the publican's flat or the back yard prevents it from being an *O*-shaped island. On occasions, especially during the 1890s, it is detached even from these and the complete island plan results (Fig. 9).

This promontory or island planning was by no means invented by publicans or pub architects. That great genius Isambard Kingdom Brunel had already worked it out in the 1840s for the railway refreshment room at Swindon (Fig. 10). The alternative arrangements that he played with can be seen in his sketchbooks. They include a double promontory of counters stretching into two separate refreshment spaces on an island site between two platforms. This was a highly practical arrangement for the circumstances. There were no dining cars on the trains of the 1840s; passengers on the Bristol express were allowed a ten-minute stop for refreshments at Swindon, during which the train disgorged them into the station and they swallowed what they could in the time. So quick turnover was an essential. A completely circular island bar was published in 1853 as an intended feature of the Crystal Palace Hotel, Sydenham (a hotel rather than a pub), which was never built. It probably derived from what seems to have been a similar bar in the waiting room at Euston Station, designed about 1847.[6]

Publicans were slow to adopt this arrangement; but then pressure on them began to be felt only as a result of the 1869–72 legislation. Even then promontory bars developed comparatively slowly. Although the Horse and Sacks, Harrow Road, designed by Alfred M. Ridge in 1877, had a serving bar which was five-sixths on the way to being an island,[7] it was not till the late eighties that fully developed promontory bars became at all common. From then until the end of the century they were replacing the earlier types all over London (Fig. 11). They proved

TRUMAN
LONDON STOUT
GOMM'S

endlessly adaptable to different social inflections; if suitably embellished they fitted well into the deal and sawdust of an unpretending dockside pub or the mahogany and lincrusta of a smart West End establishment (Plates 42, 43, Colour Plate II).

The space served by these improved arrangements was seldom an undivided one. Big, undivided bars were becoming increasingly uncommon. As has been described, some of the bars of the 1850s were already subdivided by partitions, and partitions were on the increase through the sixties, seventies and eighties. A witness to the Parliamentary commission of 1877 described a pub in Whitechapel Road with six compartments.[8] As the number of bars increased they were differentiated into public and private. A public and private bar had been shown in the plan of Tarbuck's 'first class tavern' in 1855, but here the private bar had been for orders only; later it would have been called a jug-and-bottle compartment. This use of the same term for different parts of the pub in different generations is a common and confusing aspect of pub history. By the 1870s at least, the term 'private bar' was being used in quite a different sense: it was literally a bar in which people went to be private. Not only was it screened by partitions from the other bars but another screen separated it from the barmaid behind the counter; the drink came through at a gap below eye level. For this privilege of privacy customers paid a little extra for their drink. By the end of the 1870s it was quite common for pubs to have a couple of public bars and a couple of private ones, perhaps a larger and a smaller one of each. By now even the public bars often had benches, as is shown in a snug pub interior drawn by Du Maurier in 1879 (Plate 44).

42, 43. (facing page) De luxe and economy versions of the promontory bar counter: the Crown and Sceptre, Great Titchfield Street (*c.* 1898), and Admiral Blakeney's Head, Cable Street (B. J. Capell, 1895), both photographed in the 1940s

44. A Victorian pub interior of 1879 as depicted by George du Maurier

In the course of the 1880s the number of bars proliferated. The Noah's Ark, Blackfriars Road, designed by John Toner (not a professional pub architect) in 1885, had nine compartments, four very small ones to either side of the promontory bar counter, and a biggish public bar at the end, facing the bar parlour. The Dun Cow, Old Kent Road, by J. C. Reynolds (1887), and the Equestrian, Blackfriars Road, by T. H. Smith (1888), both had eleven bars, on a similar plan to the Noah's Ark except that there were no bar parlours (Fig. 12). The Green Man, opposite the Dun Cow in the Old Kent Road (Bruce J. Capell, 1891), had ten bars. Lady Henry Somerset refers to a pub 'near Fitzroy Square' with 'fifteen compartments'.[9] In all these pubs the small bars were served off a corridor running along the outside wall of the pub. The original plans of the Dun Cow, Equestrian and Noah's Ark do not distinguish between public and private bars, except for the big public bar at the end. In the plan of the Green Man the small bars are all labelled 'private'.

45. 'Boxes' in the Barley Mow, Dorset Street

The Duke of York, Southwark Bridge Road (W. G. Bower, 1888), had four very small bars along one side of the counter only; one, slightly larger than the others, is labelled 'jugs' on the plan, and the others are called 'boxes'. The fashion for small compartments seems to have been at its height in the years around 1890; the Green Man is one of the latest examples I know with a large number of them, but its neighbour the Thomas à Becket, designed by Richard Willock in 1897, still had three (and eight compartments in all) also labelled 'boxes'.[10]

'Box' is the perfect descriptive word for these little cubicles. They were compared at the time to the similar arrangement in pawnbrokers' shops, which was perhaps their inspiration. From the late 1890s, bars gradually became larger and larger and fewer and fewer, until by the 1950s fashion had come back in a circle to the one-bar pub. As a result very few boxes have survived; the only ones that I know of in London are the two very simple ones in the Barley Mow, Dorset Street (Plate 45). This was never a lavishly done-up pub, and the boxes in the Equestrian, Dun Cow and Green Man almost certainly had more elaborate joinery.

Small private bars of railway compartment instead of tablecloth size have survived rather better in London, though they are in continual danger. There are good examples at the Prince Alfred, Formosa Street, the Argyll, Argyll Street, and the Lord Nelson, Old Kent Road. Until a few years ago there was an especially attractive one in the Boleyn, Barking Road, the only survivor of two or three (Plate 46). It was exactly like a railway compartment in size and shape, and fitted out like one with comfortable benches full length to either side, and a door in the centre; to be in it, sheltered from the outside world and cocooned in elaborately engraved glass, gave one a curiously festive feeling, as though one were setting out on a journey to an unknown but enjoyable destination.

The term 'snug' is a confusing one, because it is used in a number of different ways. It seems originally to have been applied to very small rooms, sometimes little better than cupboards, completely detached from everything else. According to R. Hall, a Lincoln magistrate who gave evidence before the Peel Commission in 1897, 'My memory goes a long way back, and the snugs were originally meant for young people who used in olden times to go for the supper or dinner ale, and they could go into this small place . . . without mixing with the general company.'[11] The potentialities of this were obvious, and not only for young people. In February 1894, in the Lion Hotel, Lincoln, a seventy-year-old man was robbed by a prostitute of nineteen in a snug.[12] Music-halls in the 1860s had 'snuggeries or small private apartments, to which bashful gentlemen desirous of sharing a bottle of wine with a recent acquaintance may retire'.[13] Boxes and little private bars were in effect old-fashioned snugs attached to the bar counter, and it is not surprising that the term 'snug' was sometimes attached to them. In Lancashire, on the other hand, parlours were sometimes called snugs. The term was much bandied around at the Peel Commission, where its suggestion of potential sex seems to have aroused a good deal of prurient excitement in the members. Although E. Maitland, solicitor to the Licensed Victuallers' Protection Society, thought that 'a few persons in one place at a time . . . is high conducive to good order', many licensing magistrates were against them.[14] In Hull, in spite of the magistrates' efforts, snugs proliferated,

sometimes five, six or seven in a row. In a 'very large house in a very prominent street in Hull', a robbery was committed in a snug and 'in this case there were little square doors . . . about 3ft. 6in. high in all the partitions with spring locks on them and the witness used the expression that the man "ran through them like

46. A screen moved from a private bar in the Boleyn, Barking Road, East Ham

a rat'', ran all round'.[15] These little doors were put in to facilitate cleaning the compartments, which otherwise were often accessible only from the street; there are still examples at the Prince Alfred, Formosa Street, and the Lord Nelson, Old Kent Road.

The people who disapproved often seemed vague as to whether they meant old-fashioned self-contained snugs or snugs attached to the counter. The latter should have been easier to supervise, but often were not, because of the counter screen. In Hull these screens were described as having 'just room underneath to get the glasses in between all the way along, and unless he [the publican] stoops right down and looks under he cannot see who is in the snug'. In Plymouth the openings were described as 'like a railway ticket booking office'.[16] This was obviously popular with the customers, but had its disadvantage for the publican, who was liable to be fined and possibly lose his licence if he allowed drunkenness, prostitution, the

47. Snob-screen in a private bar in the Prince Alfred, Formosa Street, Maida Vale

passing of bets on his premises, and the serving of drink to a drunk or to a policeman in uniform.

One case was widely reported at the time. In April 1896 a lance-sergeant in the Coldstream Guards went into a private bar in the Coach and Horses, Lower Sloane Street, and ordered two glasses of beer, one for himself and one for a constable who had come in with him. The bar had a frosted glass screen and an opening under it 'the height of a quart pot'. The barman served the drink, a police inspector, who had seen the constable go in and followed him, took note of it, and the landlord was summonsed and fined.[17] The solution, which kept the customers, the publicans and the law happy, was a frosted glass screen with hinged panels instead of fixed glass. These 'snob-screens' seem to have been introduced in the 1890s, and still survive in some numbers (Plate 47). Fixed screens are much rarer, but at least one remains, marooned by later alterations, at the Holly Bush in Hampstead. The Markham Arms in the King's Road, Chelsea, used to have an intermediate arrangement, in the form of a fixed but transparent screen of lushly wrought bronze (Plate 48).

Small bars may on occasion have been used for illicit sex, but it was certainly not their only use. They were extremely popular with women, on their own as well as accompanied by men, and respectable women as well as, and probably more than, prostitutes. Women were said to like slipping into these bars because their

48. A wrought-metal snob-screen formerly in the Markham Arms, King's Road, Chelsea

husbands could not see them;[18] some bars in the 1890s were for ladies only, and a few are still labelled as such, like the small bar at the Prince Alfred, Formosa Street. Lady Henry Somerset, who ran a home for inebriate women, thought that little compartments were one of the causes of an increase in drunkenness among women which was an undeniable feature of the 1890s.[19]

As James Moore, agent for the Missions to Seamen, put it in 1897, 'The idea is now to make the place a sort of little snuggery, or secret place where three or four can drink together.'[20] Apart from its particular uses, the snug, box or private bar marked the furthest swing of the pendulum away from the big open bars jammed with standing people, which were so very far from being 'secret places'. London in the mid-nineteenth century, below the upper social layers, was a raw and tough place. By the 1880s it was noticeably less so, and the plan of the pub reflected the change.

Multi-compartment pubs went out of fashion in the 1890s because of the saloon bar. This was very much an 1890s feature, though it first appeared in the 1880s. It is tempting to see it as being developed to cater for the increasing proportion of white-collar workers in late Victorian London. The term may originally have been applied to something rather different from a saloon bar in the later accepted sense, as so often happened in pub history. The earliest use of it I know is on the plan of the Britannia, Peckham, designed by George Treacher in 1881. This shows a small saloon bar with no fireplace; it is little more than a passageway between the rest of the downstairs bar space and the stairs up to the billiard room. It may have been called a saloon bar because it was the bar on the way to the billiard saloon. A bar in a similar position, but bigger and with a fireplace, is on the plan of the Stirling Castle, Camberwell, a Watney's pub designed by C. W. Bovis in 1882; but the bars are not named on the plan. In 1888 the George, Monmouth Street, had a 'salon' with fireplace, and the Equestrian, Blackfriars Road, a 'bar saloon', also with fireplace and with the stairs up to the billiard saloon leading off it (Fig. 12). The two variations on 'saloon bar' suggest that the term was still a relatively unfamiliar one.[21]

Although the 'bar saloon' in the Equestrian was the biggest of its ten bars except for the public bar, it was by no means large. But these small saloons of the 1880s were the cuckoos which would gradually push out all the other bars.[22] In the Fox and Hounds, Sydenham, designed less than two years later by the architect of the Equestrian there was a considerably larger saloon bar, leading to a ground floor billiard room, and only three other bars (Fig. 13). This was to become the standard arrangement. The tendency in the nineties was for saloon bars to get larger and the total number of bars smaller. It was only a tendency, however: a total of seven or eight bars was still very common. Saloon bars very often communicated directly with a billiard room, because the development of the saloon coincided with a sharp increase in the number of billiard rooms in pubs, adding up to a two-handed campaign to bring in custom. In 1896 Thurston's, the billiard table manufacturers, promoted an annual Licensed Victuallers' Billiards Tournament, and the licensed victuallers' magazines started to have regular reports of billiard matches and the

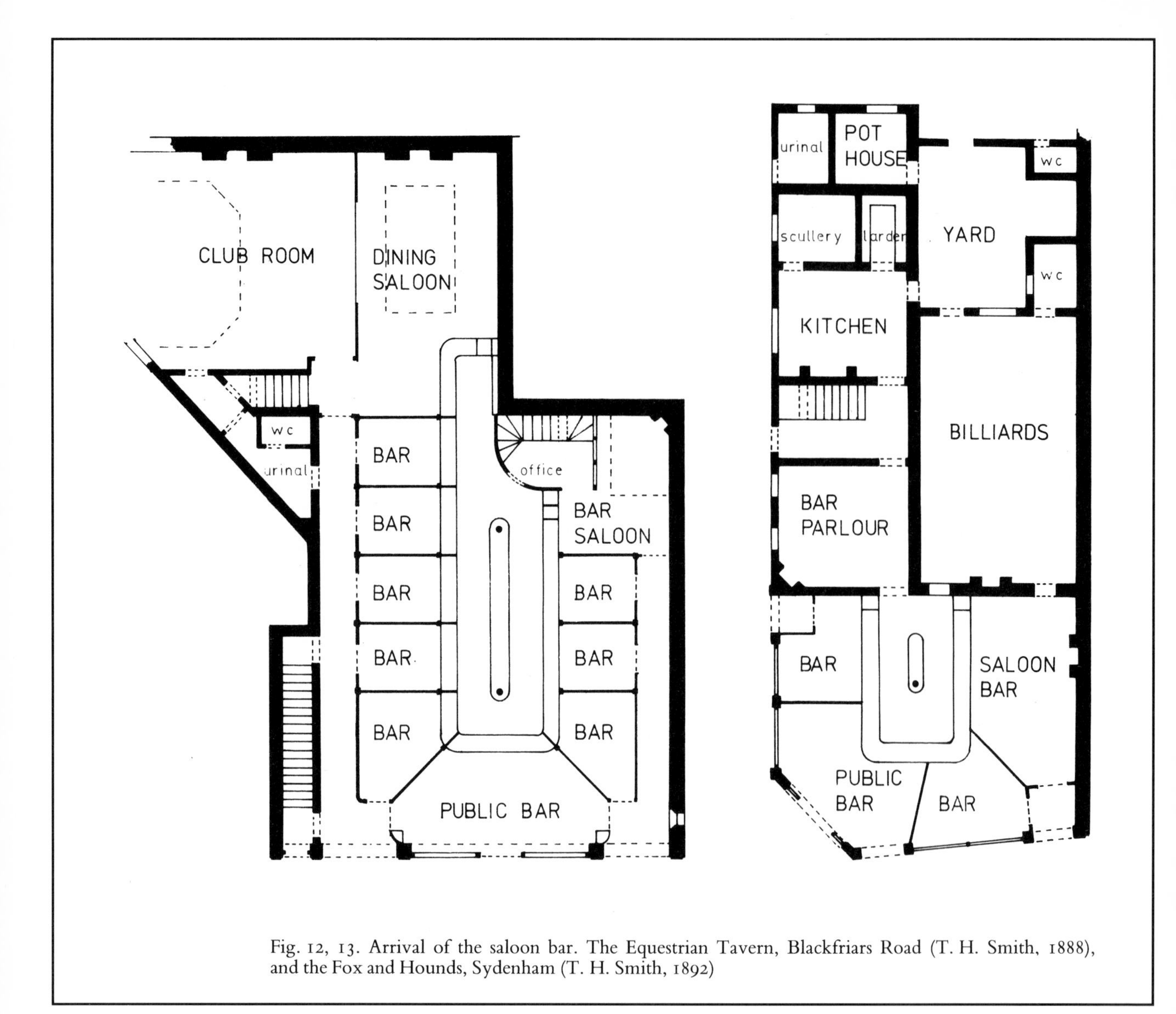

Fig. 12, 13. Arrival of the saloon bar. The Equestrian Tavern, Blackfriars Road (T. H. Smith, 1888), and the Fox and Hounds, Sydenham (T. H. Smith, 1892)

opening of billiard saloons all over London. Billiard matches were often combined with some kind of floor show, and the saloons were often extremely handsomely decorated. The majority have since been converted into bars; a sad recent loss was the opulent if somewhat battered billiard saloon at the Crown, Aberdeen Place (Plate 49), which retained its original billiard tables and fittings until 1974.

The combination of saloon and billiards, however, though very common was by no means invariable; although the term 'saloon bar' may originally have meant a bar on the way to the billiard saloon, it soon came to mean just a bar bigger than the private bars and especially comfortably furnished, always with a fireplace (unlike the other bars), often with a carpet, comfortable leather or plush upholstered

III. Design for the City of Salisbury, Tooley and Fair Street, Southwark, by C. Fitzroy Doll, 1881 (demolished)

CITY OF SALISBURY. P.H
FAIR STREET
MESSrs HOLT & Co
OFFICIAL
241
NUMBER
L.C.C.
To be returned to the
ESTATES AND VALUATION DEPARTMENT.
624
Elevation
Chas. FitzRoy Doll
Architect
64 Cannon Street
London. E.C.

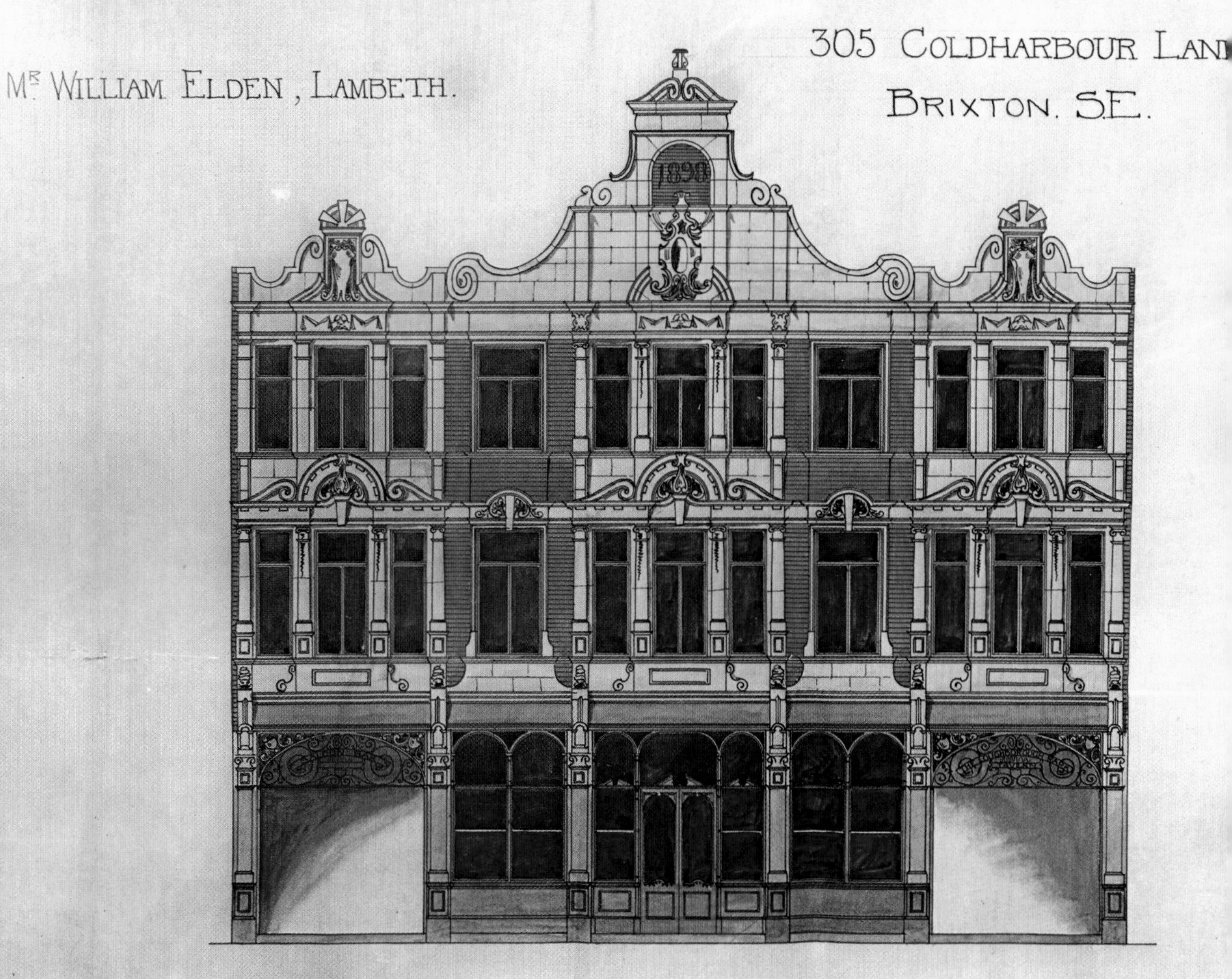
THE LOUGHBOROUGH PARK TAVERN
305 COLDHARBOUR LANE
MR WILLIAM ELDEN, LAMBETH.
BRIXTON. S.E.
1898
FRONT ELEVATION

seats, tables, vases of flowers or ferns, pictures and wallpaper (Plates 50, 51). Initially the saloon bars usually had a screen on the bar counter, as in the private bars, but this tended to be omitted; saloon bars became the local haunts of a regular lower middle-class clientele, who liked to chat across the bar. In a pub with an island serving-bar, removal of the snob-screens tended to make patrons in the saloon bar too visible from the public bars for their taste. A number of pubs of the late nineties were accordingly planned so as to have the saloon bar in a separate room with a serving-bar communicating through an arch with the rest of the serving space. Social exclusiveness was not confined to the saloon and private bars, however. Pubs of any size were likely to have at least two public bars, one for the superior artisan (a class which in the mid-century had probably patronized the tap room) and the other for labourers. Public bars had their own way of welcoming customers by enveloping them in a warm nest of rich brown, pitch-pine boarding; in small unpretentious houses this treatment sometimes extended throughout the pub. It was a style of decoration little commented on at the time but it provided (and in a few cases still provides) a remarkably sympathetic atmosphere to drink in (Plates 41, 52).

49. Billiard saloon at the Crown, Aberdeen Place, St John's Wood

IV. (left) Design for the Loughborough Park Tavern, Brixton, by Eedle and Meyers, 1898 (demolished)

An article of 1907 contains a description of a 'typical suburban pub'. It has half a dozen compartments. Omnibus drivers and conductors are in the 'four-ale' bar, 'horny handed sons of toil and lady customers' in the bar opposite, and more women in the bottle and jug, as the publican refuses to allow children. Prices are higher in the private and saloon bars than in the rest of the pub. 'The customers whose desire is to escape the "mutable many" will patronize the former; the latter is affected by the "lads of the village" and their ladies. The saloon bar is the ante-chamber of the billiard room, the habitués are mostly known to the landlord, and often address the barmaids by their Christian names.'[23]

At this stage pub-planning had come a full circle from the 'traditional' plan of the early nineteenth century. The saloon bar was close to the original parlour, the public bar to the tap room, the private bar to the snug or private room, and the jug-and-bottle department to the shop. The difference lay in the counter, which now served all the public space, allowing the publican to exert much easier supervision and making waiter service unnecessary. In between lay the wide open spaces

50. (top left) The saloon bar of the Horse and Dolphin, St Martin's Street, Trafalgar Square, in 1899
51 (left) The saloon bar of the Cantons, Cambridge Circus, in 1899
52. The Grape Vine, Mile End Road, in the 1940s

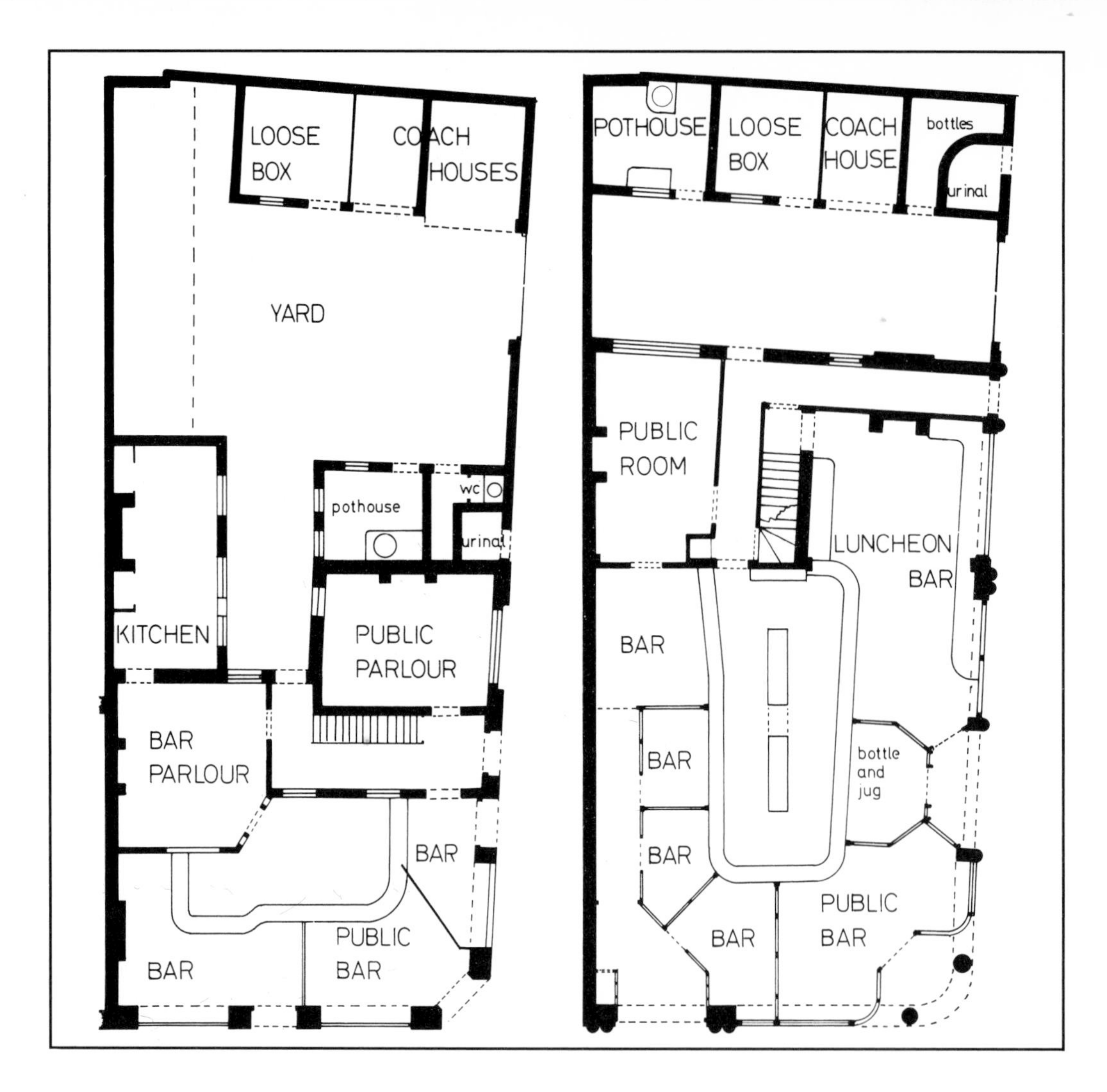

of the mid-nineteenth-century gin palaces with one bar and no seats. What had originally been the result of tough time-and-motion study had been humanized.

In fact the one-bar type had never swept the board: many pubs continued to have parlours and tap rooms until the end of the century. What was happening was a merging together of two types, the one-bar pub accepting seats and increasing numbers of partitions, the old-style pub allowing the counter to push into the tap room and parlour, and both accepting a higher standard of decoration. One result of this was that respectable women started coming to pubs for the first time in their history;[24] the clientele of taverns of the eighteenth and early nineteenth centuries, although they reached much higher up the social range, had not brought their wives with them.

Modernized pubs, saloon bars and billiard rooms attracted more people, and as the ratio of pubs to population changed there were potentially more people for each individual pub to attract anyway; the result was that an enterprising London publican in the 1890s could be confident of drawing in as many people as his pub could deal with. So in addition to improving the plan of the serving-bars, every effort was made to use existing space more efficiently and to increase the size of

Fig. 14. The Queen Victoria, Southwark Park Road, before and after alterations by J. J. Alexander in 1891. The pub has been extended over the back yard, the bar parlour eliminated and the counter extended.
53. (right) A bar stillion of 1899 in the demolished Elephant and Castle, Newington Butts

the pub as much as possible. Kitchens, if they were still on the ground floor, were more and more often moved up to the first or even the top floor. Rooms not served by a counter were got rid of; tap rooms and parlours had already been disappearing fast, and now bar parlours began to follow them; bar parlours were going down like ninepins in the 1890s (Fig. 14), replaced, if at all, by a small office behind the bar counter. The serving space behind the counter, which had often been unnecessarily large, was reduced to the minimum; the ideal was a central island serving-bar around a central island fitting, known as a 'wagon' or 'bar stillion', draped with bottles and glasses and with kegs along the top, so that everything was immediately to hand for the bar staff (Plate 53, Colour Plate II).

And pubs swelled in every possible direction (Plate 54, Fig. 14), They put on an extra storey; if they had a front garden they spread over it; if they had a back yard (and many pubs had large yards, relics of the days when they used to stable horses) they spread over it; if they could buy the next-door property they expanded into it. Sometimes these expansions were combined with a complete rebuilding, but often they were not; additions made over the front garden, usually at ground floor level only, are still easy to spot in many pubs as one walks round London today.

54. (above and right) The Hampton Court, Crampton Street, Newington, before and after rebuilding in 1893 on an extended site to the designs of F. A. Powell

It seems, at first sight, curious that the licensing magistrates, who were conducting a fairly rigorous policy of reducing the number of pubs, were prepared to allow the ones that remained to expand; in fact, the total drinking area per person in London was reduced far less than the decline of pubs per person might lead one to expect. There were two main reasons why publicans got away with it. The first was that the law was by no means clear. Sir H. B. Poland, a lawyer who specialized in licensing law, thought that a publican had a legal right to enlarge his premises within reason, and what he considered within reason was very generous:

'if having a corner house he were to take the two next houses and knock them into one, that would not be the same house; but if he built some room on the back yard, or having a large house took in a small house, it might be considered as the same . . . If it is in substance the same house, he does not require a new licence and the renewal takes place.'[25]

Many licensing magistrates did not agree with him, and managed to keep a tight hold on alterations and enlargements in their district. But enlargements frequently got through because magistrates did not, on the whole, represent the Temperance lobby, which wanted pubs reduced in order to give people fewer opportunities for drinking. Magistrates wanted to weed out small old-fashioned pubs in favour of fewer, larger and more up-to-date ones which would be easier to supervise. The big new-style pub of the nineties, with a central serving-bar from which the publican could overlook the entire drinking space, suited their purpose very well and they were not going to discourage it.

55. A private bar at the Mitre, Chancery Lane, in 1892

56. (right) *Summer*, one of a series of paintings of the seasons in the Tottenham, Oxford Street

'Tis Beer, as is to statesmen known,
Supports the Altar and the Throne,
'Twas Beer this Parliament returned
And the great Tory triumph earned
Sir Wilfred Lawson on the 1896 election

4 Politics and Money

MUCH more can be discovered about the pubs of the 1880s and 1890s than about their predecessors. This is partly because many more plans and drawings have survived, partly because the printed sources are better; the licensed victuallers' periodicals in the 1890s, for instance, are far glossier, better illustrated and more informative about contemporary pubs than earlier numbers.

But it is also because, in spite of the enormous amount of change, rebuilding, and redecoration that has taken place, pubs of the eighties and especially the nineties survive in considerable quantities, and not only their exteriors survive but their interiors as well. The popular idea of a Victorian pub interior is derived almost entirely from this period, for earlier examples are almost non-existent.

They are non-existent because so few of them lasted out the nineteenth century. The late eighties and the nineties saw a pub boom which had never been equalled before and was never to be equalled again. By hundreds and probably thousands, London pubs were rebuilt or at least completely reconstructed at ground floor level. The remodelling was carried out with a lavishness of gilding, decorated glass, painted tiles, mosaic floors, wrought metal lamps and elaborate mahogany fittings that immediately made the pubs of the previous twenty years, let alone the early Victorian gin palaces, seem dowdy and second-rate.

The boom was only partially caused by a general rise in standards of living accompanied by a rise in purchasing power. The immediate and principal cause was that the redevelopment of pubs had become a rewarding form of property speculation. It had become so because of a curious mixture of politics, economics, and morals.

Drink was a major moral and political issue in the eighties and nineties. Up till the 1870s the Temperance movement had not been identified with either of the main political parties. Support for licensing bills came from both sides of the house, although usually more from the Liberals than the Tories. Wellington's Beer Bill of 1830 was supported by the Whigs and opposed by the high Tories in his own party. The Beer Bill of 1869 was introduced by a Tory private member and supported by both parties. The Liberal Aberdare Bill of 1872 was voted for by many Conservatives and opposed by many Liberals. It had more support from the Liberals than the Conservatives, however; and the great heat engendered by the licensing question in 1871–2, especially by the abandoned bill of 1871, started a polarization of the political parties which steadily increased in the next decade. By the 1880s the Conservatives were the accepted friends of the drink interest, and the Liberals its dedicated enemies. The Conservatives started to deal out peerages to rich brewers in the 1880s, and gibes about 'brewing barons' and 'the beerage' became a commonplace in the Liberal press.

The division was not an absolute one between prohibition and permissiveness. The Conservatives agreed that the number of public houses should be reduced; they were even ready to improve on the braking power introduced by the legislation of 1869–71 and to legislate for the planned reduction of licensed houses, with compensation for those who lost their licences. The drink interest was prepared to accept this; a combination of compensation for the dispossessed and more business for the pubs that survived was not without its advantages.

But what it refused to swallow, and fought against with all the means of publicity and pressure at its disposal, was the Liberal policy. In 1891 the Liberals had lined up with the United Kingdom Alliance, the leading Temperance organization, and had accepted local option. 'Local option' meant handing the regulation of drink over to local government; it was part of a general Liberal policy of decentralization, of which Home Rule was only one aspect. Licensing was to be handed over from magistrates to local councils; a two-thirds majority among the ratepayers would allow them to thin out or even completely abolish licensed premises; and no compensation would be paid to those who lost their licences, on the grounds that a licence was not a piece of property but something which was granted annually at the discretion of the licensing authorities. Moreover the Liberals, or at least the extremely strong non-conformist and prohibition element within the Liberals, made it clear that the potentiality of areas of the country going completely dry was one that appealed to them. A Local Option Bill was introduced in 1893, postponed because of the Home Rule crisis, and re-introduced in 1895. It would probably have become law if the Liberals had not unexpectedly lost a minor motion in June and been disastrously defeated at the General Election that followed. The Conservatives, who had the support of the entire drink interest, came in with a majority of 152, and the Liberals remained out of office until 1906.[1]

The result of this political situation in terms of pub architecture was that far more pubs were rebuilt or remodelled under the Tories than under the Liberals. More was also drunk under the Tories (Figs. 16, 17). The drink boom and the building boom were interconnected. Publicans and brewers built more because they felt more secure about keeping their licences, or at least being compensated if they lost them, but also because their takings were going up as people drank more. People drank more because the fact that the drinker's party was in power spread a mood of euphoria through the bars,[2] and also because rebuilt and redecorated pubs pulled in more people.

The increase in drinking is shown by statistics; the increase in the building of pubs was much commented on at the time[3] and is supported by the evidence of the tenders in the *Builder*. The annual fluctuation of pub contracts of £1,000 or over recorded in the *Builder* between 1880 and 1899 almost exactly correlates with the political situation (Fig. 18). The Liberal ascendancy of 1880–6 is a bad period for pub contracts, which are at a low point of 21 in 1886. By 1887, with the Conservatives in, they are up to 36 and reach a peak of 62 in 1891. They collapse once more to a low point of 21 during the Liberal government of 1892–5, and zoom up again when the Conservatives come back to a record peak of 84 in 1898.

But there are two aspects of the building fluctuations which can be explained only by going outside the immediate political situation. One is the fact that the second Tory boom is much bigger than the first one; the other is its disastrous collapse in 1899, when the Tory government still had seven years to run. To explain both these features one has to turn one's attention from the politicians to the brewers, and examine the curious and ultimately disastrous history of the 'brewers' war' of 1896–9.

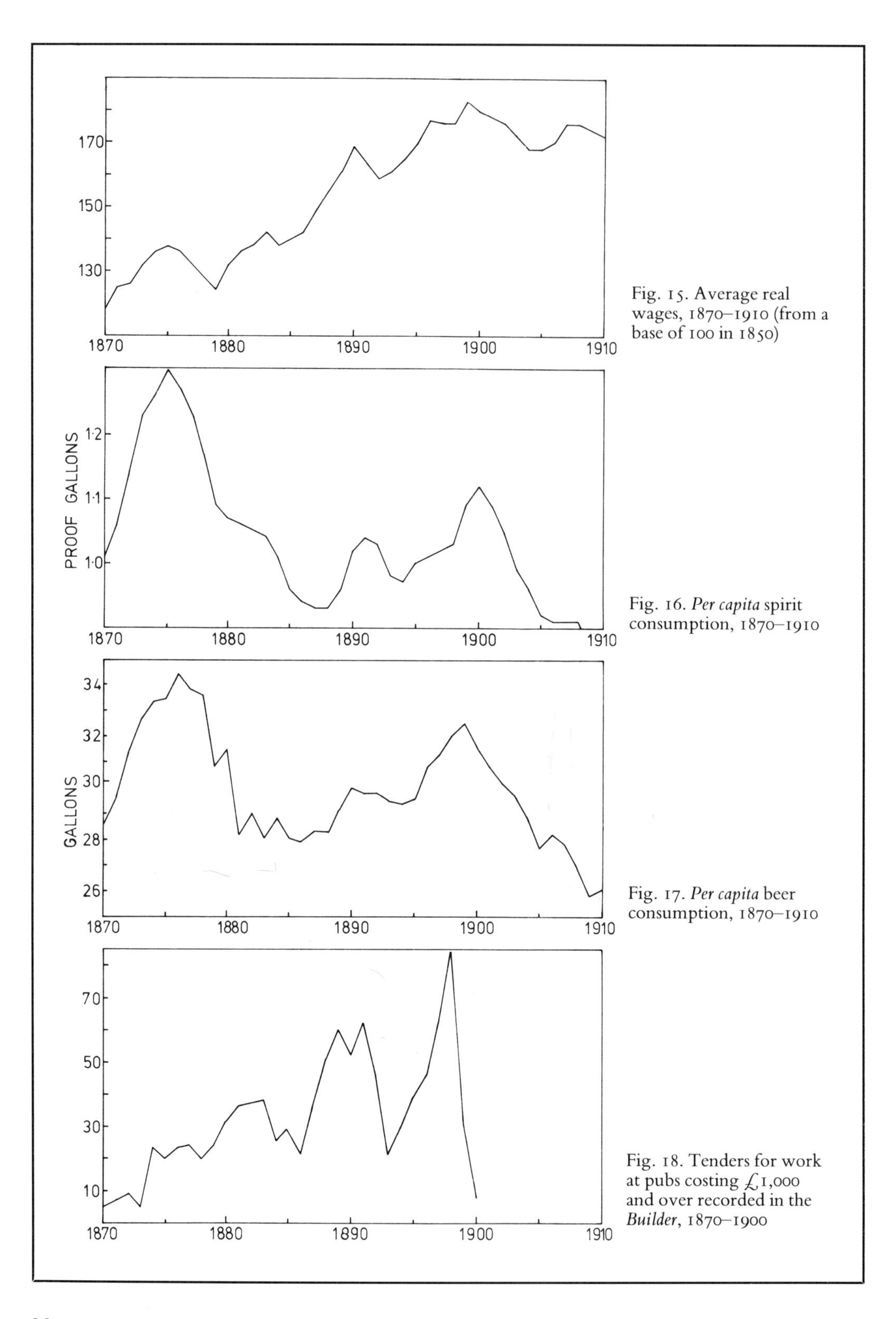

Fig. 15. Average real wages, 1870–1910 (from a base of 100 in 1850)

Fig. 16. *Per capita* spirit consumption, 1870–1910

Fig. 17. *Per capita* beer consumption, 1870–1910

Fig. 18. Tenders for work at pubs costing £1,000 and over recorded in the *Builder*, 1870–1900

Brewers have been mentioned very little so far because, as far as the building of London pubs was concerned, they were comparatively unimportant until the 1890s. In 1892, after a slow increase in the number of pubs owned by them over the century and a spurt of buying in the previous five years, they still owned only about 2,100 out of the total of about 7,100 pubs in London.[4] This was a substantial holding, but nowhere near approaching the monopoly which they were to acquire later. The situation was transformed in the next fifteen years.

There were three main reasons why brewery ownership had remained low in London, much lower than in the rest of the country. In the first place property was more expensive in London, and the brewers did not have the assets to embark on large-scale buying. Secondly, a high proportion of London pubs were leasehold not freehold, and the brewers were unwilling to invest in a diminishing asset. Finally they had an alternative system which worked very well.

This was what was known as the 'London custom' or the 'London system'. A publican or would-be publican who wanted to acquire a public house would borrow a large proportion (70 per cent was common) of the money needed from a brewer. On this he would pay 5 per cent interest and agree to buy the brewer's beer. The agreement was not binding, but if the publican started buying beer elsewhere the brewer would call in his loan. The big breweries which dominated London had a gentlemanly agreement not to try to tempt trade away from each other. Most London pubs were financed in this way. In 1892 E. N. Buxton, a partner in Truman, Hanbury and Buxton, reckoned that, of the capital invested in non-brewery-owned pubs, 57 per cent was lent by the brewers and 23 per cent supplied by the publicans.[5] The rest came from various sources, including loans from distillers, who lent money on the same kind of agreement as brewers but usually in smaller amounts.[6] It was difficult for publicans to borrow money outside the drink trade, because the value of a pub depended on its licence, and anyone lending money risked losing it if the licence was removed. The brewers were prepared to run the risk, because in addition to their 5 per cent they were getting an outlet for their beer.

The London custom began to run into difficulties in the 1880s for a number of reasons.[7] In the first place, brewers were having to lend out more money in order to sell less beer. Beer consumption was falling steadily between 1876 and 1885, a phenomenon for which the Temperance lobby took the credit[8] but which was probably due more to the industrial slump of the late seventies and the agricultural slump of the eighties. But the price of pubs, and therefore the amount publicans needed to borrow, was going up; London property prices were rising generally and pub prices faster than the average, because as the number of pubs remained static and the population rose, natural market forces were operating. Between 1869 and 1879 Whitbread's sales fell slightly but their loans to publicans rose from £450,000 to £600,000. Between 1879 and 1889, their loans had gone up by half to £900,000, and although their sales had risen by a third, most of the increase was due to free sales, not sales to tied houses. By 1897–8 their loans were up to £2,000,000.

Meanwhile the publicans and the London brewers had fallen out. London publicans in the seventies and eighties found that their costs were rising. Not only were pubs becoming more expensive to buy; rates were up (revalued every five years after an act of 1869) and licences, which were based on rates, rose with them. As far as individual pubs were concerned, the fall in drink consumption probably more or less cancelled out any benefits from the increasing ratio of pubs to people. Publicans reacted, in the time-honoured way, by watering their beer. This was made illegal, for the first time, in 1885. In 1887 the London brewers announced that they would call in the loan and refuse to take on the custom of any publican convicted of diluting. This infuriated the publicans, who looked for alternative sources of capital, and began to find them.

A system of 'vendor's mortgages' was developed by which a publican selling a pub left a large portion of the purchase price as a loan to the publican who bought it. The Licensed Victuallers' Mortgage Association, which lent money to publicans, without ties, was formed in 1887. A few institutions not connected with the drink trade, such as the Birkbeck Building Society, started to lend money to London publicans.[9] Perhaps most important of all, so did the Burton brewers.

The appearance of Burton as a major source of capital for publicans was an unpleasant shock for the London brewers. Burton beer was their great trade rival. Up till the middle of the nineteenth century the staple drink of London pubs was 'porter' or 'entire', dark, heavy beer similar to, but not quite as strong as, stout. Light or pale ale and its draught equivalent, bitter, were the invention of the Burton brewers, using the water of the Trent, which was very hard and highly charged with gypsum. Light, clear sparkling ale in glasses (as opposed to dark, heavy porter in tankards) swept the London markets. London brewers retaliated by starting branch breweries in Burton; ultimately they found they could treat their own water and produce as good bitter and light ale in London.[10] But the Burton brewers had the initiative; by the end of the nineteenth century their share of the London market was a large one, and if the London brewers lost control of their tied pubs, it was likely to become even larger.

It was not surprising that London brewers started to secure their markets by buying up pubs. But to establish their security they needed more capital than at first they had available. The way out was demonstrated by Guinness's. In 1886, for reasons quite separate from any need to buy up pubs (for Guinness was the only brewery to operate in independence of tied houses), Guinness went public. The issue of £6,000,000 was oversubscribed many times. The British public had revealed an insatiable and, as it turned out, misplaced enthusiasm for investing their money in the drink trade.

Over the next ten years breweries went public in shoals. They raised many millions of capital and proceeded to lavish them on public house property. It was an escalating situation. Buying was held in check during the Liberal government of 1892–5, but broke out again with redoubled fury when the Conservatives came back in the summer of 1895. In London the younger or smaller breweries were the most aggressive, and unlike the big established firms they had no gentlemanly scruples about poaching on others' preserves. The big breweries were forced to step up their buying in self-defence. Prices soared. The buying of public houses developed from a competition to a war, and from a war to a panic. In 1896–8 the prices that were being paid were crazy.

Pubs in key positions, or in the newly developing suburbs where the licensing authorities kept licences to a minimum, went for the biggest sums. In December 1898 the Crown, Cricklewood Broadway, was up for auction. The agents advertised it in the following enthusiastic terms: 'Valuable freehold with possession of this very successful establishment and driving a trade of great magnitude, which has increased by leaps and bounds during the past two or three years. The extraordinary development by the building of new streets and thoroughfares renders this situation one of the most remarkable. The unopposed position of the property is unique, there not being a licensed house between it and Willesden Green. Plans for the rebuilding have been passed by the magistrates, the present structure being quite inadequate to supply the wants of the public . . .'[11] When this small suburban pub, which had gone for £2,000 in 1873, was sold for £86,000, no one was especially surprised. The pub had been resold four times since 1873 and its price had risen at each sale from £2,000 to £5,000, £15,000, £32,000 and £42,000.[12] The final price, though high, was not a record.

The purchaser was the Cannon Brewery, of St John's Street, Clerkenwell. The Crown was one of the last, and the most expensive, of its purchases in a campaign of buying that had started in the mid-1890s. The Cannon Brewery had been one of the smaller breweries. It was founded in 1845 and was in a bad way by 1890, when it was rescued by two enterprising, fox-hunting managing directors, Andrew R. Motion (MFH of the East Essex) and William Musgrave Wroughton (MFH of the Pytchley). They pursued pubs like foxes, and helped the hunt along by going public in 1895 and raising a million in share capital. According to a contemporary account, 'Business developed rapidly . . . you could see it grow.'[13] They bought two varieties of public house property: leases of pubs, or freeholds with vacant possession, which they bought for the immediate benefit of their trade; and freeholds occupied by leaseholders who had some years to run, which they bought much cheaper, as a long-term investment. Whenever they had vacant possession of a freehold pub they rebuilt it with splendid effervescence, to the designs of one of the liveliest firms of pub architects, Shoebridge and Rising (Plate 57). They spent £250,000 on rebuilding pubs over six years.

In the years 1893–8 they also spent £1,363,010 on buying 125 pubs.[14] Expenditure in 1892 had been only £4,100. In 1893 and 1894 it jumped to £25,400 and £99,860. By going public in 1895 the brewery greatly increased its capital resources, and its expenditure in 1895–8 was £217,545, £443,645, £416,140 and £160,420. In these years the price that had to be paid for pubs had gone steadily up; the maximum prices paid in each of the six years from 1893 were £23,000, £24,500, £28,200, £55,000, £50,000 and £84,000. It was the aggressive entry of smaller breweries like the Cannon which forced the big breweries to join the battle, escalate their buying policy and buy up pubs at increasingly inflated prices.

REBUILT
1899

Allsopp's, for instance, buying largely outside London, spent £3,230,000 between 1896 and 1900 'in an almost feverish desire to buy licensed houses'.[15] The highest prices were mostly paid in 1896, when the fever was at its highest. The record was that of the Victoria, King's Cross, sold in November for £98,000. The Chippenham, Shirland Road (Plate 58), was sold in May for £95,000; it had fetched £17,500 in 1880, since when about £3,000 had been spent on it. The Volunteer, Kilburn, was sold in July for £32,000. It had been sold for £13,000 in 1892 after which £2,000 had been spent on it. The Railway Tavern, West Hampstead, went for £52,000, as compared to £7,000 in 1884. The general average of prices dropped slightly in 1897 and 1898, but very high individual prices continued to be paid. In 1897 the Royal Oak, Bishop's Bridge Road, went for £80,000; in 1898, as already described, the Crown, Cricklewood Broadway, fetched £86,000.[16]

These prices were out of all proportion to what had been paid for pubs before,[17] or, indeed, to what has been paid since. In some cases the pubs would be unlikely

57. (left) The Rising Sun, Euston Road (Shoebridge and Rising, 1899)

58. The Chippenham, Shirland Road, Maida Vale, sold in 1896 for £95,000

to fetch the same price if put on the market today, and the 1890s prices should be multiplied at least by thirty to give their modern equivalent. They were recorded in the papers at the time with the same kind of hushed astonishment with which soaring property prices have been recorded in recent years.

The breweries were by no means the only buyers. The spiralling market was irresistibly tempting to private speculators. To buy a pub, improve it, work up its trade and sell it at a good profit had been a recognized way of making money right through the nineteenth century. Once the numbers of pubs began to decline relative to the population in the 1870s, it became increasingly attractive financially, because the value of pubs was rising irrespective of anything the publicans did to improve them. An astute and hard-working publican could work his way up from a small pub to a large one, and from a single pub to a string of them. When the brewers' war sent potential profits soaring, publican speculators began to engage in the buying and selling of pubs with the same kind of frenzy as the brewers engaged in buying them. Almost all their business was done on borrowed money. Much of this was lent by the brewers, who in the madness of the moment continued with one hand to prime the pump that was forcing up the prices of pubs which they were buying with the other.

Pubs now tended to change hands at least every five years and often more frequently. Although it might seem that all the buyer had to do was to wait and collect his profit a few years later, a great many improved their purchases either by complete rebuilding or by extensive redecoration. They may have done this partly in order to give themselves something to do, but it was also arguable that the money spent in improvements was more than recouped in the next sale. A thoroughly up-to-date house doing a good business would fetch a good price not only because of its business but because of the political situation. It was less likely to lose its licence—without compensation under the Liberals and with it under the Conservatives—if any drastic political reduction of licensed houses was embarked on; and of course if it survived the purge its value would increase proportionately. The risk was greater under the Liberals, and the figures of public house building reflected it.

By no means all publicans indulged in this continual buying and selling, but it was the ones that did who set the pace. The pubs which they improved were likely, even if they were not rebuilt, to have their ground floor completely remodelled, with new bar fittings, a new lavishly appointed saloon bar, probably a new billiard room, and all the trimmings of engraved glass, mirrors, monstrous lamps and ceilings rich with lincrusta on a new scale of lavishness. Other publicans were under strong pressure to do the same to keep up with them; so for that matter were the brewers. The mini-boom of 1886–92 was followed by the maxi-boom of 1896–9, with the brewers' war increasing the pace and the Conservative government providing the background feeling of security. There were few pubs which escaped without at least an internal remodelling; very often a pub that had been rebuilt or remodelled in the mini-boom was done over a second time in the maxi one.

Contemporary sources are full of information about the way publicans borrowed money with which to buy pubs. They are curiously silent about where the money came from with which to rebuild or alter them. Certainly in some, and possibly in many, cases this money was also lent by the brewers or distillers. The interior splendours of the Elgin, Ladbroke Grove (Colour Plates X, XIII), for instance, are due to William George Dickinson, who acquired it in 1892, redecorated it with sprinklings of his own initials and sold it again to Smith Garrett and Company, the brewers, in 1895. He borrowed £10,000 from, apparently, a private individual, William Nesbitt of 16 Waterloo Place, and £4,000 from Courage and Company, £3,500 of which was specifically advanced 'for the purchase of the Elgin Arms and alterations and improvements effected by him in and about the same'.[18] No doubt there were many other examples of this kind of loan. In any case publicans seem to have had little difficulty in raising the money.

From time to time publican speculators rise dimly to the surface of the licensed victuallers' papers. There was, for instance, Richard T. Davies, born on a farm in Carmarthenshire, who 'has bought and sold some three score licensed houses'. There was W. C. Guider, who commenced business in 1875 with the Pemberton Arms, Bow, sold it in 1877 leaving himself with capital of £1,000 and between then and 1900 bought and sold some thirty to forty pubs. There was W. J. Goddard, 'formerly of the Aberfeldy, Poplar, the Royal Hotel, Mile End Road, the Blackstock, Seven Sisters Road, and other well-known houses (at least thirty in number) too numerous to mention'.[19] But a few of the bigger operators can be given rather more identity.

The best known and for many years the most successful of these were the celebrated Baker brothers. The brothers were William Henry Baker (1841–99) and Richard Baker.[20] They came up from Minehead in Devon as young men with a few shillings between them, and started business as licensed victuallers in the 1870s. In the 1880s they established themselves at four large and important pubs, the Angel, Islington, the Cock, Highbury, the Victoria, King's Cross, and the Falstaff, Eastcheap, a pub-restaurant in the City. In 1888 they launched Baker Brothers Ltd, a limited liability company with a share capital of £120,000 in £5 shares of which the Baker family owned just over half. W. H. Baker was chairman and Richard Baker managing director. In 1890 the brothers bought one end of the pub chain belonging to Charles Best, in the form of the massive and prestigious Horse Shoe, Tottenham Court Road, and the little Flying Horse and an adjacent tobacconist across the road. They enlarged and redecorated E. L. Paraire's brassy Horse Shoe and rebuilt the Flying Horse and its neighbouring premises (where they had their offices), renaming it the Tottenham (Plate 59).

Their financial progress then became infinitely complex. The brothers and their families performed a mysterious ritual dance, individually and in different combinations. In 1896 Baker Brothers Ltd sold the Cock, Angel and Victoria for such enormous sums (£74,000 for the Angel and £98,000 for the Victoria)[21] that they were able to pay their shareholders £4·10 in the pound and to reconstitute the company. It now owned only the Horse Shoe and Falstaff with £24,000 capital in ten shilling

59. The Tottenham, Oxford Street (Saville and Martin, 1892)

shares, of which over 80 per cent belonged to the Bakers. The Tottenham had never been part of Baker Brothers Ltd; it was run independently by the brothers, trading as Henry and Richard Baker, until they sold it in 1897 and, as Baker Brothers, unlimited, acquired the Old Bell in Fleet Street. Meanwhile William Henry Baker on his own had bought and sold the Trafalgar, Notting Hill, and then bought the Shepherd and Shepherdess, Aldenham Street, NW. Richard Baker on his own bought the Load of Hay, Praed Street, in 1890, and settled his wife Emily at the Queen's Arms, Kilburn High Street. His son W. R. R. Baker was at the Duke of York, Victoria Street, and Punch's Tavern, Fleet Street, by 1893 and the Grecian Restaurant, Strand, by 1895. During the 1890s Richard Baker, his wife and son coalesced into Baker and Company, which rapidly swelled to impressive proportions. By the end of the century Baker and Company's properties included the Queen's Hotel, the Hotel and Grand Café de l'Europe, the Garrick Hotel, Challis's Royal Hotel and the Globe Restaurant, all in or around Leicester Square, the Albion Hotel, New Bridge Street, and the Norfolk Square Hotel, Paddington. Much the grandest of these properties were the Queen's Hotel and the Hotel de l'Europe, rebuilt by Baker and Company in 1894–7 and 1896–9.

Unlike many of their fellow publicans the Bakers seldom aimed at a rapid turnover; they selected their pubs carefully, spent time and money on them and kept the more important of them ten or twenty years. They liked large pubs with a restaurant or hotel department, and pubs close to railway stations; the Victoria

was next door to King's Cross, the Load of Hay to Paddington, and the Duke of York to Victoria; the Cock straddled North Islington railway station, described in 1888 as a 'local Charing Cross', and the station refreshment rooms were in its basement. Completion of its alterations and enlargement in 1888 was celebrated by a dinner,[22] a convivial speech-laden evening, with toasts of 'Success to Messrs Baker Brothers' such as was often reported in the late Victorian press. Among the guests was Mr E. Pollendine of Messrs Nicholson and Company, the gin distillers; Nicholson's had invested £20,000 in Baker Brothers Ltd, and later provided a mortgage of £40,000 on the Horse Shoe. A dinner to celebrate the Horse Shoe's redecoration in 1893 was presided over by W. H. Bailey, the London representative of Bass, and by Mr Buchanan, of the whisky distillers, both presumably providers of further dollops of capital.[23]

With the support of the liquor trade (and, in the case of W. H. Baker, at least, numerous other financial irons in the fire) the Baker brothers rose to become the aristocrats of the public house world. Richard Baker graduated from a house in Highbury to Norfolk Crescent, Bayswater. His brother (Plate 60) became a Lieutenant-Colonel in the Honourable Artillery Company, with a house and family in Cumberland Terrace, Regent's Park, and a mistress and second family in Gordon Square. 'Colonel Baker', as he was always referred to, was described as 'a rather dandified man'; his brother, 'Dicky', was flashier, financially closer to the wind and, in later years, probably more hard-working. He used to visit each of his many

60. The aristocrat of the public house world. Colonel Baker in Hong Kong in 1898

businesses once a day; there were fourteen of them by the end of the 1890s. He claimed that if he had sold out in 1897 he would have been left worth £120,000. Unfortunately he did not sell out; and his business ventures, like those of many of his fellow publicans, ended in disaster.

The Baker brothers' empire is a largely vanished one. The massive and ornate blocks of the Queen's Hotel and the Hotel de l'Europe, flanking either side of Leicester Place, still dominate the northern side of Leicester Square, but they have long ceased to be hotels. The Horse Shoe was entirely redecorated in the 1930s; the charming interiors of the Garrick, rebuilt in 1892 with ninetyish wall decorations showing scenes of eighteenth-century life, were ripped out some years ago. The only relatively complete survival is the little Tottenham, with its gay and elaborate striped facade of stone and red brick surmounted by a Flemish gable, its sumptuous panels of engraved and coloured glass and its painted panels of plump allegorical figures (Plate 56, Colour Plate v). The architects of the Tottenham were Saville and Martin, a firm which specialized almost entirely in pubs. Like many publicans the Bakers remained loyal to the same firm through its various metamorphoses as Arthur W. Saville, Saville and Knight, and Saville and Martin.[24] They deserted it only for their last project, the Hotel and Grand Café de l'Europe.[25] The changeover perhaps reflects their transition from publicans to hoteliers and men-about-town, for their new architect was Walter Emden, a fashionable designer of restaurants, capable of more sophisticated effects than Saville and Martin could hope to provide.

Saville and Martin were also the architects for Deakin and Crimmen, a typical publican pair who sometimes operated on their own and sometimes in partnership. The Macclesfield in Macclesfield Street, Soho (for Crimmen, 1890), is a handsome example of one of their pubs.[26] Charles Deakin, as chairman of the Licensed Victuallers' Association, figured prominently as a witness at the 1896–8 Royal Commission on the Liquor Licensing Laws. There were a good few of these often-shifting publican partnerships, like that of William Poole and Venner, who bought and sold pubs in considerable number and employed the architect R. A. Lewcock to do them up.[27] Their pubs included the Royal Vauxhall Tavern, where in the 1970s the performers in a nightly drag show were to use Lewcock's curving bar counter as a stage. Another well-known publican-speculator, James Kirk, had a second line in music-halls. His architects for both types were Wylson and Long, best known for the famous Oxford Music Hall (1893), in which Kirk had an interest.[28]

But Wylson and Long were not very interesting architects. A much more lively figure who was also closely tied up with one particular public house speculator was the immensely prolific William Mortimer Brutton. He was consistently employed by the—in speculating terms—equally prolific William Grimes. Brutton was the zaniest of Victorian pub architects; Grimes, at once omnipresent and elusive, was one of the most successful of publican-speculators: between them they exude an atmosphere of music-hall raffishness and vigorous vulgarity epitomizing the pub world of the 1890s.

Grimes was born in Kennington in 1849.[29] His father was a pigeon owner and

61. William Atherden, partner in Grimes and Company

dog fancier; in view of his son's later career one wonders if he had any connection with the Grimes who owned the Oriental Music Hall, Poplar, in the 1860s.[30] As a boy William Grimes travelled all over the country flying his father's pigeons; for a time he was an office boy on a national newspaper; he was then apprenticed as a signwriter, grainer and artistic decorator 'and becoming accomplished in his profession embellished the interior of some of the handsomest taverns in London and the provinces'. His next step was to take a tobacco shop in Westminster Bridge Road, and build the business into a chain. Many late Victorian tobacconists ran a bookmaking business on the side; certainly Grimes at this period owned an interest in a few racehorses and moved in racing circles.

About 1888, in fact at the beginning of the first Tory boom, he embarked into the pub world and bought the Union Tavern, Union Road, Clapham. After that he never looked back. As the *Licensed Victuallers' Gazette* wrote in 1898: 'I am safe in saying that Mr Grimes has been connected with more licensed houses in his time than any publican in London.' But Grimes's activities are hard to follow because his turnover was so fast and it is difficult to distinguish his pubs from those of the various people who were at one time or another partners in 'Messrs Grimes and Co.' and its short-lived offshoot Grimes Ltd.

Albert Mathams and William Atherden seem to have been Grimes's particular cronies. Mathams, the youngest of the three,[31] was the son of a publican, a piano-playing athlete over six feet tall who had trained as a singer and toured in light opera in Australia and America. He started speculating in pubs in 1896 and two years later it was said that dozens of houses had already passed through his hands. Atherden (Plate 61), who was born in 1859, was the son and grandson of a publican and married a publican's daughter.[32] He was apprenticed as an engineer on the Great Eastern Railway, but at the age of eighteen he went into music-hall as a dancer and singer. For two years he took the chair at the Forester's Music Hall, Brentwood, which was attached to his father's pub; then he toured the provinces (with visits to Paris and the United States) doing pantomime sketches and 'showing extraordinary activity' in acrobatic feats through the 'star traps', 'vampires' and 'funny posts'. In 1883 he left music-halls for pubs, starting off at the King's Head, Willesden Green.

The whole Grimes set-up remained closely tied up with the music-halls. From 1892 Grimes's headquarters was the New Crown and Cushion in Westminster Bridge Road, which he rebuilt in partnership with Atherden. This was not a very large pub, but it had a small music-hall attached to it and was 'a favourite house of call' for music-hall artists. Here Grimes amiably presided over meetings of the Grand Order of Jays,[33] a music-hall society which ran its own orchestra and baseball team (Grimes was an amateur athlete, rower and boxer). Grimes also, at one time or other, had interests in the South London Music Hall and the Empress Music Hall, Brixton.

His photograph (Plate 62) shows him dressed in riding breeches, boots and Newmarket cap carrying a crop and looking like a music-hall artist got up in sporting togs and about to burst into song:

> I'm all dressed for riding in the park
> Riding in the park
> Riding in the park

The photograph dates from the short period during which he retired from the New Crown and Cushion, and from actually running pubs as opposed to buying and selling them, and set up in a villa with the suitably flashy name of De Montfort House, Streatham. But either pubs were in his blood or, more probably, he had overreached himself financially, and by 1898 he was back as an active publican, in the Spread Eagle, Oxford Street.

William Atherden served only Worthington fine pale and Burton ales in the pubs which he personally controlled. It would be interesting to know if this was the case with all Grimes and Company pubs. If so, it would suggest that they were being financed by the Burton brewers and were deliberately cocking a snook at the London brewery establishment. Certainly there is an element of brashness and cheekiness about the Grimes pubs which would go well with this. All that are documented were designed by the same architect, William Mortimer Brutton, and it seems likely that Grimes and his gang used him constantly throughout.

Nothing definite is known about W. M. Brutton's background or training, but he was almost certainly a relation, and possibly a brother, of Reginald Henry Brutton, who with William Henry Burney was a partner in Brutton and Burney, wine and spirit brokers of Great Tower Street, EC3.[34] The partners owned pubs as a sideline and were directors and shareholders in Grimes Ltd, a company incorporated

62. William Grimes, partner in Grimes and Company

in 1897 to run two of Grimes's more ambitious purchases, the Yorkshire Grey, Theobald's Road, and the Gaiety Restaurant in the Strand. W. H. Burney was also in partnership with Grimes as joint owner of the Empress Music Hall, Brixton. W. M. Brutton worked at pubs belonging to both partners, and in 1897 was appointed consultant to the Griffin Music Hall (later better known as the London) in which they had an interest.[35] His first recorded appearance as an architect was in May 1891 at the Old Friends, Lower Woolwich Road, which was being rebuilt by the New London Brewery Company. Between then and 1904 he can be connected with sixty-five new or altered pubs. His best year was 1897, when twenty-one new jobs came his way. His known jobs for Grimes were the New Crown and Cushion, Westminster Bridge Road (1892–3), the Red Lion, Camberwell (1895), the Telegraph, Brixton Hill (1896), the Earl Russell, Wells Street (1897), the Union Tavern, Camberwell New Road (1897), and the Swan and Horseshoe, a pub-restaurant in the City (1897). Other big new pubs designed by him were the King's Head, Upper Tooting Road (1896), which is perhaps his masterpiece; the Fitzroy, Charlotte Street (1897); the Loughborough, Loughborough Park (1899); and the Princess Victoria, Uxbridge Road (1899). He also worked on at least three music-halls: the Griffin, Shoreditch High Street, in 1893, the Hammersmith Theatre of Varieties in 1898, both of which had pubs incorporated in them, and perhaps the best-known music-hall of all, the Alhambra in Leicester Square, for which he designed a new Grand Entrance in 1897.[36]

Brutton was the supreme music-hall artist among pub architects, disguised in an amazing variety of costumes but always recognizable by the rakish cock of his hat, the infectious vulgarity of his walk and the brashness of his repartee, with a wickerwork trunk of architectural effects out of which he could put on act after act. Some of his many acts were more successful than others. The demolished New Crown and Cushion, which was perhaps his first important pub, was roughly speaking Gothic, a kind of mini-church of drink, culminating in a fan-shaped pediment with open arcading hanging in festoons to either side and pinnacles and little devils sprouting out on top (Plate 65). There was usually a good deal going on on the skyline of a Brutton pub. The glorious King's Head is less a mini-church than a mini-palace for a fat boozy king, with a canopied balcony for him to wave from to his loyal subjects and a series of scrolls and urns leading the eye up to a top-piece of arches, scrolls and kings' heads in front of a plump mansard roof with a little dome sprouting like a nipple on top (Plates 63, 64). The King's Head must have been justly popular, for the Union Tavern and Princess Victoria are recognizably in the same manner, gaily caparisoned with mansard roofs, balconies, towers and, in the Union Tavern, an absurd little cupola (Plate 66). The Earl Russell (now a dress shop) has a bust of the earl throned on the skyline above an arcade of fat

63. The King's Head, Upper Tooting Road, Wandsworth (W. M. Brutton, 1896)
64. (top right) The gable of the King's Head
65. (bottom left) Design for the New Crown and Cushion, Westminster Bridge Road, by W. M. Brutton, 1892–3 (demolished)
66. (bottom right) The Union Tavern, Camberwell New Road (W. M. Brutton, 1897)

THE
KINGSHEAD

New Crown & Cushion

COURAGE
UNION

dwarf columns (Plate 67). The Fitzroy (which became a famous Bohemian pub in the 1920s) is elaborate but a little fussy. The Loughborough is 'Queen Anne' in front and Second Empire behind. Perhaps best of all was the Hammersmith Theatre (or Palace) of Varieties, incorporating the Hammersmith or Palace Tavern on its ground floor, both, alas, no more. It had scrolls crawling like worms up an enormous crowning parapet, a facade below running a kind of syncopated beat of arches and triangles, and a cupola like no other cupola that ever was (Plate 68). The nervous, slapdash style of draughtsmanship in Brutton's original drawing seems in complete sympathy with the architecture.

The surviving plans of Brutton's interiors show that he liked his bar counters and bar windows to curve as boldly as the scrolls on his facades. The Union was

67. (left) The gable of the former Earl Russell, Wells Street, Marylebone, now a shop (W. M. Brutton, 1897)

68. Design for the Hammersmith Theatre of Varieties, by W. M. Brutton, 1898

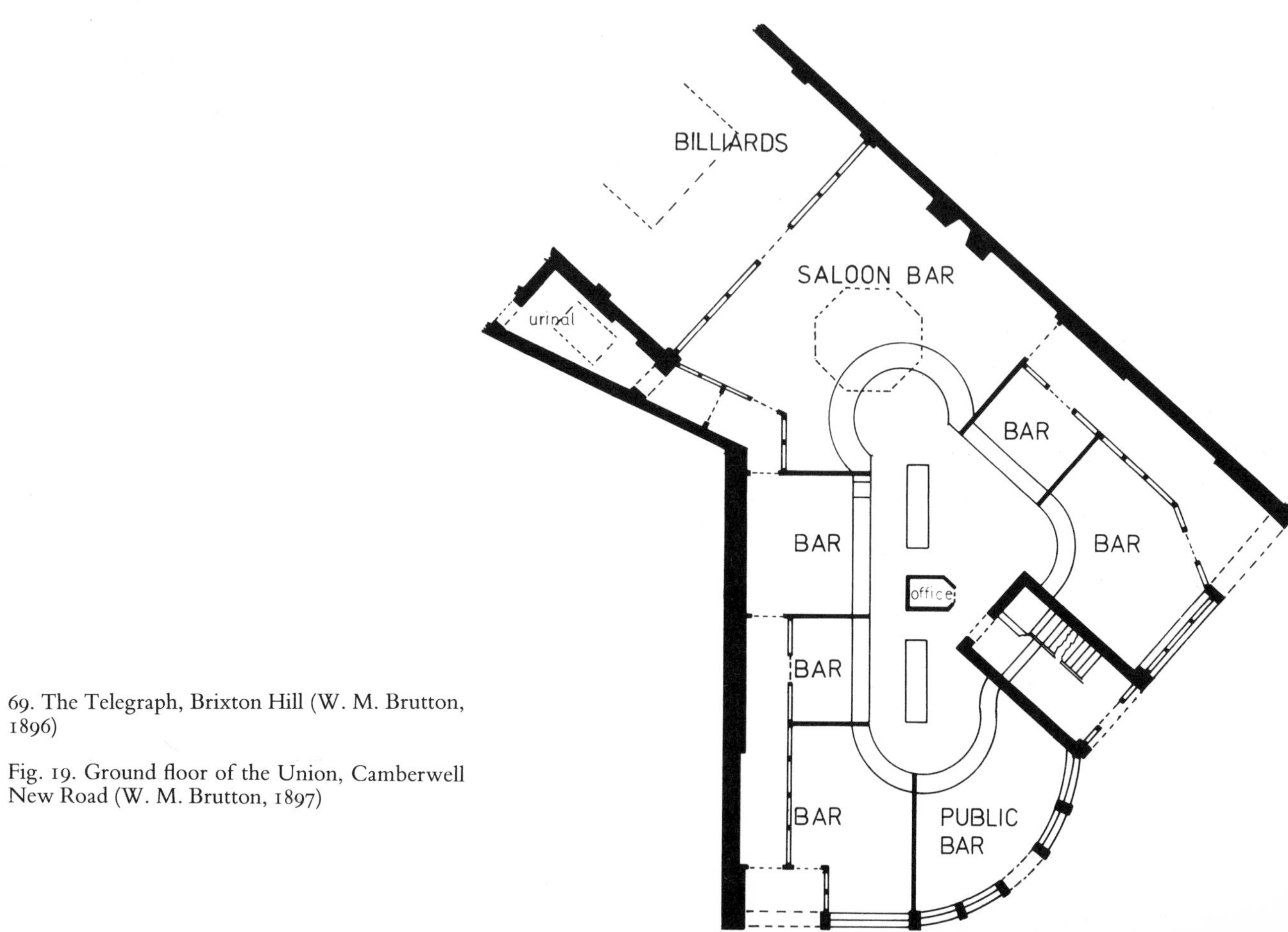

69. The Telegraph, Brixton Hill (W. M. Brutton, 1896)

Fig. 19. Ground floor of the Union, Camberwell New Road (W. M. Brutton, 1897)

an especially vigorous example of his planning (Fig. 19) with an almost complete island serving-bar curving and wriggling through a series of compartments and becoming a near-circle under an octagonal lantern in the big saloon bar.[37] It has long since been redecorated and all the original fittings have gone. The Telegraph, Brixton Hill (Plate 69), has also been completely redone, but was lyrically described by the *Licensed Victuallers' Gazette* in 1898, when Albert Mathams was the publican: 'As you enter the saloon buffet you will be struck with the loftiness of the vast apartment, its velvet pile screen curtains, the collection of valuable oil paintings upon the walls, the beautifully arranged electric light chandelier and brackets, the richly upholstered lounges . . .'[38]

70. Corridor in the King's Head, Upper Tooting Road, Wandsworth

The best surviving Brutton interior is at the King's Head, though even here there have been quite a few changes. Its roomy and animated bars show how Brutton gave his clients the full works, in the way of engraved and embossed glass, patterned tiles and wrought ironwork of almost Art Nouveau design (Plate 70). Better still was the interior of the Goat and Compasses, Euston Road, redecorated by Brutton in 1896,[39] and fortunately photographed before it was converted into a warehouse (Plate 71).

71. A corner of the former Goat and Compasses, Euston Road, now a warehouse (W. M. Brutton 1896)

72. (right) The elephant at the Elephant and Castle, Vauxhall Bridge (*c.* 1875)

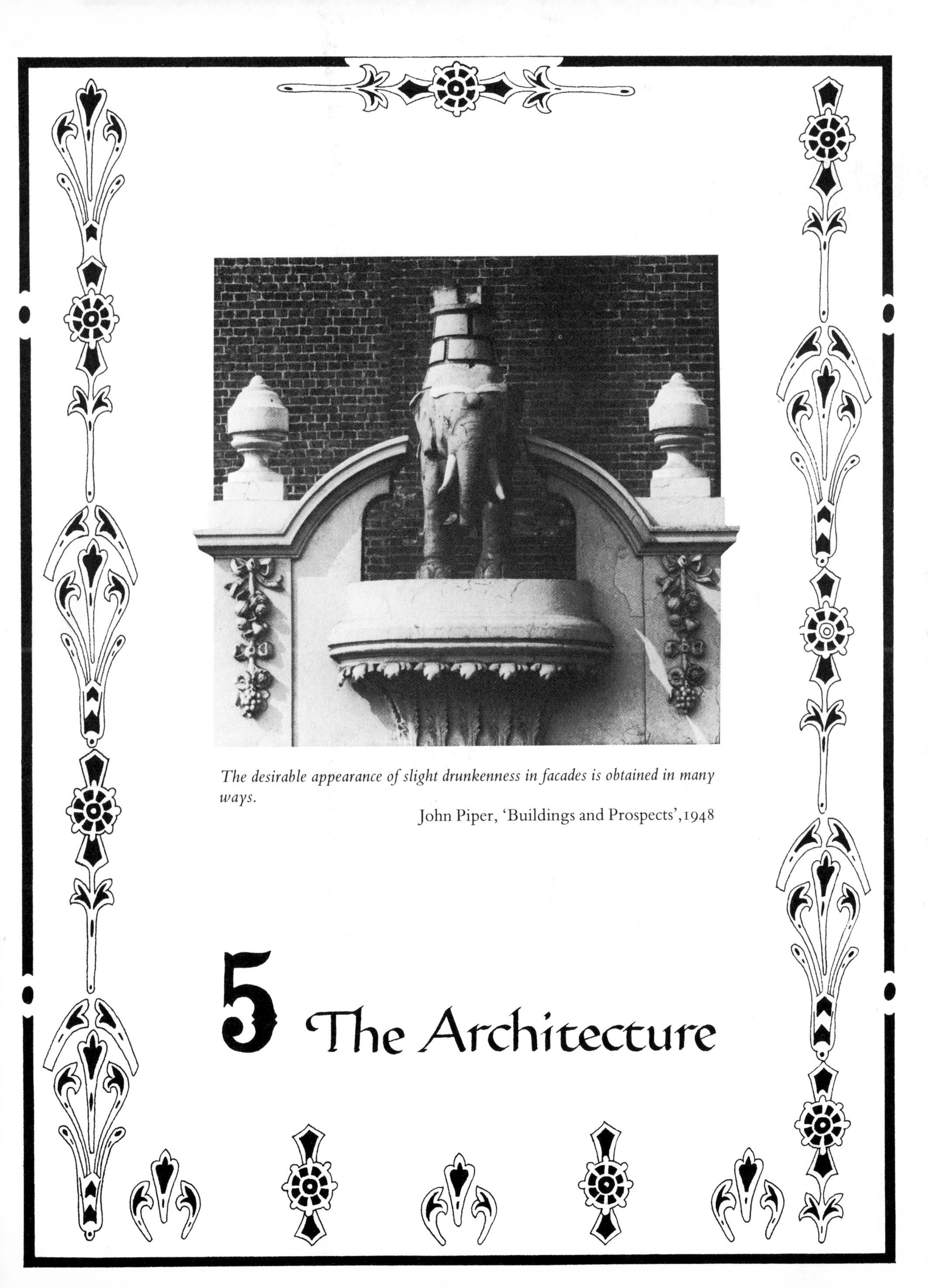

The desirable appearance of slight drunkenness in facades is obtained in many ways.

John Piper, 'Buildings and Prospects', 1948

5 The Architecture

ONE can spend an agreeable half-hour (if one enjoys that kind of thing) analysing the stylistic background of Victorian pubs. Brutton's King's Head, for instance, suggests the result of a visit to the seaside, tea in a station hotel, and a sharp walk round the neighbouring terraces of Balham and Tooting. Saville and Martin's Tottenham clearly has a different pedigree: by Norman Shaw out of E. L. Paraire, perhaps. The mixture is different but the results have much in common; both buildings are unmistakably pubs. Generally speaking, even when they have been converted to other uses, Victorian pubs are easily recognizable. To that extent there is a pub style, although perhaps it is less a style than an attitude.

The attitude is the opposite of gentlemanly. The pubs were in every way the antithesis of the clubs for which the middle classes had abandoned them. In the clubs everything was discreet and padded: thick carpets, soft tablecloths, silent servants and low voices. In the pubs it was all glare, glitter and rattle; and barmaids, as fat and vulgar as the lamps that hung outside, answered back across the bar. Pubs were popular architecture. Most of them were commissioned by publicans rather than breweries, and designed by architects who knew their public and were more likely to be found in the saloon bar than the Arts Club. They exuded an especial air of bravado because they were disapproved of and could afford to ignore it. By 1910, when the drink trade was on the run, pubs desperately tried to look respectable; in the 1890s when money was plentiful and the drink trade was organized and belligerent, they could blow raspberries at the establishment.

The architecture of London pubs was popular but also commercial. Their main purpose was to make money for the publican. They had to attract the attention of the passer-by, persuade him to come inside and keep him inside when he got there—for long enough, at any rate, for him to spend his money. The exterior of every pub was an advertisement. In addition to obvious advertising devices, such as the boards and fascias which plastered their facades and announced the brand of goods sold inside, a tower on the corner, an enormous gable, an inflated mansard roof or an elaborate tablet on the skyline were all methods of proclaiming their identity from the farthest possible distance. So were huge lamps, abundant ironwork, elaborate window surrounds, and as much carving as the publican could run to.

As the passer-by came closer, the ground floor facades of pubs performed their function of attracting him inside. The earlier Victorian pubs had done this fairly crudely by the use of large sheets of plate glass set between columns or in arches, with a row of gaslights on polished brass rails burning brightly behind each window. The later ones were more sophisticated. In the daytime as well as by night their curving fronts and much more richly decorated glass suggested an exciting interior; lit up at night they were (and still are) irresistibly seductive. Pub entrances, too, became increasingly enticing, as the fronts were set back at the corners at ground floor level to form lobbies lined with decorative tiles or painted glass and with wrought-iron grills over the upper halves, miniature foretastes of the elaborate decoration inside. Once through the swing doors the customer was rapidly insulated from reality by glittering mirrors and extravagant woodwork (Plate 73); the many

73. The Crown, Leytonstone High Street (E. C. Beaumont, 1888)

bars gave him the choice of privacy or company, cheapness or class; but one lushly figured ceiling over-sailed the whole pub, so that glimpses of the other bars and noises over the partitions suggested an enjoyable and exciting world, in which it was a pleasure to linger and to spend.

Victorian London pubs are not examples of folk art, though they are sometimes talked about as if they were. Folk art implies hereditary, self-effacing craftsmen repeating the same motifs for generation after generation. The same motifs are found over and over again in Victorian pubs not because they were traditional but because the decoration of most Victorian pubs dates from the same ten to twenty years. Pubs were designed by identifiable architects, even if they were sometimes architects hanging on to the fringes of the profession, and were fitted up by commercial firms who followed the fashions, even if they were a decade behind. The successive stylistic waves that flooded through London all reached the pubs in the end and were cheerfully adapted, misused or distorted by their architects. They included the Greek and Roman stucco architecture of the 1830s and 1840s; the Barry Italianate (big cornices, rich window surrounds, and no orders) of the 1840s and 1850s; the Gothic Revival in all its various stages; the High Victorian eclecticism that flourished in the 1850s and 1860s; the French mansard roof style of the 1860s and 1870s; the 'Queen Anne' of the 1870s and 1880s; the brick and terracotta Flemish of the 1880s and 1890s; and the Art Nouveau of the turn of the century.

Of these the influence of High Victorian eclecticism, 'Queen Anne' and Flemish was especially apparent in the pubs of the golden age of the 1890s. High Victorian eclecticism had already appeared in previous chapters, in the pubs of E. L. Paraire and Lewis Isaacs. It was an attempt to produce a 'modern' architecture by mixing motifs with complete disregard of historical scholarship, and to infuse the result with the aggressive qualities of 'vigour' and 'go' which the mid-Victorians admired. The result was a very curious selection of buildings which fail to comply neatly with any set of descriptions. But the elements that tended to go into the mix included structural polychromy, elaborate naturalistic carving, an abundance of notches and chamfers, fat pillars and pilasters, window surrounds of no obvious stylistic derivation and mansard roofs borrowed from 'Modern French' style. Openings were often neither round-arched, flat-headed nor pointed, but a mixture of the three.

Although High Victorian eclectic shaded imperceptibly into both Gothic on the one side and classic on the other, the stricter Gothicists and classicists disapproved of it. The Gothicists had their own answer to the question 'Has the nineteenth century a style of its own?': it was, or ought to be, Gothic. The eclectics, on their side, thought of the Gothicists as a precious and impractical crowd. They were the no-nonsense men, trained, many of them, at the Architectural Association, a stronghold of eclecticism in the fifties and sixties, busy designing multi-coloured villas and multi-storeyed commercial buildings, and getting a lively kick out of breaking all the rules and ignoring all the conventions.[1]

In the early years of the 1870s the new phenomenon of 'Queen Anne' broke on the architectural scene and rapidly dominated it.[2] But 'Queen Anne' was only the architectural expression of the great decorative revival of the later Victorian period, the result of the middle classes becoming house-proud. By the 1870s England was having an economic boom, the culmination of decades of growing prosperity which was the pay-off of the country's pioneer role in the Industrial Revolution. The middle classes had increased vastly in numbers, wealth and sophistication. They looked at their houses and, with some prompting from the critics, decided that they were hideous. The next twenty years or so saw an irruption of architects, artists, writers, books and magazines on house decoration, greenery-yallery, Japanese screens, blue-and-white china, sunflowers, aesthetics, wallpaper by Morris, tiles by De Morgan and children by Kate Greenaway, which rolled in an enormous aesthetic flood through the houses of the land and made them beautiful.

'Art' and 'artistic' were the key words of the time. The artist was called in to cure the philistinism of the householder and the bad taste of the manufacturer. A new generation of designers and craftsmen who had been trained in the new government-sponsored schools of design found easy employment in existing firms or started up new ones of their own. 'Art' was tacked on as an adjective to everything. There were 'art metalworkers', 'art potteries', 'art tile manufacturers', 'artists in stained glass' or just 'art workers' without number. The work they produced varied very much in quality, and the movement certainly generated a good deal of absurdity and pretentiousness; but it is being increasingly realized that much that was really good and much more that was agreeable was produced to satisfy the insatiable interest of the middle classes in doing up their houses. And it was not only their houses; the restaurants they ate in, the hotels they stayed at, the shops where they shopped were all decorated to satisfy their lively visual awareness.

When they built, rather than decorated, they built in the 'Queen Anne' style. 'Queen Anne' had relatively little to do with Queen Anne; it was as eclectic as High Victorian eclecticism but in a very different way. It was the result of a group of the younger Gothicists becoming fed-up with both the Gothic and the toughness of the 1860s. They thought up an ingenious new formula: Gothic bones, classical flesh. But the classicism which they favoured was not the monumental classicism of the grand manner, but the vernacular classicism of Dutch canal-sides and eighteenth-century provincial towns. The resulting buildings were asymmetric with high, prominent roofs, gables, oriel or bay windows and turrets, like Gothic buildings; but the gables were decorated with pediments and scrolls in the Dutch or Flemish manner, the oriels were made of wood with small-paned sash windows, the turrets ended in little classical domes and were enriched with ornamental panels of rubbed and moulded brick. The motifs were often classical, but included sunflowers, lilies, pomegranates, and even touches of Japanese ornament, spilling over from the artistic interiors. As the architects who created 'Queen Anne' were a lively and gifted group, out of this curious mixture of sources they produced something that was both delicate and pretty.

Norman Shaw was the best known of the group, and as far as London architecture was concerned much the most important. But once they had broken away from Gothic neither Norman Shaw nor his associates could stay in one place for very

long. 'Queen Anne' maintained some sort of consistency for about ten years and then began to produce stylistic offshoots. Ernest George discovered that if one isolated the Flemish element that had always existed in 'Queen Anne' and served it up strong and hot in very hard brick and very shiny terracotta, the results were highly gratifying. Others, including Shaw himself, found that the whole elaborate and pompous ritual of the classical orders could be treated as lightheartedly as the classical vernacular. Columns could be made stumpy or bulging, pediments bent or broken, and features which would usually come in the middle could be placed at the corner. The results, very popular for libraries and town halls in the nineties, were called 'free classic'.

In the 1870s any prosperous middle-class family with progressive views and artistic aspirations was likely to be buying or building a 'Queen Anne' house. In the 1880s the style spread to a much wider clientele as a result and is to be found in shops, terraces, banks and, inevitably, pubs all over London. But in sinking down the social scale 'Queen Anne' tended to lose much of its Kate Greenaway daintiness. To commercial architects used to High Victorian eclecticism it offered a new range of effects which they could combine with the old ones. This mating of the High

74. Design for the Elephant and Castle, Newington Butts, by John Farrer, 1897

Victorian bulldog with the Queen Anne poodle might have been expected to lead to uncouth results. Very often it did; but sometimes it produced jovial fantasies or gay extravaganzas and the best late Victorian pubs were among them.

In addition to a new stylistic repertoire, pub architects had the benefit of the decorative revival, of the firms and craftmanship which it had produced, and of the increasing cheapness of mass-produced ornament. So the pubs of the eighties and nineties are the result of commercial architects splashing on 'Queen Anne' colour but retaining their High Victorian approach and traces of their High Victorian vocabulary; of firms which made refined goods for artistic drawing rooms in one department modifying their wares and styles for the popular market in another department; and of motifs from these same artistic drawing rooms being adapted to decorate the bars.

The windows of the Tottenham would not have looked out of place in an 1860s villa, but its gable derives from Norman Shaw's ultra-fashionable design for Scotland Yard (Plates 80, 84). Much of the Elephant and Castle, Newington Butts, is recognizably 'Queen Anne', but the bulbous dome is a generation older (Plates 74, 75). The embossed birds that perch on twigs on the glass panels of snob-screens

75. Detail of the Grosvenor Hotel, Victoria (1860)

76. Stork panel at the Carlyle Mansions, Chelsea Embankment (1886)

77. Stork mirror at the Bunch of Grapes, Brompton Road, Kensington (*c.* 1890)

and the storks that stand in the bulrushes on the back-painted mirrors along the bars are commercial variants of the birds which the Japanese craze scattered over the homes of artistic housewives (Plates 76, 77, 78, 79). The patterned mosaic floors that gave style to public house lobbies also gave style to the entrance hall of Leighton House, the home of the president of the Royal Academy. Norman Shaw's favourite

78. 'Bird on Twig' panel at the Goat and Compasses, Euston Road (1896)

79. Plate from 'Sparrow and Bamboo' service, registered by Wedgwood in 1879

80. (left) Norman Shaw plus High Victorian eclectic. The Tottenham, Oxford Street (Saville and Martin, 1892)

81. (above) High Victorian eclectic at its most belligerent. The Logs, Hampstead Heath (J. S. Nightingale, 1868)

82. (left) Ernest George. House in Cadogan Square (1886)

83. (above) Norman Shaw plus Ernest George. The Rising Sun, Euston Road (Shoebridge and Rising, 1899)

84. (right) Norman Shaw. New Scotland Yard (1888)

85. Saloon bar fittings by James Yates, Birmingham, 1896

contractor, W. H. Lascelles, was equally prepared to pepper the slopes of Campden Hill and Hampstead with elegant artists' houses designed by Shaw or to stud the suburbs with pubs designed by much less reputable architects. W. B. Simpson, who tiled and wallpapered fashionable drawing rooms by the dozen, tiled pubs by the hundred. The many-storeyed overmantels bristling with peacock feathers and loaded with blue-and-white china that dominated the same drawing rooms reappeared only slightly changed as the centrepieces of bars, loaded with mugs and glasses and glittering with bottles (Plates 85, 86).

The wood-and-glass bay and oriel windows with which architects like Shaw and E. W. Godwin adorned their houses for the artistic upper middle classes are the direct forerunners of the fancifully shaped and glazed windows that divided late Victorian bars from the street (Plates 87, 88, 89, 90). The transformations could be strange but were by no means always for the worse; a pub like the Prince Alfred, Formosa Street, where slim columns of cast iron do all the structural work, leaving flamboyant glass and slim balusters of wood free to curve and glitter without any

86. (right) Drawing room mantelpiece by H. W. Batley, 1883
87. (following page top) The Clarence, Whitehall (1896)
88. (following page bottom left) Window by E. W. Godwin. Chelsea Embankment (1878)
89. (following page bottom right) New Zealand Chambers, Leadenhall Street (Norman Shaw, 1871–3)

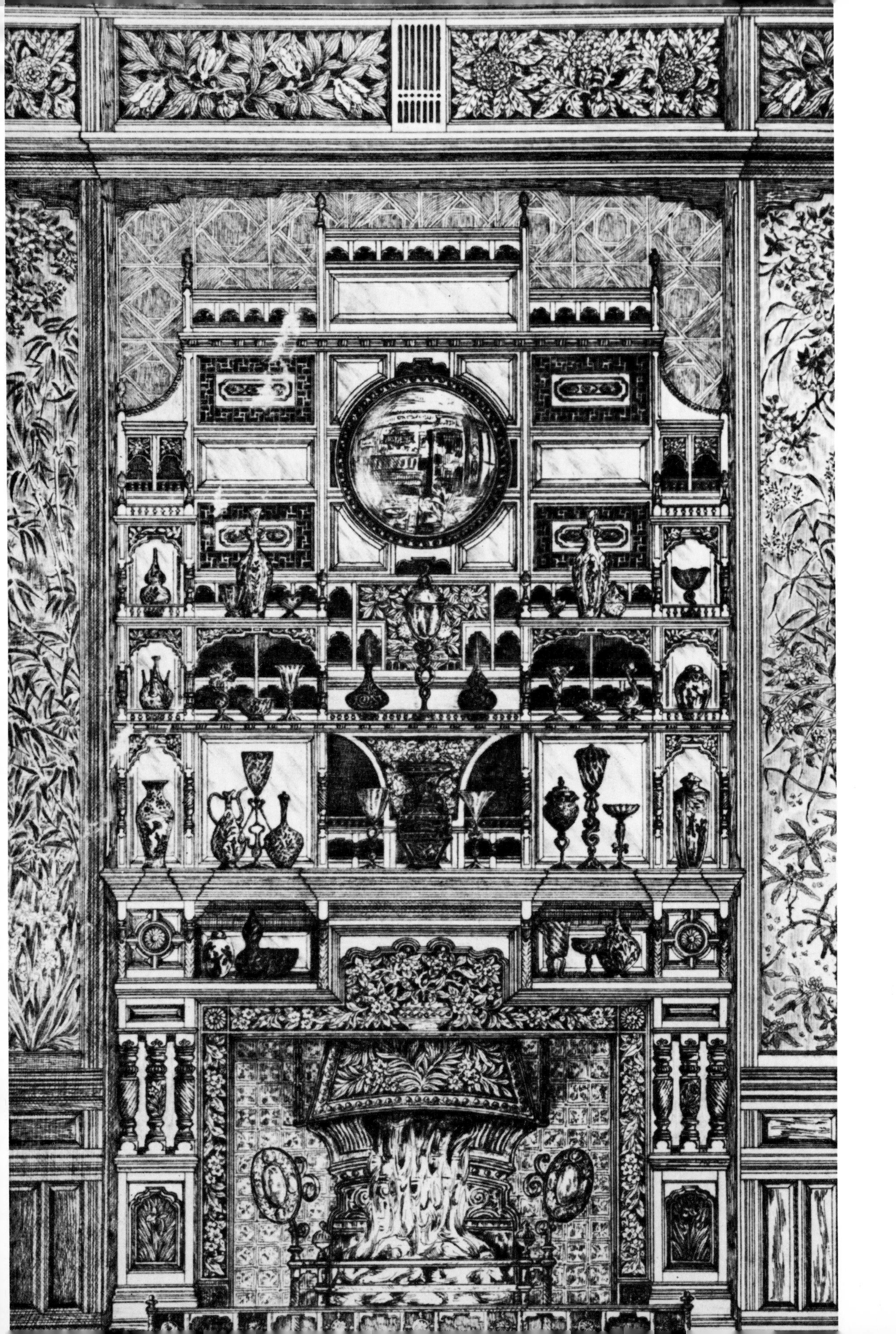

Saloon
Evening News
THE CLARENCE
SNACK BAR NOW OPEN
AVAILABLE BY THE GLASS
The Evening News on sale here

NCE ALFRED
IND COOPE

90. (previous page) Detail of windows at the Prince Alfred, Formosa Street, Maida Vale (*c.* 1898)

91. Windows at the Prince Alfred

structural constraints behind them, is in its way more daring than anything that Shaw ever did (Plate 91). Many late Victorian pubs, on the other hand, however genial their general effect, are the work of architects who, too busy or insensitive to worry about making a coherent whole, ordered fancy pieces from the catalogues and threw them together in a hurry. It is time to discuss just who these architects were and what the catalogues had to offer them.

92. (right) Dome of the Boston, Fortess Road, Tufnell Park (Thorpe and Furniss, 1899)

Mr. H. I. Newton, Architect and Surveyor, begs to inform his clients he has removed from 27, Great George St. to 17 Queen Annes Gate.
Plans, Specifications &c. prepared for Public Houses, Rebuilding, Alterations, Repairing &c. (Vacancy for a pupil)

'Morning Advertiser', 4 May 1885

6 The Architects

WHO has ever heard of H. I. Newton? And yet as an architect he did documented work at no fewer than ninety-six pubs. Who has heard of Bird and Walter, or Saville and Martin, or Treacher and Fisher, or Wilson, Son and Aldwinckle, or Alexander and Gibon, or Thorpe and Furniss? The Victorian pub architects of the eighties and nineties are a completely forgotten body of men. Why did they so often hunt in pairs? What did Shoebridge say to Rising, or Treadwell to Martin, or Fletcher to Migotti? Did J. W. Brooker and Eedle and Meyers, both with offices in Railway Approach, London Bridge, meet and swap ideas in the Southwark saloon bars? What row made Wilson, Son and Aldwinckle part company? What caused Frederick Ashton's fixation on female breasts?

They are not only forgotten but, apart from their buildings, largely irrecoverable, for they existed below the print line. Their pubs were occasionally illustrated in the building magazines; but those great sources of information about Victorian architects, the obituary columns of the *Builder* and the *RIBA Journal,* are almost completely silent about them. A few were members of the RIBA; many more belonged to the Institute of Surveyors, for they worked on the borderline between surveyors and architects. One can presume, but seldom prove, that they were trained in the offices of surveyor-architects as obscure as themselves. About the dates of their births, deaths and marriages almost no information is available. Faceless and obscure, they flit in and out of the pages of the Post Office Directory.

There is one exception. Thomas Wayland Fletcher (1833–1901), who on his own reckoning did work at seventy-seven pubs, wrote an autobiography and diary which survive in manuscript in Tower Hamlets Public Library. If a pub architect was to reveal himself in this way one might have chosen almost anyone but Fletcher, who was a failure and a hack and did much of his work before the great age of the Victorian public house. But his autobiography is a curious and interesting document. It gives a vivid picture of the Pecksniffian background out of which at any rate one pub architect emerged, and of the hazards of his practice which ultimately submerged him.[1]

Fletcher was the son of a milliner and a language teacher. He was articled at the age of fifteen. His parents were unable to afford the kind of premium required by an architect of any reputation. His first employers—Campin and Clements, John Burges Watson, 'Mr Humber', Gribble of Torquay, Bracebridge of Poplar—were dim, eccentric or dishonest, and sometimes all three. Much of his training consisted of copying the plates in the *Builder*; J. B. Watson, the most sympathetic of his early employers, taught him perspective. His leisure time he spent drinking, dancing, whoring or doing the theatres with his more dissolute fellow clerks. Already by the age of sixteen 'I was tall for my age and mounted a chimney pot hat, rough pilot overcoat, with the large buttons then in fashion, and these supplemented with stick-up collar and stick with the head carved like that of a greyhound soon established me in my coveted appearance as a "fast man".' By 1864, when he was married and trying to go steady, he was 'really a very smart young man, used to dress well with white hat and flower in button hole, etc.' By then he had left Bracebridge and gone as assistant to Robert Parker, the Surveyor to the Poplar

Board of Works. In 1866 he left the 'droning life' of this cushy job to set up in partnership with W. A. Hills, his predecessor as assistant surveyor. In his autobiography he described Hills as 'my reptile of a partner' with a 'little priggish mind', but the partnership lasted until 1887. In that year he was joined by his wife's nephew, Alphonzo Migotti, and this partnership continued until his death.

As Fletcher put it in his own analysis of his character, 'united to a strong sensual disposition were fine poetical feelings'. On the one hand he was 'so devoted a worshipper of Venus'; on the other 'I was a great reader of poetry . . . and adjourning as I many times did in the summer evenings for a swim in the Serpentine, I used to take my book with me under the trees in Kensington Gardens, read my book before bathing, afterwards smoking a quiet weed.' It was not easy for a Victorian to reconcile his idealistic and sensual aspects, and Fletcher notably failed to do so. The resulting struggle made him a sympathetic but disastrously unsuccessful character.

In 1861 he experienced religious conversion and resolved that I MUST FIGHT SIN. He joined a series of Baptist chapels, became a Ragged School and Sunday School teacher, ran a Young Men's Improvement Society and was secretary to the Chapel building fund. He published a pamphlet, *Remarks on the Unbelief of the Age*, of which, to his chagrin, no one took any notice. He is, in fact, a warning against drawing too firm a line between those Victorians who frequented chapel and those who frequented pubs. Fletcher did both, but neither he nor his fellow chapel-goers were happy about it. There was a Band of Hope attached to the chapel and most of the Sunday School teachers were abstainers who cannot have approved of his profession. Fletcher, for his part, found aspects of chapel life distasteful: 'talk the simple goody goody stuff that young Dr. Cummins did to the children in his class I felt I could not'. But he always had 'the most chivalrous feelings' toward the girls in his Sunday School classes; 'it is something for an old gay Bird to be able to say this'. Away from Sunday School the gaiety would break out and be bitterly repented.

Fletcher's connection with pubs may originally have started through his first employer, Mr Clemens, who had a connection with William Laxton, editor of the *Civil Engineers Journal*. Laxton was the 'architect having had great experience in fitting up public houses' who designed the suburban public house in Loudon's *Encyclopaedia*. Later, when Fletcher was working in Poplar under Parker, one of his colleagues in the office, George F. Holt, was the son of a publican. He had already done work at seven pubs before setting up in the partnership with Hills which he later so regretted. 'I am afraid I did not consult God in prayer or I might have withstood, more particularly when one of the inducements was the work likely to spring from Whitbread's Brewery of which Mr. Hills' father-in-law Mr. Cluse was one of the resident directors.' In fact very little Whitbread's work ever materialized, but Fletcher had other public house connections through G. F. Holt, through his brother-in-law Girado Migotti, who was a publican, and through Cole, a publican whom he met as a result of joining the Volunteer Rifles: 'I used to go once or twice a week to convivial meetings held at the Railway Tavern, West India Dock Road, where Serjeant Cole was manager, too frequently I imbibed too much.' About 1877 he became surveyor to Smith, Garrett and Company, the East End brewers of Bow Brewery. In partnership with Hills he designed the offices of the Poplar Board of Works and a few factories and housing schemes. After 1866 he worked on at least seventy pubs; much of this work consisted of small alterations and the surviving pubs designed by him are very dim (Plate 93).

Other pub architects may have entered with zest into the public house and music-hall world, but Fletcher, as a result of his chapel life, was filled with guilt and disapproval, at any rate on paper. He was prepared to concede that people could be 'good industrious citizens without being abstainers', and commented of publicans that, 'despite the no doubt questionable character of their business and surroundings, I have by no means found them worse than the generality of other men'. But he was bitterly ashamed when money troubles in 1879 forced him to give up his house and move in with his brother-in-law at the Clarence, Gray's Inn Road. It was a 'very rough house' frequented by 'low Irish . . . this was a drop in the world and I felt it most acutely . . . Girado and his wife used to have terrific shindies, knives occasionally being thrown.' As for music-halls, they were 'thrice cursed places . . . One existed in the East India Road and our servant Mary Wingfield used sometimes to go. I cautioned her about it, telling her it would be her ruin, so it was and after she left us she went on the streets.'

In 1888 he observed how Hills's cousin, R. W. Crawley, who worked for John Hudson, the surveyor to Ind Coope, 'had acquired a taste for drink . . . he now appears to be a confirmed dipsomaniac, with shaking hands and bloated face, an awful contrast to the slim sentimental youth he was when first I knew him'. But Fletcher himself was to slip steadily downhill in the next ten years, lose his Smith, Garrett surveyorship, and end up as a poverty-stricken old man, cadging loans and picking up hack surveying jobs. It was a sad end for the cheerful, dissipated young swell of the 1850s. He blamed it on the connection of his practice with pubs. While walking on the parade at Margate in 1895, he met and escaped from two publican ex-friends and it led to an outburst in his diary: 'Booze, Booze, nothing but Booze. Archer was down at the sea side because too much "Scotch" had injured his liver, and his doctor had advized it. Thank God I am out of the horrid, horrid, circle. When I come to think of the 16 years torture I spent while surveyor to the Bow Brewery, I wonder however I weathered it. Unquestionably it dulled my mind, got me into wrong tracks, kept me back from actively serving my Saviour.'

One probably should not judge Fletcher from the tone of his autobiography without bearing in mind the other side to his personality. Fletcher at Cremorne or the Rosherville Gardens or in the saloon of a pub or out with the Volunteers or at a smoking concert at the Bow and Bromley Social and Literary Club ('ever since I joined I have been going down, down, down') was probably scarcely recognizable as the Fletcher with pen in his hand moralizing and repenting next morning. An entry in his diary for November 1895 can serve as his epitaph: 'Went out for some lunch, had some at the ABC company's branch Gracechurch St., glass of milk and piece of cake $2\frac{1}{2}d$. How are the mighty fallen and old Brewer's Surveyor come to this!!!'

Fletcher's disastrous combination of drink and Dissent may have been peculiar to him; one can hope that other pub architects were less guilt-ridden, and many were certainly more successful. But a lower middle-class background, articled pupilage to a surveyor-architect, training that consisted of being taught perspective and copying plates from the *Builder*, and relationship to, or a connection with, someone in the drink trade were probably a fairly typical pattern. Practices of the Fletcher variety, doing a certain amount of other work but largely specializing in pubs, dominated the late Victorian pub world. Owing to the changed patterns of licensing, the earlier pattern of builders putting up pubs as part of new housing developments and selling them off when built and licensed to a publican or brewer, was by now comparatively unimportant. The typical client was the publican-speculator, moving quickly from pub to pub, converting or rebuilding them and then selling them, and often remaining loyal to the same specialist pub architect for ten or twenty years.

Enough original designs survive to make it clear that architects worked out the plans of their pubs in considerable detail, and that their drawings were usually competent and a great deal more decorative than they would be today. The surviving designs were almost all made for presentation to the licensing justices or the local authority, who did not require detailed drawings of the internal fittings. Sections

93. The African Tavern, Grundy Street, Poplar (T. W. Fletcher, *c.* 1860)

drawn by specialist pub architects such as T. H. Smith, Shoebridge and Rising, and F. A. Powell[2] show enough of the interiors to make it clear that architects were prepared to design them in some detail; but it will probably always remain uncertain how much was left to the cabinet bar fitters and high-class joiners who fitted them out. As far as the architectural evolution of pubs is concerned, their number was so enormous and the surviving plans, especially in the seminal period, comparatively so few that it is impossible to award firsts with any certainty. There are no giants, no obvious Norman Shaw of the pub world. Pub architects, one gets the impression, cribbed from the architecture of their better known contemporaries more than from each other.

Several architects held a brewery surveryorship, as Fletcher did for Smith, Garrett. Some, like J. G. Ensor of Watney's, seem to have been salaried brewery architects who did no other work.[3] But the majority of pub work was still being done for publican clients. Even in the pubs which they did build, the brewers were not, on the whole, the pace-setters for the rest; the exception is the Cannon Brewery, a newly refurbished firm anxious to put across its image, which helped to popularize the Flemish style for pubs in the 1890s. In contrast, Watney's, the biggest brewery builder of pubs, produced buildings that were extremely efficiently planned but stylistically old-fashioned and rather staid; they came nearer than most late Victorian pubs to being in good taste. Perhaps this was deliberate. Although there are exceptions, the jazziest and gayest late Victorian pubs were built for the publicans; they wanted something to catch the eye, for in almost every case, they were planning to sell again at the first good opportunity.

Some of the pub practices that had started in the 1860s and the 1870s continued to flourish up till the end of the century. The oldest-established was Bird and Walters. It was started up by J. Bird in or before 1862, became Bird and Walters about 1866, and was still going strong in 1898 with documented work at seventy-four pubs to its credit. Its stylistic development followed the conventional path: lushly classical in the 1860s (Britannia, Clarendon Road, Notting Hill, 1867), still High Victorian eclectic in the early 1880s (Father Red Cap, Camberwell Green, 1883) and Flemish in the 1890s (Cow and Calf, Eastcheap, 1892).[4] Edward Brown, who set up practice in 1863 and took his son into partnership about 1898, was an almost equally prolific pub architect; up till the 1880s he was still producing old-fashioned and rather stodgy brick-and-stucco classical pubs, but in 1879 he designed the richly Gothic Railway Hotel, Hackney (Plate 40), alas no more.[5]

George Treacher, who is first heard of in 1872 and became Treacher and Fisher in 1889, may have been related to W. J. Treacher, of New London Street, Mark Lane, Wine Merchant. He produced delightful semi-naive drawings for his cheerful classical pubs of the 1870s and 1880s (Plate 94). His bar facades, with their chunky joinery and elaborate cast-iron ventilating grills and railings, are especially charming; unfortunately they have almost invariably been removed as a result of the later remodelling of the bars, but the well-known front of the Red Lion, Duke of York Street (by the otherwise unknown W. H. Rawlings, 1871), is of a very similar type (Plate 96). Treacher's most elaborate 1870s pub was probably the Opera

94. (top left) Design for the Britannia, Peckham High Street, by George Treacher, 1881
95. (top right) Design for the Stirling Castle, Camberwell, by C. W. Bovis, 1882
96. (right) The Red Lion, Duke of York Street, St James's (W. H. Rawlings, 1871)

14
THE STIRLING CASTLE
14

IND COOPE
RED LION
Red Lion
Ind Coope
PUBLIC BAR
PUBLIC BAR
Red Lion
Ind Coope

SIR
SIDNEY
SMITH.
MEUX'S
Original London
STOUT
GIN
GIN

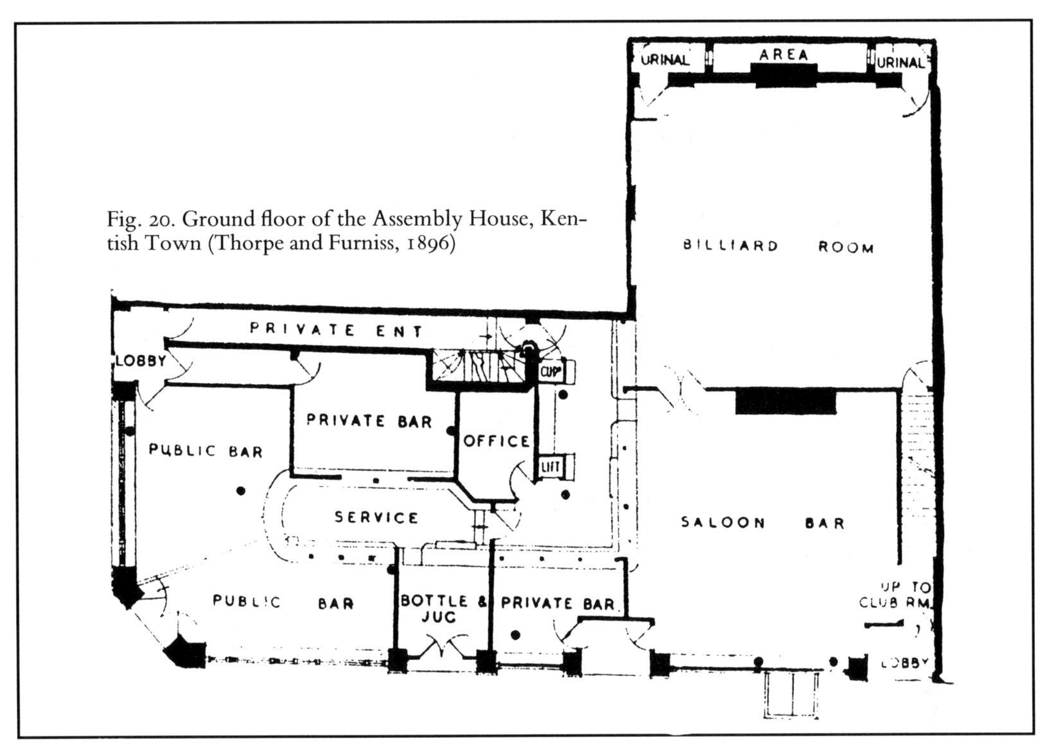

Fig. 20. Ground floor of the Assembly House, Kentish Town (Thorpe and Furniss, 1896)

Tavern (1879) opposite the Drury Lane Theatre, still a nice example of vulgar stucco classicism, though without its original bar front. In the early 1880s Treacher went French, as in the Sir Sidney Smith, Chester Way (1884), which brought an unexpected whiff of a French *hôtel de ville* to a quiet street in Kennington (Plate 97). In the 1890s new ideas were introduced, no doubt by Fisher; the Freemason Arms, Long Acre, is Flemish but lacks the panache of its predecessor, the Opera Tavern, around the corner.[6]

Treacher's buildings have a certain individual flavour, but it is hard to find one in the work of the indefatigable H. I. Newton, whose advertisement heads this chapter. He worked at his ninety-six pubs between 1873 and 1891. The total is less impressive than it sounds, for Newton seems to have taken care to inform the *Builder*'s tender department of every job he did, however small. Surviving pubs by him include the Artichoke in Lower Marsh, Lambeth (1878), and the Adam and Eve, Petty France (1881), both unassertive and agreeable in white brick, and the big commercial 'Queen Anne' George and Dragon, St John Street, Clerkenwell (1889), considerably more assertive and rather less agreeable in red brick, with a little tower.[7]

The Artichoke and Adam and Eve were designed by Newton for Watney's, along with a number of other pubs in the 1870s. Watney's seem to have continued to pass on conversion jobs to him, but from 1880 had their own full-time architect for new pubs: C. W. Bovis from 1880 to 1886 and J. G. Ensor from 1887 to 1897. A few of Bovis's own drawings for solid old-fashioned classical pubs survive (Plate 95), and his style is easily recognizable in many existing Watney's houses.

97. The Sir Sidney Smith, Chester Way, Kennington (George Treacher, 1884; demolished)

Ensor began classical, turned French and ended up very moderately 'Queen Anne': his most ambitious pub is the French mansard-roofed Archway, still a prominent object marooned on a traffic island at the foot of Highgate Hill.[8]

Two practices which established themselves in the 1870s were those of J. R. Furniss (Thorpe and Furniss from about 1887) and Wilson, Son and Aldwinckle. Thorpe and Furniss had their offices in Camden High Street and were extremely prolific producers of pubs, mainly in north London. But the firm was not at all a lively one until Thorpe arrived on the scene. His distinctive style still provides the major landmarks on a drive from Camden Town to Tufnell Park. He strapped up his buildings in pilasters and entablatures like Christmas string round a parcel. At the Brighton, Camden High Street (1889), the parcel is on its own (Plate 98); at the Assembly House (1896) and Boston (1899) it comes with a tower, closing the vistas up Kentish Town Road and Fortess Road, respectively.[9] Both pubs are on corner sites; the Assembly House tower is in French chateau style, with a candle-snuffer roof; the expensive Boston (Plates 92, 99) is tied up with Portland stone trimmings instead of stucco ones, and the tower is pulled out like a telescope and ends with a clock and a dome. The Boston and Brighton retain nothing Victorian inside. The Assembly House has superb glass by William James of Kentish Town (Plate 132), ironwork by Jones and Willis and joinery by W. A. Antill and Company (Plate 155); although a number of partitions have been removed, it remains one of the best Victorian pub interiors in London.

Wilson, Son and Aldwinckle did numerous pubs from about 1875 onwards, but the death rate among these has been very high. It is a pity, because they were a capable firm. They also designed a number of lively public baths in the Flemish manner and, as surveyors to the Leathersellers Company, an exuberant set of almost

98. The Brighton, Camden High Street (Thorpe and Furniss, 1889)

99. (right) The Boston, Fortess Road, Tufnell Park (Thorpe and Furniss, 1899)

BOSTON ARMS
WHITBREAD

Celtic wrought-iron gates for the Leathersellers Hall in 1879.[10] The firm seems to have split up in the late 1890s, when Aldwinckle and Wilson, Son went their own ways. Aldwinckle was an FRIBA and one of the comparatively few pub architects to push his head a little out of the sea of personal anonymity.

Another RIBA pub architect, J. W. Brooker, of 13 Railway Approach, London Bridge, was given a fullish obituary in the *RIBA Journal* when he died in 1904.[11] It gives the impression of a successful Fletcher: he was a non-conformist (he designed Penge Tabernacle) architect of south London villas (at Grove Vale, Dulwich, Herne Hill, Brockley and Lewisham) and an occupier of one himself (Durlstone, Brockley Park), with a small line in offices (around London Bridge and in Shoreditch) and a bigger line in pubs (twenty-one between 1877 and 1898). As tended to be the case at the time, the fact that he was an FRIBA did not mean that he was a higher class, or even a more literate, architect than the many architects who were not. His work can be represented by an early example, the Yorkshire Grey, Theobald's Road (1877), and a late one, the Half Moon, Herne Hill (1896), one bastard classical, the other 'Queen Anne' of the most commercial variety. He had a fondness for

100. The tower of the Spanish Patriot, Lower Marsh, Lambeth (J. W. Brooker)

101. The Equestrian, Blackfriars Road, Southwark (T. H. Smith, 1888; demolished)

little corner cupolas, the nicest of which is perhaps that at the Spanish Patriot, Lower Marsh, Lambeth (Plate 100), in different coloured stripes of brick like a piece of liquorice allsorts.[12]

Before moving on to the pub architects who made their name in the 1890s it is worth briefly mentioning two architects who designed important and typical pubs in the eighties, although pubs were not their main line. Thomas Halliburton Smith worked from Basinghall Street and his speciality was late Victorian offices, which he designed in large numbers in the City and elsewhere (also, possibly as a side-kick from these, a house in Park Lane for Barney Barnato, failed music-hall star turned diamond millionaire, in 1895–7).[13] His four principal pubs were the Goat in Boots, Fulham Road (1887), the Equestrian, Blackfriars Road (1888), the Fox and Hounds, Sydenham (1889), and the George and Dragon, Blackheath (1890).[14] Engravings of the first three appeared in the building magazines (Plate 101), complete with plans. They were not especially lively buildings, but their finishes were more expensive than were customary at the time, and they probably helped to establish commercial 'Queen Anne' and the multi-compartment pub as the norm in London.

The firm of G. R. Crickmay and Son originated from Weymouth where they had a big West Country practice, especially church restorations and housing estates at Weymouth, Dorchester and Swanage. (Thomas Hardy worked for them from 1869 to 1872, before he abandoned architecture for writing.) In the 1880s they set up an office in London and were responsible for more housing estates in the London suburbs and the south of England.[15] In 1886 they provided designs for rebuilding the Horns in Kennington, a famous pub with a big assembly room attached. They designed at least three more London pubs, the White Swan, Shoreditch (1896), the Prince Albert, Weedington Road, NW (1899), and the Six Bells (1898), prototype of the 'olde worlde' pub, with a pseudo-Sparrows-House, Ipswich, facade which is a familiar landmark on the King's Road (Plate 178).[16]

The Horns, and possibly other pubs, were designed by Crickmays for Messrs Nicholson, the gin distillers. The William Nicholson for whom Crickmay designed Nos. 1 and 2 South Audley Street in 1884[17] must surely have been a member of the firm, for these extraordinary French and 'Queen Anne' mishmashes, lavishly got up with more in the way of wrought iron, modelled brick, frescoes, gilding and plasterwork than one would have thought it possible to be squeezed into a single house, are a remarkable example of the public house manner at its most expensive adapted for domestic use.

Pubs like the Equestrian and the Horns set new standards of lavishness in the 1880s, but in the boom of 1895–9 this kind of elaboration became almost a commonplace. For a few glorious years pub architects had more work than they could cope with. Their numbers increased, and many can only be mentioned in passing. Bruce J. Capell designed Gothic and 'Queen Anne' pubs with distinctive window glazing, some for publicans, and others for Truman, Hanbury and Buxton.[18] R. A. Lewcock's rather boring exteriors tend to be richly decorated inside with superior touches derived from the Aesthetic movement.[19] Horace M. Wakley, the architect

member of a publican family, produced even more elaborate interiors and liked to pepper his exteriors with coloured faience columns and little cupolas; two cupolas on his Cantons (now the Spice of Life) of 1899 in Cambridge Circus (Plate 102) cheekily echo the two bigger ones on the Palace Theatre next door.[20] J. T. Alexander's Flying Horse, Walworth Road (1888), Noah's Ark, Oxford Street (1890, Plate 1), and Old Leather Bottle, Leather Lane (1891), have (or had) the mixture of cheerfulness and craziness that distinguishes the best Victorian pubs.[21] The work of four firms—Eedle and Meyers, Shoebridge and Rising, Treadwell and Martin, and Frederick W. Ashton—can be examined in more detail.

Eedle and Meyers have been selected, not because their pubs are, with a few exceptions, very original or even especially recognizable, but because they had unusual stamina—they lasted longer than any other pub firm—and because their decorative and gaily coloured drawings seem to show exactly the right approach to pub architecture. F. J. Eedle first appeared in 1885 and Meyers came into the partnership in 1890. Their office from the beginning was at 8 Railway Approach, Southwark, and the firm was still there when it finally closed down in 1946, specializing in pubs to the last. In the 1880s they seem to have had two design styles

102. The former Cantons, Cambridge Circus, now the Spice of Life (H. M. Wakley, 1899)

103. Dome of the Angel, Islington (Eedle and Meyers, 1901-3)

running side by side, a rather old-fashioned but cheerful polychromatic classical (Dover Castle, Little Surrey Street, 1888; Larkhall Tavern, Clapham, 1889) and a more up-to-date and equally cheerful commercial 'Queen Anne' (Railway Hotel, Putney, 1888), turning Flemish and terracotta in the 1890s (Loughborough Park Tavern, 1898; Angel, Islington (Plate 103), 1901–3).[22] The two styles make one wonder whether Meyers was in the office before he became a partner and whether he was responsible for the 'Queen Anne' side. The firm's drawings are immediately recognizable and a pleasure to look at, because pure bright colours are splashed on to them with such a gaily abundant hand. Best of all, perhaps, is the elevation of the Loughborough Park Tavern (Colour Plate IV), which, after a period as a West Indian jazz pub, was demolished in the 1970s.

Treadwell and Martin are the exact opposite of Eedle and Meyers; they designed comparatively few pubs but had a distinctive personal style so suited to everything a late Victorian pub stands for that one can only regret there is not more of it. Their pub masterpiece is the Rising Sun (1896) in Tottenham Court Road (Plate 104).[23] The style of this is, if anything, Gothic, not the chunky heavyweight Gothic of the 1860s but the delicate late Gothic that was in fashion in the 1890s.

104. The Rising Sun, Tottenham Court Road (Treadwell and Martin, 1896)

But curious and delightful things have happened to it. The facades are divided up by delicate mouldings into panels in the Perpendicular manner, but these are enriched with playful Art Nouveau foliage and sprout out at the top into little concave gables each topped by miniature pediments. Best of all, playing among the Gothic ribs are a row of rising suns with corkscrew rays. The facade was originally of stone, but by a stroke of genius the brewers exaggerated its already festive and confectionery character by painting it green or blue and white—alas, later altered to an anaemic cream.

The same enjoyable style was employed for what was originally Scott's Restaurant (now an amusement arcade) in Coventry Street (1894) and for the demolished offices and spirit vaults built by J. Buchanan and Company, the whisky distillers, on the corner of Holborn and Fetter Lane. This was a bigger brother to the Rising Sun, with three big gables and an amazing tower. The style appears again on a smaller but still lively scale in the Old Shades in Whitehall (1898), and very much subdued in the Old Dover Castle (1894), now an employment exchange, in Westminster Bridge Road.[24]

The Old Dover Castle, along with the Leicester in Coventry Street, was built in 1894–5 to Treadwell and Martin's designs for Charles Best from the proceeds of selling the Horse Shoe, Tottenham Court Road, and the adjacent Tottenham to the Baker brothers. Best had set new standards of public house lavishness when he originally built the Horse Shoe in 1875; at the Leicester and Old Dover Castle he went even further, and although, for instance, in the wine bar at the Leicester he was clearly aiming at a class of client above the average, even the public bars were furnished with considerable splendour (Plates 105, 106). The Leicester has been demolished and the Old Dover Castle gutted, but both were fortunately photographed in detail by Bedford Lemere in 1895.

Treadwell and Martin were architecturally rather more respectable than most pub architects; Treadwell, at any rate, was considered to merit an obituary in the *Builder* when he died at the early age of forty-nine in 1910. From this it appears that his full name was Henry John Treadwell, that he was at the Architectural Association in 1886 and that he was a Fellow of the Surveyors' Institute. The firm also designed a number of small office buildings, as gay and inventive as their pubs. Shoebridge and Rising, another and more prolific firm with a line in pubs, were in a similar bracket, and when Henry Whitebridge Rising, who seems to have been the dominant member of the partnership, died in 1937 his obituary in the *RIBA Journal* was a full one. He was born in 1857, was articled in Lowestoft, worked for eighteen months with a builder studying joinery and set up his own practice in 1887. About 1896 he went into partnership with W. G. Shoebridge. In 1900 he married Catherine Gandy, the great-niece of Soane's pupil J. M. Gandy. He moved to Reading in 1910 as a partner in Albury, Rising and Morgan, and ended up in retirement as librarian to the Reading Architectural Society.[25]

Rising designed churches in Bristol, Wolverhampton and outer London, but the principal item in the list of his buildings given in his obituary is 'many works for the Cannon Brewery'. From other sources these are known to include the King

105. Bar at the Old Dover Castle, Westminster Bridge Road, in 1895 (Treadwell and Martin, 1894–5; remodelled)
106. Wine bar at the Leicester, Coventry Street, in 1895 (Treadwell and Martin, 1894–5; demolished)

SPECIAL SCOTCH
JAMAICA RUM
PALE BRANDY

BOLEYN

William IV, Leyton High Street (1897), the Boleyn, Barking Road (1899–1900, Plates 46, 107, 108), and the Crown, Cricklewood Broadway (1899). These are stylistically so similar to the Rising Sun, Euston Road (1899, Plates 57, 83, 109), the Black Horse, Catford (*c.* 1898), the Great Northern Railway Tavern, Hornsey (1897), and the Red Lion, Whitehall (*c.* 1896), all Cannon Brewery houses, that there is little doubt that Shoebridge and Rising did all the architectural work for 'that enterprising firm' in their campaign of buying, rebuilding and refurbishing pubs during the 1890s.[26] But they were clearly prepared to work for other pub clients as well, for their delicately drawn designs for the Feathers, Broadway, Westminster (1898), now hang in its bar, and show that it was designed jointly for William Maitland Edwards and the New Westminster Brewery Company.

Shoebridge and Rising were a perfect choice to satisfy both the Cannon Brewery, which probably wanted rather more literate architecture than most publicans, and the potential users of the pubs, who wanted to feel that they were having an evening out. Each of their pubs is noticeably different, an appetizing ragout of Norman Shaw and Ernest George—spiced up only in the case of Norman Shaw, for by the 1890s it was impossible to spice up Ernest George. Their tastes ran to the Flemish end of 'Queen Anne' and the freer end of free classic. They liked elaborate Flemish gables, concave pediments, columns or pilasters rusticated half the way up, oval windows, plenty of stripes, and turrets with saucy little domes. Rising had profited

107. (top left) The Boleyn. Barking Road, East Ham (Shoebridge and Rising, 1899-1900)
108. Billiard room ceiling at the Boleyn
109. Office and bar screen at the Rising Sun, Euston Road (Shoebridge and Rising, 1899)

from his eighteen months of studying joinery, and the joinery of the firm's windows and bar fittings is always enjoyable and individual. Typical and especially charming is the office in the Rising Sun, with its arched and oval windows (Plate 109). The firm's interiors always had the full range of pub splendours; they liked saloon bars semi-separate from the rest of the pub and went in for especially lavish billiard rooms (Plate 108).

From Shoebridge and Rising to Frederick W. Ashton is a considerable jump in architectural literacy; though perhaps one has to know the period to realize that, whereas Shoebridge and Rising mixed their motifs according to the accepted standards of the time, Ashton mixed his with a wildly personal eccentricity. His office was in Bow, and he worked on at least forty-five pubs, almost all in east or north-east London. His best hunting ground was in the working- or lower middle-class suburbs which spilled over from London into Essex in the 1880s and 1890s—Barking, Ilford, Upton Park and East and West Ham.

Much of Ashton's work was done for William Langman (b. 1854), the son of a Trinity pilot who after a short spell as a pilot himself went into business as a publican in 1887. He bought and sold pubs with increasing success, and after fifteen years on the East Ham local board was on the LCC by 1898. Langman seems to have had a fondness for dukes, especially royal ones, for his pubs included the Duke of Edinburgh (his first), the Duke of Fife, the Duke of Clarence, and the Duke of Portland.[27] He clearly liked girls as well as dukes. At the Duke of Fife, Upton Park (Plates 110, 111), F. W. Ashton provided him with no fewer than thirty-three caryatids, all with prominently exposed stomachs and breasts. Nine of them, with hands on their hips and elbows touching, surround the cupola at the corner; twenty-four more, in groups of four, support basket capitals above the entrances. Lurking in the frieze above the first floor windows, cupids carry shields decorated with William Langman's initials.

Busty caryatids appear again on at least two more of Ashton's pubs, the Two Brewers, High Street, Ponders End (1896), which was another job for Langman, and the Britannia, Church Road, Barking (1898), for W. G. Kitson. Although these are both less distinctive than the Duke of Fife, the caryatids would make one attribute them to Ashton even if the *Builder* did not supply the necessary evidence. But the White Hart, Upton Park (1897), is equally clearly by Ashton, though caryatids are lacking.[28] The common factors of his more elaborate pubs are a lavish overabundance of stucco ornaments and a reckless mixture of speculative builder's classical, 'Modern French' and 'Queen Anne' motifs. The results have the eccentricity of W. M. Brutton's pubs without their skill, and once their curiosity value has worn off they become a little tedious.

Three large and in their time famous pubs remain to be discussed because they seem to epitomize all the best qualities of the pubs of the 1890s. Yet curiously, they were designed neither by professional pub architects nor for any of the big-time publican speculators. These are the Elephant and Castle, Newington Butts, unhappily demolished to make way for a traffic roundabout, and the Salisbury Hotel, Green Lanes, Harringay, and Queens Hotel, Crouch End, still happily much alive.

The Elephant and Castle was a long-established pub standing on ground belonging to St Mary Newington Charity. In July 1897 Algernon Meekins bought an eighty-year lease of the pub and adjoining houses for £30,000 at a rent of £2,850 a year. Designs for rebuilding the pub on a very much larger scale were submitted to the licensing justices in the same month (Plates 74, 112, Fig. 21). The pub, together with an adjoining block to contain nine shops, offices and flats, went out to tender at the end of the year; the lowest tender was for £35,933. The foundation stone of the pub was not laid until December 1898; the presence of Mr Read of

110. The Duke of Fife, Upton Park (F. W. Ashton, *c.* 1895)

111. Cupola of the Duke of Fife

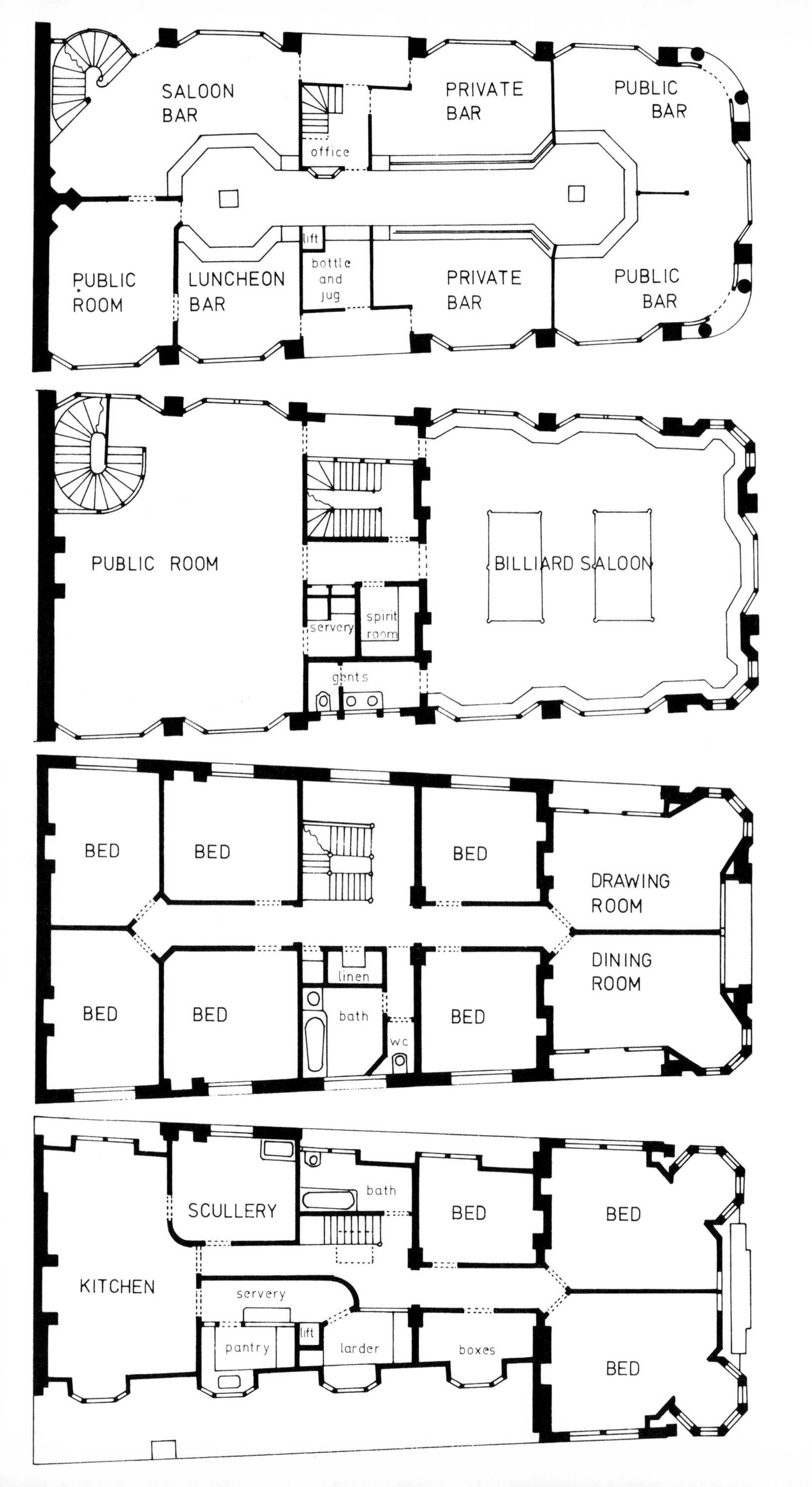

Fig. 21. The Elephant and Castle, Newington Butts
a. Ground floor
b. First floor
c. Second floor (the drawing room and dining room were for hotel guests)
d. Fourth floor

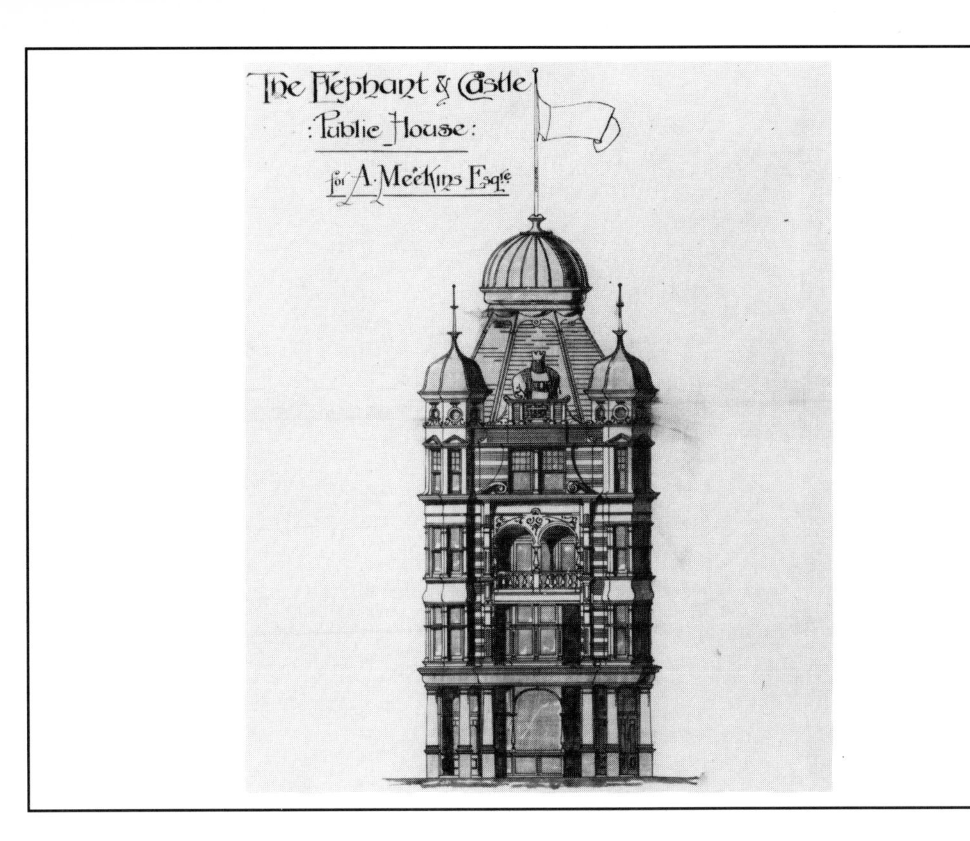

112. Design for the Elephant and Castle, Newington Butts, by John Farrer, 1897

the Capital and Counties Bank and of a representative from Truman, Hanbury and Buxton suggests where most of the money had come from.[29]

Algernon Meekins is said to have had previous experience as a licensed victualler, but the London Post Office Directory provides no information. He lived out at Eltham, and the Elephant was run by a manager. His architect, John Farrer, of 20 Finsbury Pavement, was an equally obscure character. The pub they built was a beauty. The Victorians, unlike architects of the present day, had unfailing resourcefulness in making the best of a corner site. Six roads intersected at the Elephant and it presided over them like a striped cathedral of drink. An immense inflated cupola was tethered like a balloon between two little domed turrets. Underneath, a kind of inset baldachin of columns, balcony and pediment led the eye up to an elephant and castle sculpted on the parapet between the turrets. Similar motifs were repeated along the side, but crowned by gables instead of elephants. On the ground and first floors the windows rippled in and out like a series of lanterns. The cupola was an exaggerated version of W. M. Brutton's cupola on the King's Head, Upper Tooting Road; the rest of the detailing was in the Shoebridge and Rising manner, but somewhat cruder and jollier. Inside, an enormous island serving-bar shaped rather like a dog bone served rather fewer and larger bars than it would have done six or seven years earlier. The first floor contained a big public room and a billiard room with two tables; the original plans showed a two-storey basement with cellars in the lower storey and a seven-table billiard room in the upper, but as built there was only one basement, shared between cellar and billiard room. The few surviving photographs suggest that the interior fittings were as lavish as the facades would lead one to expect (Plate 53).

The Salisbury, Green Lanes (Plate 113), has a cupola which must have been inspired by that of the Elephant and Castle. It was designed a year or so later (it opened in the summer of 1899) and was perhaps intended to be its north London counterpart; but it was even bigger and more lavishly fitted out. It was built by neither a brewery nor a professional publican but by a successful north London builder, John Cathles Hill. Hill built two London pubs (or rather pub-hotels), the Salisbury and the Queens Hotel, Crouch End;[30] both were intended to serve neighbourhoods he himself had helped to develop, and to this extent were more reminiscent of the methods of the 1850s than the 1890s. Hill's career was a remarkable one.[31] He was born in Scotland in 1858, the son of a line of cartwrights and wheelrights. After a spell in Glasgow he migrated to London in 1879 and took a job as a joiner. In 1881 he set up on his own and started a joinery and building business active in speculative development in Highgate and adjacent parts of north London. In 1889 he decided to make his own bricks, and acquired a brick field at Fletton on the outskirts of Peterborough. He developed this side of his business into the London Brick Company, even in his lifetime an immense concern covering 1,300 acres of brick fields and brickworks, including the famous 'Napoleon' kiln, in its day the biggest kiln in the world. Hill was largely responsible for introducing Fletton bricks to London and himself built some 2,000 houses in and around London. His career ended in disaster, for he went bankrupt in 1912 with gross liabilities of over a million pounds. He died in 1915.

In the late 1890s he was at the summit of his career. He was clearly a man of enormous energy; although the two pubs were only a sideline to his other business interests, he pushed the projects through with speed and determination. Both pubs were on new sites and needed new licences; difficult though these were to obtain in the late nineties, Hill overcame considerable local opposition and won over the licensing magistrates. The Salisbury cost £30,000 (raised outside the breweries) and was opened in 1899, with W. A. Cathles, presumably a relation of Hill's, as the manager; the Queens Hotel was planned in 1899 and opened about 1901.

Hill was his own architect at the Salisbury and probably also at the Queens: the bar fittings were made to his designs in his own workshops. At the Salisbury (Plates 114, 115, 124, 140) in addition to a large billiard room and far more spacious bars than was usual, there were a restaurant and concert room on the first floor, both long since disused. Cakebread, Robey provided splendid glass and the Mural Decoration Company lavish fibrous plaster work. Halfway through fitting out the bars, Hill moved over from the standard 1890s pub detailing to the Art Nouveau which proliferates in both the glass and the joinery. At the Queens the glass and metalwork are Art Nouveau throughout (Plate 163, Colour Plate XII). Both pubs have saloon bars divided off from the rest by arches, with enticing glimpses through them to the other bars, and little mirror-lined snuggeries under the staircases. Outside, the Salisbury is ringed by immensely jolly black marble columns of elephantine size; the Queens Hotel has a corner tower amazingly cantilevered out over a circular lobby lined with Art Nouveau glass (Plate 116). They are a wonderful pair of pubs, which worthily round off the century and deserve to be better known.

113. The Salisbury, Green Lanes, Harringay (J. C. Hill, 1898–9)

114. Saloon bar at the Salisbury in 1899

CHARRINGTON
THE SALISBURY

115. Bar fittings of *c.* 1900 at the Salisbury, Green Lanes, Harringay

116. The Queens, Broadway Parade, Crouch End (J. C. Hill, 1899–1901)

117, 118. (right) Lamps by Biggs and Company, Southwark, and D. Assersohn, Commercial Road, as advertised in 1899

Mirrors, coloured glass, massive brasswork, flashy furniture and encaustic tiles tend more to please the eye than satisfy either the palate or the stomach.

'City Press', 1 September 1897

7 The Fittings

ALTHOUGH there was a good deal of criticism of them at the time, it is the fittings of Victorian pubs of which most people think today when they grow enthusiastic or nostalgic about them. It has been suggested in the last two chapters that the architects of Victorian pubs are an identifiable body deserving more attention than they have received. But the fact remains that much of their work consisted of choosing and piecing together fittings designed and supplied by others. It was the richness and variety of fittings available, and the superlative quality of their manufacture or craftsmanship, which made the pubs of the eighties and nineties possible.

Perhaps the best way to approach Victorian pub craftsmanship is from the outside, by way of the immense wrought-iron pub lamps that feature so prominently in old photographs, though a rusting, broken-off stump is likely to be all that remains of them today. Dickens wrote about 'immense lamps' in 1836,[1] but as in so much to do with the early gin palaces their immensity was only relative. Even Cruikshank's cartoons show lamps of ordinary street-lamp size outside gin palaces. With the occasional exception (Parker's in Walworth Road (Plate 18) is the only example I know of, and the artist may have exaggerated) the pub lamps shown in early trade circulars and in photographs are comparatively modest, though there are often a good many of them. The facade of the sumptuous Eagle, City Road, when it was engraved in 1841 (Plate 20), was lit by six standard lamps of ordinary size. As the engraving makes clear, however, the streets around it had no form of lighting at all. The great increase in size and elaboration of pub lamps was partly to keep step with a general increase in the richness of pub decoration, but also to assert the pubs against the competition of steadily rising standards of street lighting.

Typical lamps of the sixties and seventies, as shown in numerous old photographs, are circular or square with ogee domed tops, often bracketed out from the columns

119. Refitted gas lamps of *c.* 1870 at the Brownswood Park Tavern, Green Lanes, Harringay

on the bar facade (Plate 119) rather than suspended from the wall above it. The first really ostentatious show of outside lights that I know of (and even these may have been later replacements) is (or rather was) the splendid double ring at the Alfred's Head, Newington Causeway (*c.* 1870), an inner ring on pedestals above the fascia of the bar front and an outer on standards along the pavement (Plate 32). If the pub is correctly attributed to E. L. Paraire, the original lamps were probably supplied by Thaddeus Hyatt, Pavement Light Maker of 9 Farringdon Road, EC, for 'Hyatt's Lights' on pavement standards are marked on Paraire's plans for the Admiral Keppel, Shoreditch, and the Duke of York, Clerkenwell, both of the late seventies.[2]

Hyatt does not seem to have done pub work in the eighties and nineties. The once omnipresent but now completely defunct hanging pub lamp was evolved in these decades and reached its final heights of fantasy in the late nineties, when *S*-shaped scrolls ornamented with foliage and flowers began to rear in ranks of three or more out of the first floors of pubs like rows of enormous insects supporting huge floating Chinese lanterns of iron and glass.

The leading producer of these glorious monsters was Biggs and Company of the Bee-Hive Works, Borough Road, Southwark, maker of the 'Solar Eclipse', 'Biggs' New Hexagon', 'Essex', 'Goldhawk' and other lamps (Plate 117). The firm was founded in 1828 and in 1899 claimed to be 'the oldest established licensed victuallers' gas and electrical lamp maker and fitter' in existence. John Biggs, who ran the business in the 1890s, was a craftsman himself and made his own designs. He advertised 'magnificent lamps, chandeliers, pendants, brackets, hot water urns, etc.' His firm's masterpiece was a hanging centre lamp big enough for four men to stand inside, the chief exhibit at its stall at the Licensed Victuallers Exhibition of 1899.[3] In the same year D. Assersohn, established at 37 Commercial Road since about 1897, was taking out full page advertisements for his 'Registered Design no. 341,929' (Plate 118), of which he was justly proud, for it was perhaps the gayest and most inventive of the nineties lamp designs.[4] Other lamp makers were W. Winn of Union Street, Southwark, and J. Ungar and Company of Danbury Street, Islington. The latter firm, which had existed since at least 1888, advertised in October 1899 an 'illuminated grill' which projected only eight inches and 'cannot be rejected by Parish Authorities or County Council'.[5] The background of this and similar advertisements was that earlier in the year the LCC had forbidden private bracket lamps projecting more than a limited distance above the pavement. Their attempt to force publicans to take down existing lamps met with indignant protests and seems to have been abandoned, and their writ anyway did not extend to the City or the outer boroughs. But even so the edict meant the ultimate death of the monster hanging lamp; it was one of several nails which the LCC hammered into the coffin of the Victorian pub.

Pub standard lamps, of the Alfred's Head type, continued to be erected either as supplements to the hanging ones or on their own. In 1893–4, for instance, Biggs supplied six standard lamps, four on the kerb and two to either side of the main entrance, for the Elgin, Ladbroke Grove; the publican's correspondence with the

vestry about them is still in existence.[6] They have all been removed, but a few kerb-edge pub standards survive, sometimes truncated of their lamps, like those outside the Prince Alfred, Formosa Street. A superb pair of standards still flank the main entrance of the Warrington Hotel in Warrington Crescent.

Biggs, Assersohn and probably other lamp makers also provided light fittings for the interiors of pubs. These could be bracketed from the wall or the back fitting, be supported on standards around the counter, hang from the ceiling or, very commonly, run in a row along rails fixed a few feet above the sill of each window so as to blaze brightly from the outside as well as the inside (Plate 120). Sometimes a pub had all four arrangements, for the ideal was to obtain the maximum of glitter. Interior light fittings were usually of brass, with their supports boldly scrolled or ornamented in the same manner as the outside lamps, though seldom as elaborately. The Ten Bells in Commercial Street, Spitalfields, had lion's-head brackets of unusual and attractive design (Plate 121). Some of the grander pubs of the late 1890s went in for special effects, like the wine bar of the Leicester in Coventry Street (1895) which had Louis XV wall brackets with candle-bulb electric light fittings, and further electric sconces supported by swirling white biscuit-porcelain nymphs (Plate 106). Similar lamps supported by bronze nymphs and marking the divisions between the plush upholstered benches are still a feature in the Salisbury, St Martin's Lane, of about 1899 (Plate 122).

120. Internal lamps photographed in an unidentified pub in the 1940s
121. (top right) Lamp brackets and Simpson tiles at the Ten Bells, Commercial Road, Spitalfields
122. (bottom right) Lamp of *c.* 1899 in the Salisbury, St Martin's Lane

Electric light fittings were nothing out of the ordinary in Victorian pubs. People probably tend to think of the Victorian pub as gas-lit, but in fact the richest and most familiar examples all date from the 1890s when electric light was spreading rapidly, and were as likely to be lit by electricity as gas. Biggs and Assersohn were prepared to fit both types. According to an article of 1893, electricity in pubs was pioneered by Baker Brothers, possibly at the Falstaff, Eastcheap, in the late 1880s. But as late as 1900 the *Licensing World* still favoured gas, on the grounds that electricity was subject to 'blinking, dazzling and modulating effects'.[7]

The mystique of the public house lamps consisted partly in their enormous and elaborately shaped lanterns but as much in the ironwork with which these were decorated and supported. But pubs had other ways of using ironwork. One can distinguish a move from the cast-iron age of the 1860s and 1870s to the wrought-iron age of the 1890s. The typical adornments of the earlier period were the decorative cast-iron frills which ran above the fascias of the bar front, or railed in the top of a mansard roof. This kind of ironwork (which can also be found on many shops of the period) went out of fashion during the 1880s in favour of elaborate wrought-iron grills enclosing the top portion of the outside entrance lobbies. The first securely documented examples of these that I know of were at T. H. Smith's Equestrian, Blackfriars Road, of 1888 (Plate 101); in the 1890s they were a commonplace (Plate 124). A fine example at the Lion Hotel, Highgate (Thorpe and Furniss, architects), was engraved at the time as an example of 'wrought iron hammered and polished brasswork lately executed by Jones and Willis'.[8] As was usually the case, the grill incorporated the name of the pub, together with roaring lions and vigorously curling tendrils and fronds in the Tijou manner (Plate 123).

Jones and Willis had made their names in mid-Victorian times as ecclesiastical furnishers. In 1894 they were advertising themselves as 'church furniture manufacturers, interior decorators, church plate, clerical vestments, mediaeval metal workers, stone and wood carvers, glass stainers, embroiderers, gas and electric fitters, manufacturers of the "Cathedral" lamp'. The firm originated in Birmingham, where its main works were located, but it had a London showroom and works in the East End which were moved in the 1890s to the Eagle Works at Hornsey. When the mid-Victorian enthusiasm for church building was increasingly being diverted into house building and house decoration, Jones and Willis, as their advertisements show, started to take on secular work. From cathedrals to pubs seems

123. Wrought-iron grill by Jones and Willis at the Lion, Highgate

a considerable jump, but they are also known to have done the metalwork for Thorpe and Furniss at the Assembly House, Kentish Town (1896),[9] as well as at the Lion, and can be presumed to have made the grills for the rest of that firm's many north London pubs of this period, and probably grills for other pubs as well. The fine grill at the Great Northern Railway Tavern in Hornsey, by Shoebridge and Rising in 1897, must surely have been their work, for the Eagle Works actually adjoined it and its metalwork sign 'Art Metal Works Jones and Willis' can be seen fixed to the wall of the pub in old photographs.

An earlier Thorpe and Furniss job, the Castle, Kentish Town Road, which they redecorated in 1889, has a lobby with no grill but with a large panel of painted tiles showing knights jousting above the inscription:

> Beneath the Castle Walls the lists are set
> Knighthood and chivalry and beauty met

Tile work was another prominent feature in the decoration of the late Victorian pub. As early as 1850 the billiard room at Gurton's in Old Bond Street had been decorated by E. F. Lambert with encaustic panels showing 'Bacchus and Ariadne',

124. Grill of 1899 over the lobby of the Salisbury, Green Lanes, Harringay

'Jupiter's Cupbearer', 'The Suttler's Booth', etc., 'not without merit', according to the *Builder* of 23 March 1850. Neither this nor any other tile work on pubs of this period survives, and it is unlikely to have become at all common before the 1880s, when tile decoration proliferated.

The jousting panel in the Castle is signed by Wm. B. Simpson and Sons of 100 St Martin's Lane. Simpson's are one of the principal firms that connect the pub world with the world of the aesthetic drawing room, which was frequently decorated with their wallpapers, fireplace tiles and tiled fire screens. The firm had been founded as housepainters and decorators in 1833, but by the 1870s they were also commissioning wallpapers, specializing in painted tiles and mosaic work and describing themselves as 'art workers'.[10] They were the London agents for Maw and Company, the Shropshire tile manufacturers who made the tiles which Simpson's decorated in London. They executed the tiled interiors of the Criterion Restaurant in 1873, and the tiles and mosaics lining the Grill and Refreshment Rooms at the Victoria and Albert Museum in 1874.

In the pub world they did work for Baker Brothers at the demolished Old Cock, Highbury, in 1888, and after that numerous tiled walls and pictorial tiled panels all over London. Their most typical pub decorations were historical tile pictures like the jousting scene at the Castle, already referred to, the 'Trial of Queen Katherine' in the Red Bull, Peckham High Street, 'Club Row in ye Olden Time' in the Well and Bucket, Bethnal Green Road (Plate 125), 'Spitalfields in ye Olden Time' in the Ten Bells, Commercial Street, and Robin Hood and his merry men at the Green Man, Old Kent Road.

Simpson's employed a wide range of artists, and the quality and style of their work is very variable. The commercial 'olde worlde' historical panels are rather too reminiscent of paintings by the less lovable Academicians of the period; but some of their work has much more vigour or charm: the classical figures of pronounced aesthetic character that accompanied 'Club Row in ye Olden Time' at the Well and Bucket, for instance, or the raised borders and friezes or panels of painted ornament that surround or accompany the tile pictures (Plate 121). A

125. Title picture of *c.* 1890 by W. B. Simpson and Sons formerly at the Well and Bucket, Bethnal Green Road

126, 127. (facing page) Tile pictures of 1890 formerly at the Clarence Arms, Plumstead Road, Woolwich

splendid Simpson interior survives comparatively little altered (apart from removal of partitions) at the Princess Louise in High Holborn. Here the firm redecorated the entire pub in 1891, subcontracting out the joinery and glass and lining the walls of the bars with a mixture of plain and ornamental tiles, culminating in sumptuously coloured panels of swags and baskets of fruit or flowers that alternate with equally sumptuous mirrors (Colour Plate XI).

But Simpson's by no means had a monopoly of tile work in pubs. There are, or were, many other tile panels in existence, signed by a variety of other manufacturers. A firm which did a good deal of pub work was Millington, Wisdom and Company, Art Tile Painters, of Shaftesbury Avenue. They signed the tiles still lining the large vestibule to the Greyhound, Sydenham, and framing Jones and Firmin's polychromatic mirrors and De Jong's plump Seasons in the Tottenham, Oxford Street (1892). Their own tile panels of the Seasons in W. M. Brutton's Goat and Compasses, Euston Road (1896), have gone (Plate 71), as have the 'Scenes of Bartholomew Fair' made in 1885 for the Jolly Butchers, Brick Lane, Spitalfields, by Carter and Company of Dorset.[11] A sad recent loss were the two panels of guns at the Clarence Arms, Plumstead Road, up the road from Woolwich Arsenal. Made in 1890 by 'GW and S Ltd.', these were signed by W. Lambert (Plates 126, 127). Surviving panels include the launching of a man-of-war in the Centurion, Deptford High Street, by William England and Sons of 2 Bury Street, Bloomsbury; a scene of the 'Hay Market in Whitechapel High Street', by Charles Evans and Company of Warwick Street, 1888, transferred from a local pub to the vestibule of Whitechapel Public Library; and the George and Dragon in the pub of that name in St John's Road, Clerkenwell, by Webb and Company of 94 Euston Road (1890).

Decorative tile work was also used on the outside of late Victorian pubs. A number had columns covered in faience, probably provided either by Simpson's, Doulton's or the Burmantoft Faience Works of Messrs Wilcocks in Leeds. A fine surviving example, probably of about 1900, is the porch of the Warrington Hotel, Warrington Crescent, flanked by the equally handsome lamps mentioned a few pages earlier; here the tiles were provided by Craven Dunhill's Jackfield Works at Ironbridge.[12] The Fox and Anchor, Charterhouse Street, of 1898, is still completely covered in tiles, with curly pilasters and scrolls around the bar front, faience monsters projecting above the first floor, a fox and anchor in coloured tiles in the gable and a strong admixture of Art Nouveau influence throughout.

Handsome though their tiles, mosaics and metalwork may be, when Victorian pubs are mentioned it is probably their decorated glass that most people immediately call to mind. Superb examples of the other types of decoration still abound in other types of Victorian buildings, but the vast majority of surviving embossed and brilliant cut glass, and all the best examples, are in pubs. This predominance used not to be so great. In 1898 a textbook of glass decoration could state that 'there is scarcely a warehouse, a bank, a shipping office, or public building throughout our great towns in which embossed or ornamental glass in some shape or another is not used'.[13] Embossing and brilliant cutting figured prominently on the side panels of tradesmen's vans and on the glass windows of hearses. Even so,

publicans were probably always the most lavish patrons of the technique and the initial predominance has been exaggerated because, great though the destruction of pub glass has been, the destruction of glass in shops and commercial buildings of the period has been even greater.

But the glass in Victorian pubs did not consist only of embossed or brilliant cut glass; gilding, enamelling, painting and staining were also to be found. The story can start with four newspaper entries in the *Building News* of 1857–8, even though none of them related to pubs. On 23 October 1857 the *Building News* described the fascia of the new shop front of J. W. Cassell, a silversmith and jeweller's shop in Camden High Street: 'the frieze is of glass, the ground of which is deep blue, in diaper pattern, on which the name &c. are gilded'. Similar shop fascias in Leicester Square are described in December. On 10 September 1858 the ceiling lights in the new coffee room of Feuillade's Hotel, Haymarket, are 'filled with embossed glass in highly elaborate patterns'. On 21 August 1857 an advertisement announces 'Bowden's Brilliant Cut Ornamental Window Glass—Architect's designs carefully executed. Mark Bowden and Co., Bristol, manufacture the above elegant article, which surpasses other kinds of Glass in beauty, brilliancy, and effect.'

These are early examples of gilding, enamelling, embossing and brilliant cutting of glass, all techniques which had been available for some years but were only just beginning to come into use since the removal of excise duty and window tax in 1845 and 1851 had cut the price of plate glass by more than half. Embossing and brilliant cutting were the equivalents of etching and engraving. Embossing, as normally practised in the earlier Victorian period in England, consisted of burning a pattern into glass with dilute hydrofluoric acid. The ground of the required pattern

128. Glass embossing workshop of Messrs Baxendale, Manchester and Edinburgh, as shown in their catalogue of 1902

Reid's

was first coated with a protective; acid was then applied and bit away the unprotected surfaces. But the embossed portions were still transparent; to bring out the pattern the raised surface had to be sprinkled with sand or emery powder and ground with a flat block of copper or glass to obscure it (Plate 129). Brilliant cutting consisted of cutting a pattern into the glass with a rotating stone wheel and then smoothing and polishing the cut (Plate 130). The process had been in use for many years as a means to decorate glassware and small pieces of glass. As it involved bringing the glass to the wheel rather than the wheel to the glass, it had been impossible to apply it to large panels. In 1850, however, Mark Bowden of Bristol installed an apparatus, which had been developed in the United States, by which the glass was suspended by an overhead arrangement of counterbalances, so that the operator could handle large sheets of plate glass with ease.

In contrast to brilliant cutting and embossing, both means of decorating glass without colour, were the processes of enamelling and gilding, Enamelled or 'flashed' glass was ordinary clear glass on to which a thin veneer of coloured glass had been blown. Ruby and blue were the colours most commonly used; green and yellow were much more expensive.[14] Gilding was applied to glass by putting on a coat of transparent size, as a key, and then applying and cutting to shape the thin sheets of gold leaf. Gold letters and diaper could be applied to the front surface of enamelled glass but better protection was given on a fascia or wall panel if the enamelling was applied to the back, the lettering or diaper embossed through the enamel to the clear glass, and then gilded, also from the back.

Enamelling, gilding and embossing probably started to appear in pubs at much the same time as in shops and hotels. The engraving of the pub in the New Cut, Lambeth, in Sala's *Twice Round the Clock* of 1859 seems to show a mirror decorated with a bunch of grapes (Plate 25). The processes were certainly much in evidence by the 1870s. James Callingham, in his *Sign Writing and Glass Embossing* of 1871, commented on how writing in gold and embossing had been 'within the last few years . . . brought to a marvellous state of development', and exampled pubs as one of the places where they were found: 'in the more tastily fitted-up public house bars of the metropolis and of the better class of public houses in the leading provincial towns it is now no uncommon thing for the inside walls of a richly decorated spirit bar to be entirely covered with glass, either embossed or written on in burnished and matt gold, the whole being the work of the more advanced sign writers'. It was to such an 'artist in glass' that John East, grandson of John East who owned the George, Southwark, and the Trafalgar, Greenwich, was apprenticed in 1873, and 'after a tour of cathedrals . . . was given a first commission to work on various panels at the Trafalgar'.[15]

The King Lud at Ludgate Circus had low panels of simple embossing in each window, as is shown in the *Builder* engraving of 1 April 1871 (Plate 38). In 1875 E. L. Paraire's Horse Shoe, Tottenham Court Road, had a Greek-key pattern in the same position; the identical frieze was continued in stone or plaster across the intervening pilasters (Plate 34). These low window panels became very common in pubs, usually with a row of gas lamps on a brass rail above them. The Horse

129. (top) Embossed glass at the Yorkshire Stingo, Marylebone Road
130. (bottom left) Brilliant cut glass at the Unicorn, Shoreditch
131. (bottom right) Combined French embossed and brilliant cut glass at the Assembly House, Kentish Town.

Shoe also had 'skylights' glazed with Hartley horticultural plate glass, on which an ornamental pattern has been burnt'; the *Building News* thought that this had a 'novel and pleasing effect'.[16] The glass was by 'Mr James of Camden Town'. This was an early appearance of William James of Camden and later Kentish Town, whose firm was to become one of the most prolific and accomplished manufacturers of pub glass.

Although the Trafalgar, King Lud and Horse Shoe are all still in existence, their embossed glass has disappeared. Surviving examples of embossed pub glass which can be attributed with any confidence to the 1870s, let alone documented, are rare. No doubt there are examples still in existence and waiting to be identified; but as a result of the more sophisticated techniques and standards of the eighties and nineties, and of subsequent alteration or destruction, the great majority have been swept away.

A modest example of enamelled and gilded glass, on the other hand, probably dating from 1873, is in the Greyhound, Sydenham. According to the *Builder*, the bar here was fitted up in 1873, with embossing by George Hollyer.[17] The Greyhound was done over again in the 1890s, and there is no surviving window glass that appears to date from the earlier period; but the original 1873 back fitting survives, and has a frieze of blue enamelled glass on which is written in gold 'Choice old foreign wines and spirits of the finest character, fine cigars'. As the firms who specialized in embossing tended to write on glass as well, Hollyer probably also did the frieze. He was one of the two Hollyers working in south London in the 1870s, the other being Joseph Hollyer of Camberwell, 'writer and embosser on glass'. One or the other of them may have been the 'Hollyer of Kennington' who provided embossed glass for a big shoe mart in Westbourne Grove in 1860.[18]

But the inconspicuous lettering at the Greyhound pales beside the panels in the back fitting of the Balmoral Castle in Pimlico (Colour Plate VII). There are three of these there today, announcing 'superior old Irish and Scotch whiskies', 'celebrated Double Diamond cream', and 'Martell or Hennessy cognac'. One or possibly two more were probably removed when the bar parlour was, at some stage, opened up into the rest of the bar (could the similar panel now in the Bride of Denmark, the 1950s bar in the basement of the Architectural Press, have been one of these?). The elaborate lettering is above a panel of green and gold diaper, and there is more ornament on glass strips set into the pilasters which frame the panels. It looks as though a combination of enamelling, gilding, painting and embossing may have been used: painting on glass in oil, with a transparent or tinted varnish as a key, was an alternative to enamelling that seems gradually to have superseded it in this type of decoration.[19] The panels can tentatively be dated to the late seventies or early eighties, when this type of 'elaborated' lettering was much in vogue and the former near-monopoly of Irish whiskey was being challenged by a vigorous campaign to introduce Scotch to London. In about 1878 the *Daily News* commented: 'to the aesthetic mind there may be nothing very beautiful in plate glass adorned with huge gilt letters setting forth the virtues of the "Dew of Ben Lomond", or the "Gatherings of Rob Roy" but to the eyes weary of a dingy workshop, or dingier

V. Mirror of *c.* 1892 by Jones and Firmin at the Tottenham, Oxford Street

VI. (left) Mirrors by Walter Gibbs and Sons at the Half Moon, Half Moon Lane, Herne Hill (1896)

VII. Advertisement panel of *c.* 1870 at the Balmoral Castle, Churchill Gardens, Pimlico

VIII. Lobby at the Salisbury, Green Lanes, Harringay (1898–9)

attick, these objects are more attractive than "red curtains and sanded floors".'[20] Sometimes these painted panels advertise beer rather than spirits; two handsome panels advertising Allsopp's are in Upton's, in Exmouth Street off Commercial Road.

The panels at the Balmoral Castle are not signed; the even more splendid mirror panels at the Lord Nelson, Old Kent Road, are signed by James Carter of 273 Gray's Inn Road. On one mirror, in a small private bar, swirling gilded grapes and foliage encircle Nelson and his men and little vignettes of kingfishers (Colour Plate IX); in a slightly larger bar are two similar panels, with Nelson replaced by storks in the rushes, together with a frieze announcing 'Finest Old Brandies, Irish and Scotch whiskies' and another panel advertising, in rich, elaborate letters, 'Mile End Distillery Co's celebrated Cream Gin'. James Carter first appears in the Post Office Directory in 1870 as a 'letter cutter' and by 1874 had moved to Gray's Inn Road as 'glass and general letter maker, sign writer glass embosser and writer, door and window plate maker, window letter advertising contractor'. The Mile End Distillery started up in about 1880, and as the panels seem to be all of the same date and style they are unlikely to date from before that year; most probably they were installed in 1888, as part of the 'improvements' introduced with R. A. Lewcock as architect.[21]

There are interesting differences in technique between the panels at the Lord Nelson and the Balmoral Castle. Those at the Lord Nelson are decorated mirrors; the Balmoral Castle panels (like those at Upton's) have no mirror glass at all. At the time they were set up there was no technique available for silvering over painting applied to the back of a sheet of glass. Coloured mirrors therefore either had to have the ornament on the front of the mirror, where it was vulnerable to wear and tear, or be made of two sheets of glass, at extra expense. In the late eighties or early nineties a process was introduced by which glass could be silvered over the painting, and what was known as a back-painted mirror resulted.

The Lord Nelson panels may be early examples of this technique; it is hard to tell without dismantling them. Another firm of glass painters, Jones and Firmin, claimed to have introduced the process.* The firm started up in Borough Road in 1878 as 'licensed victuallers glass writers and embossers and sign and fascia writers' and moved to 120 Blackfriars Road in 1883. Its business was described at some length in a *Descriptive Account of South London* of about 1893.[22] This referred to 'the new method of painting on the silvered side before the silvering is done, introduced by Messrs. Jones and Firmin, a vast improvement on the common method of painting on the face of the glass'. There are superb mirrors signed by Jones and Firmin and back-painted in brilliant colours in the Tottenham, Oxford Street, rebuilt for the Baker brothers in 1892 (Colour Plate V).

The *Pottery Gazette* of February 1887 refers to 'painted glass mirrors' as having 'lately become so fashionable',[23] but seems to know only the technique of painting on the surface. It describes the fashion as having been first revived in Rome, where designs by the artist Fornari 'are in the old Cinque Cento style, and are remarkable for the richness and variety of the flowers and arabesques used'. But the themes suggested by the *Pottery Gazette* derive from aesthetic drawing rooms rather than

*In fact the process had been known in the eighteenth century, but had apparently passed out of use.

IX. Mirror of *c.* 1888 by James Carter at the Lord Nelson, Old Kent Road

the Renaissance: apple and cherry blossoms or hawthorns with tomtits, goldfinches, butterflies and bees on the branches or above the flowers; or waterlilies, flags mixed with flowering rush, meadow sweet and purple loosestrife, with kingfishers, moorhens and dragon flies. It was subjects like these which were to proliferate on innumerable back-painted mirrors in pubs of the 1890s. Jones and Firmin's Tottenham mirrors, on the other hand, are brilliant exercises in 'the old Cinque Cento style'.

According to the *Descriptive Account*, Jones and Firmin were also glass stainers and practitioners of 'the new French or shaded embossing'. Their stained glass work included an exotic commission to decorate the 'princely bungalow' of S. D. Sassoon on Malabar Hill, Bombay. Stained glass, although it was certainly being made for pubs from at least the late 1880s, especially for skylights or small panels at the top of windows or around doors, never became a typical pub feature. But it is hard to underestimate the revolutionary effect of 'the new French or shaded embossing' in the pub world.

The earlier method of embossing, as described at the beginning of this section, etched away the glass without obscuring it; contrast of tone was obtainable only by grinding the top surface. This meant that only two tones were available, provided by the contrast between the clear and the obscured surfaces. In the second half of the nineteenth century French chemists developed and perfected a new process, involving the application of 'white acids'. White acids result from the mixture of hydrofluoric acid and various other chemicals, and when applied to glass form a dense white obscuration without depth. If hydrofluoric acid is then applied to these obscured portions it will reduce the whiteness. By forming a block design with white acid, coating parts of it with a protective and applying an etch of hydrofluoric acid, two tones can be obtained, known as 'white' and 'half-tone'. If the white and a portion of the half-tone are then protected and a second etch applied, a third tone results, known in the trade as 'bright'. In true French embossing only these three tones are used, resulting from one application of white acid and two hydrofluoric etches; but examples exist where four or more tones have been taken out of the white acid.

French embossing was first used in England in the late 1880s. Its aesthetic results were celebrated by the *Descriptive Account*:[24] 'this shaded embossing has all the softness of tone, delicacy and brilliance that the artist can desire'. But the effects were financial as well as aesthetic; as a technical manual of 1898 put it: 'the importance of this invention to the glass embosser or glass writer cannot be over-estimated, as by its use sheet glass can be used instead of plate, thus reducing the cost so materially that an extensive trade is done in a direction which before was practically closed to the general public'.[25] The price of sheet glass (very roughly speaking, because there were so many variations for different sizes and qualities) was about one-third that of plate glass.

With the new sophistications of French embossing and back-painted mirrors, with more glass available for the same sum of money, with more money to spend anyway as a result of booming sales and escalating property values, and with a

flourishing decorative tradition, it was not surprising that the 1890s were the golden age of pub glass. Large areas of sheet glass could be covered with embossed ornament for very modest sums. Those with more money to spend could indulge in the ultimate luxury of pub glass, the combination of French embossing and brilliant cutting (Plates 131, 132). Brilliant cutting, although a process available since 1850, seems to have been little used in pubs at first, perhaps because it was much more expensive than embossing. There may have been earlier examples but I have come across no mention of it in a pub context before the 1880s. In the 1890s it proliferated, even though it had become relatively even more expensive than embossing, for it could be carried out only on plate glass. It was sometimes used on its own for the relatively simple patterns of straight or gently curving lines which were all that the technique allowed. Alternatively its extra flash and sparkle could be used to frame or emphasize more complicated designs of flowers, birds or scrolls in embossed glass (Plate 134). Both embossing and brilliant cutting could be stained or gilded or combined with back-painting. A final refinement was to bend the glass to fit the curving fronts of the more exotic pubs of the 1890s. This was a hair-raising process, for it involved heating and bending massive pieces of glass which had already been decorated, with a considerable risk that the glass might break and the expense of the decoration be wasted.

The stiff geometric or repetitive patterns of the seventies tended to give way in the late eighties and nineties to the two types recommended by the *Pottery Gazette*: on the one hand, the 'Cinque Cento style', and on the other, naturalistic

132. French embossed and brilliant cut glass by W. James of Kentish Town at the Assembly House, Kentish Town (1896)

flowers or foliage on their own or combined with birds or insects. The former provided the lush scrolls and baskets or cornucopia bursting with fruit or flowers on the larger panels; birds on twigs, a hangover from the Japanese craze, were a particular favourite for the hinged panels of snob-screens (Plate 133). The two types often coalesce, with Renaissance or rococo patterns lapping and scrolling round little naturalistic vignettes of birds or bunches of flowers (Plates 134, 135).

133. (top left) Snob-screen and carved grapes at the Bunch of Grapes, Brompton Road, Kensington
134. (left) Glass of *c.* 1899 at the Salisbury, St Martin's Lane
135. Decorated mirror of *c.* 1899 at the St Stephen's Tavern, Bridge Street, Westminister

So pubs all over London glittered, glowed and sparkled as ornamental glass of every description crept over their walls and partitions, lined the shelves of their back fittings, flashed from their snob-screens, and, unless the licensing magistrates prevented it, splashed far further up the outside windows than the discreet panels of the 1870s. Magistrates were not friendly to decorated glass in pubs on the ground that it made supervision difficult. At various times the magistrates in the City, Wandsworth and Newington licensing districts (the last covering Camberwell, Peckham and Southwark) attempted to limit its use. They demanded that glass above a height of five feet and sometimes of four feet should be clear in both external windows and partitions. Clear glass in partitions was probably intended to prevent misconduct in snugs; and in the windows it enabled the police to 'spy on the customer inside', as the *Licensed Victuallers' Gazette* put it.[26] These regulations were much resented in the trade and were said to have been ineffective; it remains a fact, however, that the more elaborate surviving examples of pub glass are all in other licensing districts.

Makers of pub glass flourished and proliferated in response to the fashion for their products. A number of firms deserve to be mentioned in addition to those already referred to. One of the best established businesses was that of Walter Gibbs (later Walter Gibbs and Sons), who claimed to have started up in 1861, but first appears in the Post Office Directory in 1866 as 'Painter, writer and embosser on glass' at 123 Union Street, Southwark. In the 1870s the firm moved to works in the arches under the railway viaduct in Blackfriars Road, and in the 1880s opened a showroom in 2 Charlotte Street. After Walter Gibbs died in 1891 the business was carried on by his widow and sons.[27] In 1893 they were said to have 'quite recently . . . introduced an improved patented process of amber staining for French embossing and brilliant cutting'. A rich claret stain was also available, and examples can be seen in, for instance, the doors of the Elgin, Ladbroke Grove, the Lord Nelson, Old Kent Road, the Washington, Primrose Hill, and the Red Lion, Duke of York Street. If Gibbs and Sons had a monopoly of their process it would suggest that they did glass at all these pubs and were also responsible for the superb mirrors at the Red Lion (Fig. 136). The firm also supplied back-painted mirrors and their signed mirrors still line the wine bar at J. W. Brooker's Half Moon, Herne Hill, of 1896 (Colour Plate VI). The firm has since amalgamated with another long-established business in Blackfriars, James Clark and Son Ltd. As James Clark and Eaton Ltd (with Walter Gibbs and Sons as a subsidiary) the firm is one of the few still making embossed and brilliant cut glass.

A defunct, but in its day extremely successful, firm was that of William James of Kentish Town. The firm first appears in 1869 and by 1875 had moved to Camden High Street as 'W. James and Co, glass merchants, dealers in glass shades and articles for horticultural and domestic purposes . . . glass painters, stainers, writers and embossers'. Although there is a chronological gap between them, the firm may have been connected with W. H. James of 37 Camden High Street, who in the late fifties was advertising 'Engine-turned and every variety of enamelled window glass'.[28] About 1880 the firm moved to 72 Willes Road, Kentish Town. Brilliant cutting was first advertised in 1892; from about 1893 to 1895 there was a second

'brilliant cut glass and metal casement works' in Richmond Road, EC, but this department was later moved back to the presumably enlarged works in Willes Road. As 'Mr James of Camden Town', the firm was responsible in 1875 for the embossed glass at the Horse Shoe, Tottenham Court Road, already referred to. As 'W. James, Kentish Town' it signed the lush back-painted mirrors in the Bunch of Grapes, Brompton Road (Plate 78), and was responsible for the glass at the Assembly House, Kentish Town (1896), an unequalled example of virtuosity in the combination of brilliant cutting and embossing (Plate 131).[29] The firm failed to survive the 1914–18 War and its works in Willes Road have been ingloriously converted for the manufacture of windscreens.

The gold embossed mirrors (Colour Plate XI) in the Princess Louise, Holborn (*c.* 1892), are signed by R. Morris and Son, who first appear in 1866 as 'Richard Morris, Writer on glass' in the Euston Road and move in 1869 to Kennington Road as glass embossers. Brilliant cutting was first advertised by the firm in 1898, when they were 'Richard Morris and Son, artists in stained glass, glass embossers, and stainers, writers and gilders on glass and glass brilliant cutters'. But amongst the most interesting of the glass firms is Cakebread, Robey and Company, a firm still in existence, which has preserved a glass and leaded lights catalogue of about 1900.[30] They first appear in 1887 as 'Lead, glass and colour merchants, glass stainers, and lead glaziers' in Stoke Newington High Street (telegraph address, 'Splendour' London). By the late 1890s they had expanded and become full-scale builders' mer-

136. Glass of *c.* 1890 at the Red Lion, Duke of York Street, St James's

chants, as they remain today. In 1900, apart from pub glass, they made ribbed and fluted glass in a wide variety of patterns, glass ventilators, shop fascias, leaded lights in clear or stained glass for houses and stained glass windows for churches.

Their patterns ranged from the simplest brilliant cut stars or embossed key patterns to the full splendour of birds, swans, fruit and flowers in combined embossing and cutting (Plates 137, 138). A detailed price list enables one to work out with some accuracy how much it cost a publican to bring a pub up to date as far as its glass was concerned in the late 1890s. A plain sheet of plate glass, for instance, six feet by four, cost £3 2*s.* If embossed it cost, depending on the elaboration of the design, from £5 2*s.* to £5 16*s.*, including the price of the glass; if brilliant cut, between £7 10*s.* and £11 10*s.* The most elaborate combination of brilliant cutting and embossing brought the cost up to £15 2*s.*, and if the glass was curved as well it was likely to cost at least £20.

The catalogue contains a list of 'various important works carried out by us' at seventeen pubs all over London.* The most important survivor of these is the Salisbury, in Green Lanes, Harringay, where, in addition to brilliant cut, embossed and gilded mirrors (Colour Plate VIII) and windows, the firm also provided elaborate stained glass (since removed) in the skylight to the saloon bar (Plate 114). A contemporary description of the Salisbury in the *Licensed Victualler* refers to the firm as being 'very widely known as glass manufacturers in all its branches, but chief of them all is their stained glass work'. The stained glass in the Salisbury consisted of a classical design of cherubs and swags, but by 1900 Cakebread, Robey were also producing stained glass designs under Art Nouveau influence; to judge from their catalogue they had a strong selling line in flowers, tendrils and sailing ships for the front doors of new north London houses. There are also a few Art Nouveau-ish designs in the brilliant cut and embossed section, and some lively and

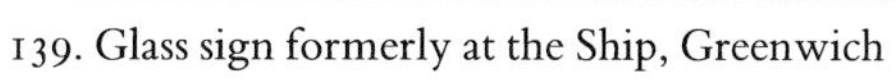
139. Glass sign formerly at the Ship, Greenwich

140. Art Nouveau glass of *c.* 1900 at the Salisbury, Green Lanes, Harringay, probably by Cakebread, Robey and Company

original examples executed for the Salisbury are probably by them (Plate 140). The firm's Art Nouveau masterpieces are the stained glass windows at the Queens, Crouch End, where fronds and flowers in brilliant colours leap, whirl and rotate across the big arched windows looking out towards the Broadway (Colour Plate XII). As the glass dates from about 1901, it was too late to get a mention in Cakebread, Robey's catalogue; but there is little doubt that it was their work, for it was made for the same publican as the glass at the Salisbury and immediately after it.

Cakebread, Robey's embossed and brilliant cut glass employs exactly the same motifs in very much the same manner as that of William James of Kentish Town. The back-painted mirrors at the Half Moon and the Bunch of Grapes could easily be attributed to the same maker if the signatures did not show that they were by William James and Walter Gibbs. As signatures are comparatively rare and only one London catalogue, and that a late one, has so far come to light, it is impossible to say who was the pioneer and who was borrowing whose ideas. Although in

*Elmhurst, Lordship Lane; Salisbury, Green Lanes; Queen's Head, Green Lanes; White Hart, Newington High Street; Three Crowns, Newington High Street; Hungerford Arms, Barnsbury; Old King of Prussia, N. Finchley; Priory, Clapton; Duke of Fife, Upton Park; Lord Raglan, Walthamstow; London Bridge, London Bridge; Black Horse, Strand; Haunch of Venison, Brook Street; King's Arms, Sloane Square; White Lion, Putney Bridge; Star and Garter, Putney; Golden Lion, Fulham Road.

137, 138. (facing page) Designs for French embossed and brilliant cut glass, stained glass, and French embossed glass, from the Cakebread, Robey and Company catalogue of *c.* 1900

1899 Walter Gibbs and Sons advertised 'Architect's own designs carefully executed', the offer was seldom taken up, to judge by the great similarity of so many of the windows. But architects or publicans must have been able to gain a certain measure of variety by ordering different combinations of frames and centres, or by fitting the device or initials of the pub into the scheme of decoration. The Ship at Greenwich had a three-masted schooner (Plate 139); the Eagle in Camden Town is full of eagles (Plate 141); huge Prince of Wales feathers proliferate on the windows of the Prince of Wales, Princedale Road (Plate 142); the bold superimposed double *S*'s in the mirrors of the Salisbury, St Martin's Lane, stand for its original name of the Salisbury Stores.

The publican who wished to economize in the considerable outlay required to line his pub with decorated glass could go in for advertising mirrors, which were presumably paid for or subsidized by the breweries and distillers whose names they bore. These lettered mirrors, though not as luscious as the painted glass panels which preceded them, were sufficiently decorative, and survive in much larger numbers. They were a speciality of the Brilliant Sign Company which established itself in Gray's Inn Road in 1893. Its stall of scrolled and gilded mirrors, advertising all the leading brewers and distillers, was a familiar and regular feature at the Licensed Victuallers Exhibition for many years.[31]

The sculptural decoration on and in pubs is neither as consistent nor as individual to the pubs as the glasswork, but it has its agreeable moments. A common inspiration for carving, as for glass, was the name of the pub. For some reason, inn signs were not popular in Victorian London (except for 'improved' pubs put up by philanthropic middle-class patrons), but many pubs had an inset carved panel or

141. Eagle at the Eagle, Great College Street, Camden Town
142. (right) Prince of Wales feathers in French embossed glass at the Prince of Wales, Princedale Road, Holland Park

a piece of sculpture on the parapet to represent their name. The phlegmatic elephant and castle on the gable of the demolished pub of that name and location has been imprisoned in the new shopping centre, but there are two smaller but very taking ones on the parapet of the Elephant and Castle at Vauxhall Bridge (Plate 143). The Yorkshire Grey in Gray's Inn Road is surmounted by an inflated tin soldier on horseback (Plate 144), carved by 'Mr Plows' in 1878.[78] The classical lady who

143. (following page) The elephant at the Elephant and Castle, Vauxhall Bridge (*c.* 1875)
144. (facing following page) Yorkshire Grey carved by 'Mr Plows' at the Yorkshire Grey, Gray's Inn Road (1878)

COOPER LONDON Ld

supports the oriel of George Treacher's Shipwright's Arms, Tooley Street (1884), is presumably inspired by a ship's figurehead and is surrounded by much lush, jolly carving (Plate 145). Later sculpture tends to be more sophisticated though not necessarily more attractive. The name panel (Plate 146) of the Jolly Gardeners in Black Prince Road, Lambeth (1890), was probably carved by Frederick T. Callcott, who seems to have had a tie up with R. A. Lewcock, its architect. He signed the relief panels of eighteenth-century scenes, very much in the manner of Simpson's tile pictures, in the bar of Lewcock's Black Lion, Bayswater (1889), and it was presumably he or a relative whom Lewcock took into partnership about 1898. Callcott also supplied hammered brass panels representing scenes in the history of Croydon at the Greyhound, Croydon, and must have been responsible for the similar panels still in the Black Lion, Kilburn (Plate 147). Both pubs date from 1898 and both were probably by Lewcock.[33]

145. Figurehead at the Shipwright's Arms, Tooley Street, Southwark (1884)

146. Gardeners at the Jolly Gardeners, Black Prince Road, Lambeth (1890), probably carved by F. T. Callcott

Much of the external decoration of the pubs of the late eighties and nineties consisted of panels of ornamental brickwork or plaster. These were a typical product of the Art movement and can be found in quantities on buildings of all sorts all over London. Aesthetic sunflowers or lilies and Renaissance cherubs and urns are especially common. Much remains to be found out about the firms who supplied them. A documented artist-manufacturer is Gilbert Seale, of 14A George Street, Camberwell, whose decorative advertisement is in the *Architect* of 7 January 1888. He describes himself as 'Modeller, Sculptor and Fibrous Plasterer, sgraffito, carton pierre, carving in wood, stone cement and brick'. He was responsible for the frieze of frolicking cherubs on T. H. Smith's Equestrian, Blackfriars Road (Plate 101), and for the carving at the same architect's Goat in Boots, Fulham Road, both built in 1888. He may also have supplied the carving at Crickmay's Horns, Kennington, in 1886 (and on the amazing Nos. 1 and 2 South Audley Street), for he modelled

147. The Black Lion, Kilburn High Road (1898), showing figurative panels probably by F. T. Callcott

the plasterwork at Holmwood, near Wimborne, a country house designed by Crickmay in 1897.[34]

The life-size plaster cherubs (Plate 148) that fill either end of the enormous club room at the Crown, Cricklewood (Shoebridge and Rising, 1899–1900), must have been modelled by someone like Seale or by the Mural Decoration Company of 50 Milton Street, EC, who were responsible for the rich fibrous plaster decoration at the Salisbury, Green Lanes (Plate 114). But what at first sight appears to be hand-modelled plasterwork very often turns out to be the work of those great standbys of the pub architect or decorator, Lincrusta-Walton, Tynecastle, and their rivals, all producing imitations of plasterwork made by various processes of stamping paper or embossing on a canvas or paper background. The results were used *ad infinitum* for coves, friezes and ceilings, and the range of designs was considerable. The ceiling of the Crown, Leytonstone High Street (1888), is imprinted with strange bearded mythological figures, but an imitation of Jacobean ribbed plasterwork was more usual. A typical example, at the Assembly House, Kentish Town, was supplied in 1896 by the Plastic Decoration Company, 'manufacturers of architectural decorations in fibrous plaster, a large stock of dry fibrous plaster slabs always in stock, papier mâché, carton pierre, etc.'[35]

Decorative painting is comparatively rare in late Victorian pubs. Even the elaborate graining with which W. H. Grimes as a boy had embellished 'some of the handsomest taverns in London and the provinces' was going out of fashion. The more lavish pubs of the nineties could anyway afford expensive woods like teak, walnut and mahogany for their bar fittings, and polished granite for their fronts. Figurative

148. Plasterwork cherubs in the former club room of the Crown, Cricklewood Broadway (1899–1900)

painting probably failed to flourish, not because it was expensive, but because publicans favoured hard, durable, washable surfaces. The best surviving examples are the bosomy ladies in the Tottenham, Oxford Street, signed F. De Jong and Company (Plate 56). The Tottenham was a Baker brothers/Saville and Martin pub of 1892, and there used to be paintings, possibly also by De Jong, in the same firm's Garrick Hotel of Leicester Square. Felix De Jong was a decorative painter, who, during the 1890s, formed a company producing both paintings and fibrous plaster decorations, and specializing in doing up music-halls, such as W. M. Brutton's Hammersmith Theatre of Varieties in 1899 and Frank Matcham's Hackney Empire in 1901.[36] The Tottenham was only a couple of doors down from the Oxford Music Hall, and must have been much frequented by its audiences during the interval.

Decorative marble, although certainly hard, durable and washable, was perhaps too expensive for most publicans. A few of the most ambitious pubs, however, had marble decorations of some elaboration, possibly in imitation of the socially slightly superior bars attached to café-restaurants. The bar at Gatti's in Adelaide Street, like the Bodega Bar in Bedford Street much frequented by actors, was known as the 'Marble Halls' because of its decoration.

Oh the Marble Halls! The Marble Halls
A place in the Strand where everybody calls
When the actor out of collar
Often raises half-a-dollar
O God bless Gatti and the Marble Halls.[37]

There was a good deal of marblework in the extremely expensive Prince of Wales (formerly the Feathers), King Street, St James's, designed by Robert Sawyer for E. Bratt in 1898, clearly in the hopes of getting a clientele socially above that of most pubs. It is now occupied by Spink and Sons, the art dealers, and the original interiors have all disappeared.* The best surviving example of a Victorian pub 'Marble Hall' is the saloon bar of the Crown, in Aberdeen Place, designed in 1898 by C. H. Worley, FRIBA, for Frank Crocker, formerly of the Volunteer, Kilburn. C. H. Worley was not a professional pub architect, and the building clearly set out to escape from the usual pub image. Fittings were not only lavish but different, and culminated in the marble-lined walls, marble counter and baronial marble chimney-piece (Plates 149, 150) of the saloon, of which the *Licensed Victuallers' Gazette* remarked, with considerable truth, 'one would fancy that it was the hall of some magnificent modern mansion rather than the saloon of a tavern'.[38]

But however great the importance of glass, tiles, marble, metal work and whatever else the publican could afford, the unifying factor of a pub interior was its joinery. It was all important as the framework which tied the interior together. It radiated out from the elaborate back or centre fitting of the serving-bar, by way of the compartment partitions, to the outer walls and windows, in a spidery skeleton of balusters, pediments and shelving, framing, supporting and fusing together engraved glass, bottles, urns, barrels, glasses, clocks, vases and light fittings.

* A more modest, though far from simple, pub interior redecorated by Bratt (probably employing Sawyer) in the 1890s survives relatively little altered at the Argyll, Argyll Street, W1.

Pub joinery of the eighties and nineties has a highly homogeneous character and is completely a creature of its age. This character is 'Queen Anne', and typical features are pediments, often broken, with urns on pedestals between the break, coves, decorative patterns of wooden glazing bars, and balusters, sometimes attenuated, sometimes short and bulbous, and often closely spaced and repeated to form screens or rails. The central feature in all pubs was the joinery of the serving-bar. In the earlier Victorian pubs this had culminated in the back fitting along the wall behind the counter. The standard form for this from the very earliest days was

149. (left) Bar fittings in the saloon bar of the Crown, Aberdeen Place, St John's Wood (C. H. Worley, 1898)

150. Chimney-piece in the saloon bar of the Crown

a framework of columns or pilasters and entablature filled with mirrors and shelves and often with a row of spirit casks along the top (Plates 151, 152).

With the changing plan of the 1870s and 1880s the serving bar pushed out from the wall in an increasingly elongated promontory, so that the conventional back fitting became increasingly inconvenient to reach for the barmen at the further end of the bar. The obvious solution to this was an island centre fitting, sometimes known as a 'wagon' or 'stillion', as a replacement or supplement to the back fitting. In an island or near-island bar there was, of course, no back fitting at all. Two centre fittings are shown on the plan of the Britannia, Peckham High Street, designed by George Treacher in 1881, but they mostly date from the late eighties and nineties. Some pubs have both centre and back fittings, like the Prince Alfred, Formosa Street (Plate 153); in the Wheatsheaf, Goldhawk Road, an abandoned and disused back fitting made by Schlater in 1886 survives against the wall since an island bar and wagon were installed by R. A. Lewcock in 1891.[39]

151. Typical mid-Victorian back fitting from an engraving by Cruikshank
152. (top right) Back fitting of 1875 in the Rose and Crown, Highgate
153. (right) Back fitting and wagon of *c.* 1890 in the Prince Alfred, Formosa Street, Maida Vale

Now
on Draught
STRONG ALE

These later back and centre fittings often gave up the old column-and-entablature formula for a new arrangement. The new inspiration was the overmantel of the late Victorian drawing room (Plate 86), and a publican with pretensions to taste could use its upper shelves for displaying objects of art rather than for practical use. The possibilities are suggested in a slim volume of *New Designs of Cabinet Bar Fittings*, published in 1896 by James Yates, 'high class barfitter' of 39–42 Coleshill Street, Birmingham, of whom more in the Epilogue. These are all in the 'Queen Anne' style and show pots of flowers and ornamental jugs displayed on the shelves (Plate 85). A dimmer London counterpart of James Yates was the firm of George Farmiloe and Sons, of 54 St John Street, Smithfield, whose illustrated advertisements for bar equipment and bar stillions were familiar features in both the licensed victuallers' and the building magazines of the eighties and nineties. Farmiloe, like Yates, advertised 'special designs on application'.

There were, in fact, four classes of firms doing cabinet work for pubs: pewterers and bar fitters, like Yates and Farmiloe, who also had a cabinet department; specialists in joinery, not only for pubs, like W. A. Antill and Company of the Mornington Electrical Joinery Works, Arlington Road, Camden Town, 'speciality high class joinery, inlaying in the solids, carving etc.'; general builders with a joinery department, like Thomas Gibbs of 10 Three Crown Square, Borough Market, 'Public House, Office, and Shop Fitter, Builder, Decorator, Sanitary engineer and Plumber'; and furniture suppliers, like N. J. Moxhay of 57 Strutton Street, Curtain Road, EC, who after sixteen years with Bowler Brothers, suppliers of furniture for pubs, set up on his own in the late nineties to provide 'saloon bar furniture, also specializes in bar cabinets, and screens'.[40]

Probably all four types could supply their own designs as well as carry out the designs of others. Athough, as discussed in Chapter VI, some pub architects were perfectly capable of supplying their own joinery designs, one cannot help wondering to what extent the dimmer or busier one relied on the expertise of cabinet bar fitters, especially when, as sometimes happened, these were of rather higher calibre than the architects themselves. It is hard to believe, for instance, that a firm with the reputation of W. B. Simpson and Sons did not have more to do with the interior decoration of the Princess Louise, Holborn, than Arthur Chitty, the otherwise unknown architect in charge of the conversion. Although the *Builder* includes many tenders for cabinet bar fittings, it much less often publishes which tender was accepted; furthermore the pubs in question have frequently been redecorated, so that it is difficult to get together a large selection of documented work for comparison in order to see, for instance, whether joinery done by the same firm for different architects is recognizably similar.

A firm of comparable status to W. B. Simpson that did even more pub work was W. H. Lascelles and Company, 'builders, manufacturing joiners, bank office and shop fitters, horticultural builders and concrete manufacturers', of the Finsbury Steam Joinery Works. Lascelles are interesting because of their close connection with Norman Shaw and his circle. They built many of his London buildings; between about 1875 and 1885 he designed furniture for them; in 1872 they published

a slim volume of buildings in the Old English and 'Queen Anne' styles, designed by Norman Shaw and Ernest Newton, 'to be contracted in the patent cement slab system of W. H. Lascelles'. They first appear in the pub field tendering for the Victory, Trafalgar Road, in 1877; thereafter they appear regularly in the tender lists and by the 1890s (by when Lascelles himself had retired) were explicitly advertising as public house fitters in the trade journals. In 1886 their tender to fit out the Archway Tavern, Highgate, was accepted; if, as seems likely, they were responsible for the clock surmounted centrepiece like a miniature clock tower that still survives there, they must also have done the joinery in the Princess Louise, Holborn (1891), where there is an almost identical clock case (Plate 154). Certainly they are exactly the kind of firm one would expect to find working with W. B. Simpson and Sons. It would be interesting to known how much influence they had in introducing 'Queen Anne' joinery of high quality into the public house bars of the eighties and nineties.[41]

Another big builder with a joinery department that frequently tendered for pubs and pub fittings was Edwards and Medway of the Kennington Steam Joinery Works, 9 Ethelred Street, Lambeth. Antill and Company, mentioned a few paragraphs previously, were clearly a high quality firm and their capabilities are still spendidly demonstrated by the cabinet work of Thorpe and Furniss's Assem-

154. Wagon of 1891 in the Princess Louise, Holborn, probably by W. H. Lascelles and Company

155. Joinery by W. A. Antill and Company at the Assembly House, Kentish Town (1896)

bly House, Kentish Town, of 1896 (Plate 155). Most of the fittings in W. M. Brutton's pubs were provided by J. Brown and Company. J. C. Hill's lavish joinery made in his own workshops for his two pubs the Salisbury, Green Lanes, and the Queens, Crouch End, was described in the previous chapter. The Hackney Furnishing Company of Mare Street, Hackney, cast an interesting sidelight on one way by which some publicans raised money to refurbish their houses; it was prepared to do work on the hire purchase system, and according to a note in the *Licensed Victualler* 'has gained a great reputation in this direction'.[42]

Once the main decorations were completed the serving-bar had to be fitted up and the rooms furnished. Beer engines were provided by pewterers and bar fitters, the biggest of whom was probably Gaskell and Chambers in Blackfriars Road—

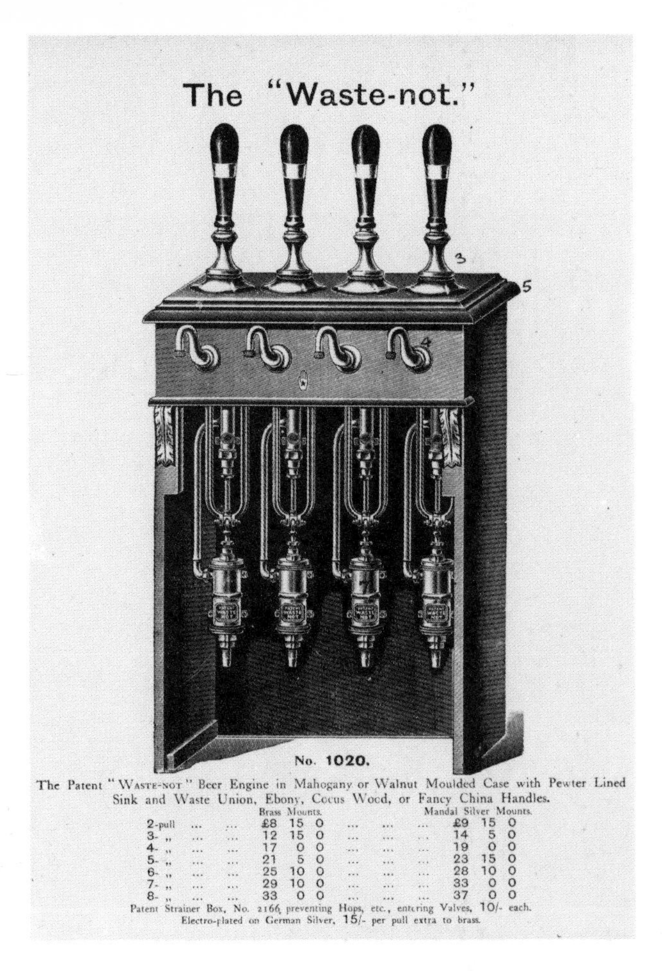

156. 'Waste-not' beer engine from a Gaskell and Chambers catalogue of *c.* 1900

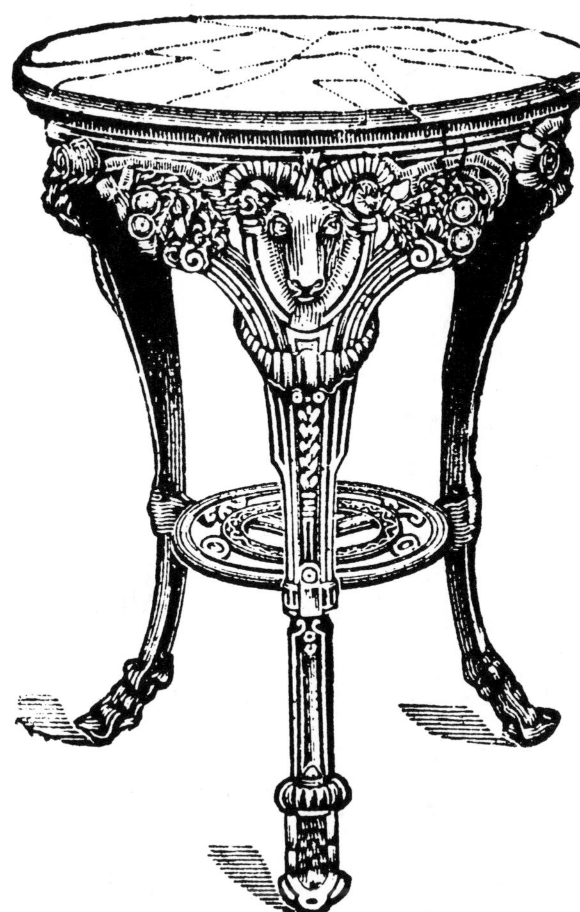

157. Iron bar table from a late Victorian catalogue

'Beer Engine makers, pertwerers, and cabinet bar fitters. Established 1797'—who survived until well on in this century and produced a handsome catalogue (Plate 156). But there were numerous smaller firms, one of which, Pringle and Son, pewterers and bar fitters, carried on business until 1972 in a Dickensian office, complete with high desks and stools, in Brick Lane, Spitalfields. One of the specialities of bar fitters was an elaborate range of china bar-engine handles decorated with different patterns and now sought after by collectors. Judging from old photographs, however, by the 1890s these were being replaced in fashion by smart and simple brass or brass-bound ones. Similarly, both the massive spirit casks so prominent behind the bar in illustrations of early Victorian gin palaces, and the familiar decorated china barrels, with the name of the spirit on them, were being replaced in the 1890s by glass spirit urns along the bar counter.

The china barrels could be obtained from E. Coaney and Company of Birmingham, or Henry Turner of the Crown Pottery, Paddington, founded in the early nineteenth century. These also supplied glasses, as did C. Paine—'The celebrated Licensed Victuallers Glass and Bottle Contractor . . . Do not be misled by prejudiced persons stating that I have discontinued business'—whose 'very beautiful show of cut and coloured glass' was a prominent annual feature of the Licensed Victuallers Exhibition.[43] A number of firms supplied glass spirit urns, but the king of them was James A. Cox of 42 Old Compton Street, a firm much

publicized in the *Licensed Victualler*. Their designer was James Cox, Junior, 'a first class draughtsman and designer in art metal work as well as glasswork'. The firm claimed to be 'sole inventor of glass whiskey urns' and in addition to individual urns supplied the Excelsior screen, the Queen screen, the Cupid stand (for sandwiches) and above all 'Mr. Cox's Combined Whisky Urn Standard and Counter Screen'.[44] In this a row of spirit urns was joined by decorative metal work in polished brass and copper, the whole supported on brass standards which sprouted out at the top with sprays of electric light bulbs (Plate 158). It thus provided drink, light and privacy, for it was designed as an alternative to the glass-panelled snob-screens: 'the inventor's idea is to entirely do away with the inconvenient and bulky mahogany counter screen now in vogue (which has at all times been an unnecessary evil)'. A few surviving old photographs, such as one of the bar in the St Stephen's Tavern, Westminster, show the glitter provided by these multiple spirit urns (Plate 159). As far as I know none survive, but there are quite a few single ones around, in private collections or as decoration in pubs, and their crystal glass and eighteenth-century profiles are extremely handsome.

The early Victorian concept that a bar was a place in which drinkers stood and that if they wanted to sit they went to the tap room or parlour (if the pub had one) had largely disappeared by the 1880s. All bars normally had seating of some kind, though of course it varied in comfort from public bar to saloon. In 1896, for instance, Ernest F. Bowler, of 29 & 31 Curtain Road, EC1, advertised seats in plushette (8*s*. 6*d*. per foot), velvet (10*s*. 6*d*. per foot), perforated wood back and seat (7*s*. to 8*s*. per foot) and mahogany (9*s*. per foot). He also provided 'marble top iron stand tables' from 12*s*. 6*d*.[45] Another frequent advertiser of these iron tables was Arighi Bianchi and Company, whose own warehouse in Macclesfield is still a notable example of early cast-iron construction. Manufacturers of bentwood furniture also advertised in the licensed victuallers' magazines, and there were firms who specialized in better quality furniture, like Swire and Company of 62 City Road, manufacturers of saloon bar furniture and fittings. Waring, not yet amalgamated with Gillow, provided furniture for the Prince of Wales in King Street in 1898 and decorated the banqueting room in Treadwell and Martin's Old Dover Castle in 1896.[46] These were two of the most expensive of Victorian pubs, and perhaps it was also Waring who provided the Empire-style tapestry-upholstered chairs and tables (Plate 106) for the wine bar in the same architects' Leicester, Coventry Street, in 1894—the ultimate remove in the hierarchy of pub furnishings from the 'perforated wood back and seat' benches in the public bar.

Another regular advertiser in public house periodicals was the Empire Furnishing Company of 154 Edgware Road. They supplied 'Household and Office Furniture, Clocks, Ornaments, Bronzes, and Fancy Goods on Easy Terms, without security at Cash Prices'. Firms like this were resorted to by publicans for the kind of objects that gave the final touch of tone to a richly upholstered saloon: 'bronzes and fancy goods' seems exactly the right description for the ornaments on the saloon overmantel of the Black Lion, Kilburn High Road, fortunately photographed in situ in the 1940s before they were dispersed (Plate 160).

158. Cox's combined whisky urn standard and counter screen, 1899

159. Bar at the St Stephen's Tavern, Bridge Street, Westminster, in 1899

Once fitted up with a drink from Cox's Combined Whisky Urn Standard and Counter Screen, and seated on a plushette or velvet bench at an Arighi Bianchi iron-and-marble table, the saloon bar customer was able to entertain himself by pushing a penny into one of the numerous brands of musical automata. In 1898 the *Licensing World* noted that 'these instruments have, within the last year or two, made rapid strides'. The biggest suppliers were Nicole Frères, of 21 Ely Place, but also of Geneva, Leipzig and New York (Plate 161). They supplied a wide range

160. Chimney-piece ornaments formerly in the Black Lion, Kilburn High Road

of models including the Polyphon in an elaborate case, 'which plays over 1000 tunes and is popular everywhere . . . In public places it can be very profitable.' These musical automata were, in fact, straightforward musical boxes operated by clockwork; insertion of a perforated circular metal disc and a penny to free the machinery would release a tinkling stream of gaily melancholic music. Other suppliers included D. Harper and Company of South Street, and Eyre and Son of Barkers Pool, Sheffield, makers of the penny-in-the-slot Symphonion.[47] The king of musical automata was the musical clock (Plate 162), of which, until it was sold in 1974, there was a sumptuous example, complete with painted panel of a nude on the clock case, in the Crown, Aberdeen Place.

161. Automata by Nicole Freres, as advertised in 1899
162. Automaton clock formerly in the Crown, Aberdeen Place, St John's Wood
163. (following page) Art Nouveau door-handle of *c.* 1901 at the Queens, Broadway Parade, Crouch End

A public house without the drink
Where men may read, and smoke, and think
Then sober home return;

A stepping stone this house you'll find,
Come leave your rum and beer behind
And truer pleasures learn.

8 The Opposition

A SIGNBOARD with the inscription quoted on the previous page swung in front of the first British Workman's Public-House opened in Leeds on 30 September 1867.[1] The Temperance lobby had conceived the bright idea of carrying the war into the enemy's country. It was sufficiently realistic to understand that the function of the pub was not only to sell alcohol: it realized that 'Persons in the humbler walks and occupations of life, who were not habitual drunkards, were often compelled to frequent the public-house, because in this class of establishments alone were supplied the ordinary and natural cravings for society, the news of the day, and a place where they could pass a sociable hour'.[2]

Coffee public houses were designed to have the social qualities of the pub with the alcohol left out. In addition, they aimed at providing what pubs in the mid-Victorian period provided inadequately, if at all—good cheap food. The movement started with a series of working men's coffee houses in Dundee, the first of which opened in 1853. But these, unlike the Leeds ones, were straightforward coffee houses, not dry imitations of pubs. The Leeds formula spread rapidly in the north and reached London in the early 1870s. In October 1872 Dr Barnardo, of the Homes, bought the Edinburgh Castle in Rhodeswell Road, Limehouse, 'widely known throughout the East-End as a resort of the most abandoned' and re-opened it in the next year as the Edinburgh Castle Coffee Palace (Plates 165, 166). He carried out a similar conversion job on the Dublin Castle, Mile End Road, in 1875–6. In 1877 'an influential committee of earnest Christian workers' opened the Rose and Crown, Knightsbridge. In 1874 the People's Café Company was founded in an attempt to place 'the continental café system before the London public' and 'serve as a counter attraction to the public house and gin palace'. The Coffee Tavern Company Ltd followed in 1876. The Coffee Public House Association, founded in 1877, made loans to those who wanted to start up houses. The lavishly produced and illustrated *Coffee Public House News* was founded in 1878. By 1884 there were 121 coffee houses of various kinds in London and over 1,500 in the British Isles. They were to be found in Ireland, America, Canada, Australia, Holland, Switzerland and Belgium.[3]

Coffee public houses provided more than coffee. Non-alcoholic drinks on sale included tea, cocoa, milk, lemonade, gingerade and soda water; food ranged from full meals to plates of beef or ham, boiled eggs, cake and bread and butter. In addition to a bar or coffee room, most had a reading room, and many a social or club room. By and large they closely followed ordinary pub lines, for the coffee public house movement aimed at providing a similar but alternative structure to the drink structure. Most allowed smoking; many provided billiard or bagatelle tables, put on smoking or coffee concerts and ran debating or discussion groups. The Royal and Antediluvian Order of Buffaloes and its fellows were paralleled by organizations such as the Original Grand and United Order of the Total Abstinent Sons of the Phoenix, who on 9 July 1898 were to be found 'assembled at the Brondesbury Station (Metropolitan) for the purpose of spending a half-day in the fields and meadows without the aid of strong drink to mar their pleasures'.[4] In place of strong drink, Temperance advocates were offered beverages that sounded

164. (previous page) Advertisement in the *Coffee Public House News*, 1 January 1885
165, 166. (facing page) The Edinburgh Castle Coffee Palace, Rhodeswell Road, Limehouse

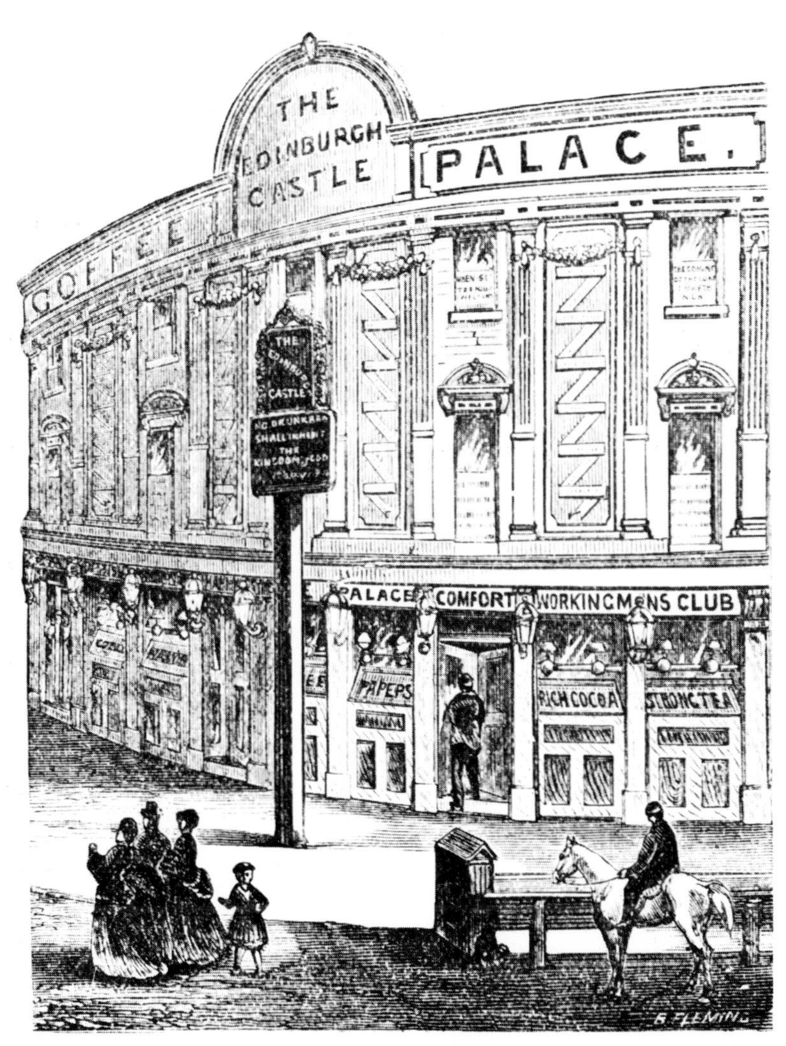
THE EDINBURGH CASTLE
COFFEE
PALACE.
THE CASTLE
NO DRUNKARD SHALL INHERIT THE KINGDOM OF GOD
PALACE
COMFORT
WORKINGMENS CLUB
PAPERS
RICH COCOA
STRONG TEA

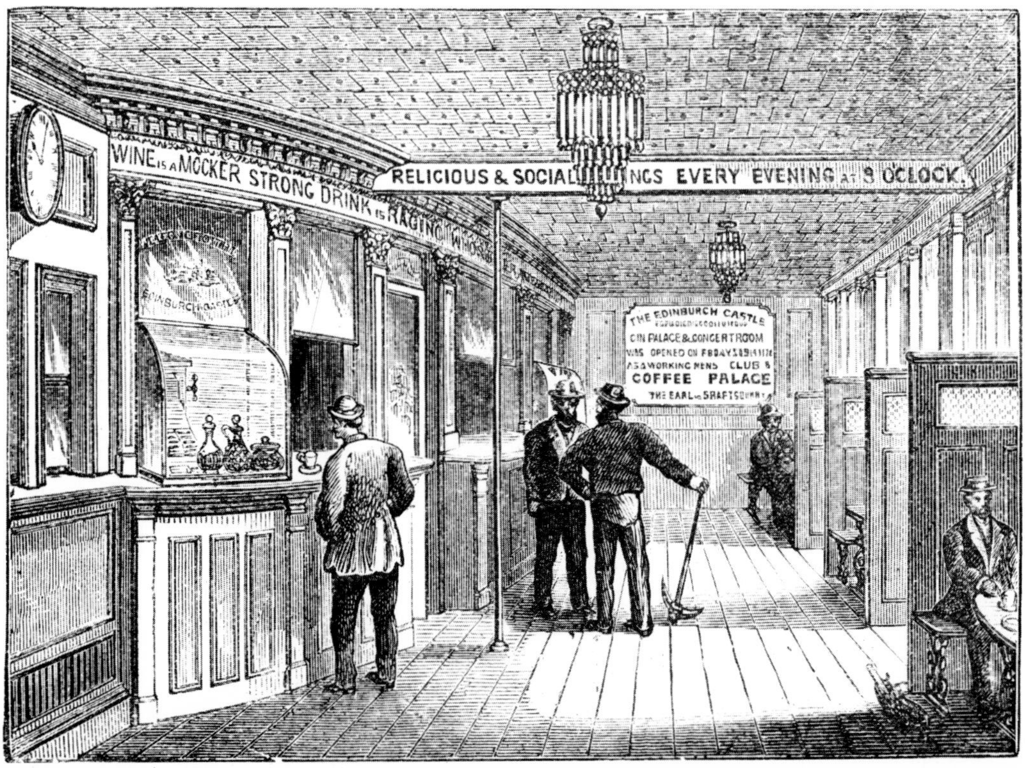
WINE IS A MOCKER STRONG DRINK IS RAGING
RELIGIOUS & SOCIAL
NGS EVERY EVENING AT 9 O'CLOCK.
THE EDINBURGH CASTLE
GIN PALACE & CONCERT ROOM
WAS OPENED ON
AS A WORKING MENS CLUB &
COFFEE PALACE
THE EARL

and even looked like it—what Charles Booth called 'Sheep in wolves' clothing'.[5] The Temperance beer was 'Cox's Anti-Burton. A Perfect Mild Ale Substitute. Awarded First Prize by Ely Diocesan Branch of Church of England Temperance Society'. The Temperance champagne was 'sparkling milk', milk impregnated with carbonic acid gas and bottled. The Temperance wine was Beckett's Winterine, 'the best non-alcoholic substitute for punch, brandy etc.'[6] A full-page advertisement for this in the *Coffee Public House News* of 1 January 1885 (Plate 164) shows a buxom barmaid ladling it out from a steaming punchbowl.

The reclaimed workman who wanted more of a night out than was involved in knocking back Winterine at a coffee concert could attend the Royal Victoria Tavern Music Hall in Lambeth. This was originally the popular low-class Royal Victoria Theatre, situated in the notorious New Cut, one of the toughest and sleaziest areas in London, notorious for its gin palaces. Suitably remodelled and supported by two neighbouring coffee public houses, the Royal Victoria devoted four nights a week to 'Variety Entertainments, after the style of the ordinary music halls, but free from any objectionable features'. Another night was given over to ballads, Saturday to children, and Sunday to religion. Under the energetic management of Emma Cons and her niece Lilian Baylis, the Royal Victoria ultimately developed into the Old Vic.[7]

The thought of a music-hall or public house reformed and devoted to good purposes gave Victorian do-gooders the same kind of pleasurable feelings as the thought of a reformed prostitute. A number of coffee public houses, like Dr Barnardo's Edinburgh and Dublin Castles, were converted pubs, retaining their plate glass and bright lights to advertise the Temperance cause with 'Coffee', 'Tea', and 'Cocoa' engraved on the lamps, and texts across the windows. New premises were often designed to resemble pubs and were deliberately sited next door to them. Those put up by the British Workman's Public-House Company Ltd in Liverpool were 'a reproduction of the old Liverpool "publics" *with a difference*'. The Rose and Crown in Knightsbridge had plate glass, gas lamps and swing doors on the pub model; inside 'reflected in mirrors behing them, coloured and other glass bottles on narrow ranges of shelves give a brilliancy and air of comfort without imitating too closely the elaborate decoration of the ordinary gin palace'. The magnificent Cobden in Corporation Street, Birmingham, designed by William Doubleday in 1883, went the whole hog in the way of imitation, with elaborate tile pictures and brilliant cut plate glass windows decorated with the arms of the city and the Birmingham Coffee-House Company.[8]

But among the promoters of the movement the desire to attract was always conflicting with the desire to improve. There was a group of coffee public houses which deliberately set out to produce a different image from that of the gin palace, and went back for inspiration to the mythical golden age of the old English inn. The most interesting and much the most decorative among these were the coffee taverns designed by Ernest George; the Cocoa-Tree, Pinner (1877–8), the Bee-Hive, Streatham Common (1878–9), and the Ossington Coffee Palace, Newark-on-Trent (1881–2).[9] Ernest George at this period was a young and comparatively unknown

167. Brick detail at the Bee-Hive, Streatham High Road (Ernest George, 1878-9)

168. The Bee-Hive, Streatham High Road, Streatham Common (Ernest George, 1878-9)

18
76
BULL

architect. He was born and brought up in Streatham and his introduction to the Temperance movement was probably by way of P. C. Cow, a Temperance rubber manufacturer who invented Cow gum, lived and had his factory in Streatham, and was the treasurer of the local organization which built the Bee-Hive. In the 1870s George was strongly under the influence of Norman Shaw. The Bee-Hive (Plates 168) is a charming design in the pure 'Queen Anne' manner, with none of the flashiness which pub architects managed to impart to it. The Cocoa-Tree is more in Norman Shaw's Old English manner, and to Victorian eyes seemed a delightful re-creation of a village inn complete with horse trough and swinging sign; besides providing non-alcoholic drink and food, it was the headquarters of the local Band of Hope and Cricket Club, and botany classes were held there twice a week.

The Bee-Hive was opened in July 1879 by Lord Cairns, the Lord Chancellor. As part of the ceremony he was presented with a copy of Ernest George's *Etchings on the Loire and Moselle*, for George combined extreme shyness with a considerable talent for self-advertisement. Within eighteen months he was to achieve even closer connection with the peerage (and future sources of patronage) when Viscountess Ossington, sister of the Duke of Portland and one of the mainstays of the coffee public house movement, commissioned him to design a coffee palace in Newark-on-Trent in memory of her husband and nephew. The Ossington Coffee Palace cost £20,000, closed the vista of the main street of the town more prominently than the town hall and contained bars, assembly room, reading room, club room and billiard room, stabling for fifty horses and a garden with an American bowling alley, designed for music and refreshments on summer evenings on the lines of a German Biergarten.

Lord Chancellors and Viscountesses were nothing out of the ordinary in the coffee public house movement. The whole weight of well-born, well-intentioned or well-heeled Victorian England was behind it. Lord Shaftesbury was president of the People's Café Company; the saintly evangelizing W. F. Cowper-Temple, later Lord Mount Temple, was president of the Coffee Tavern Company; and the millionaire philanthropic Duke of Westminster was president of the Coffee Public House Association. Vice-chairmen and directors included Gladstone, always good for a speech at an opening, the Nottingham hosiery tycoon Samuel Morley, and Tom Hughes of *Tom Brown's Schooldays*. The 'earnest Christian workers' who managed the Rose and Crown, Knightsbridge, were headed by C. E. Tritton, of the High Church banking family which also helped finance the Woodward schools and All Saints, Margaret Street. Mrs Russell Gurney, the spirituel and artistic friend of the Cowper-Temples and all the cream of Victorian do-goodery, personally bought the Walmer Castle in Seymour Street and converted it into a coffee public house.[10]

But in spite of, or perhaps because of, this weight of good intentions and great names, the movement was a considerable flop. As a correspondent wrote to the *Coffee Public House News* in January 1881, 'the tastes of the lower strata of society are so much vitiated by strong drink that "the cup which cheers but does not inebriate'' finds little acceptance at their hands'. Coffee public house companies flourished like mayflies in the summer, but many of them vanished as soon as their middle-class sponsors grew tired of forking out money to subsidize them. Others, especially in the north, where the Temperance movement was strongest, did better and even paid dividends, though one wonders how much these were invisibly subsidized by private contributions.

Few even of these survived the 1890s and few if any coffee public houses still fulfil anything resembling their original function. Many have been demolished; a few, like the Old Coffee House in Beak Street, have, so to speak, lapsed and become pubs. The Ossington Coffee Palace now houses the local council offices; the Bee-Hive, Streatham, was absorbed after its failure by the adjoining Cow rubber works and used for the manufacture of hot-water bottles.

Their failure was not only due to the vitiated tastes of the lower strata. They did not help their cause by plugging the wrong drink; while tea and cocoa consumption was booming in the late nineteenth century, coffee consumption, for reasons that remain obscure, was steadily going down. More important, many coffee public houses were atrociously badly managed under the direction of committees with no practical experience and little business sense, and of managers who were usually incompetent and often dishonest. In spite of what the propaganda would lead one to expect, their tea, coffee and food were frequently disgusting, and the surroundings they provided were gloomy and squalid enough to be compared to 'a workhouse dining-hall'.[11]

Most important of all, in spite of many good resolutions not to patronize or preach to the clientele, their well-meaning sponsors were seldom able to refrain from doing both. At the Dundee Workman's Public-House without Drink, for instance, a converted pub re-opened about 1875 by the Ladies Temperance Prayer Union, evangelistic meetings were held every Monday and Thursday and 'several young ladies in turn lead the praise, and preside at the harmonium'.[12] The Edinburgh Castle, Limehouse, announced in huge letters across the bar, 'Religious and Social Meetings every evening at 8 o'clock', and another streamer above the counter proclaimed that 'wine is a mocker, strong drink is raging'. More texts on the exterior, such as 'No drunkard shall inherit the kingdom of God' on the inn sign and 'The coming of the Lord draweth nigh' on an upstairs window, rubbed into the clientele the fact that they were sinners saved from the burning (Plates 165, 166). Pious dukes could get away with inscribing texts of this nature on the walls of their kitchens and servants' halls, but it was not a form of decoration calculated to attract independent working men looking for an agreeable meeting place.

But the coffee house movement, even if it nowhere near fulfilled the hopes of its sponsors, was not a complete write-off, for it had at least two successful spin-offs. In the first place, the subsidized do-gooding coffee public houses stimulated the growth of a great many working-class cafés, and when the coffee public houses fell by the wayside, the cafés remained and flourished. They did so because their aims were straightforward, unambitious and useful; they made no effort to improve their customers or to rival or even rather childishly imitate the public houses, but provided cheap food and refreshment in clean surroundings. The two most successful chains of working-men's cafés in London were Lockhart's Cocoa Rooms and Pearce and Plenty Ltd. The latter were started in the 1880s by John Pearce, a Temperance-pledge porter in Covent Garden who had worked his way up to them by selling coffee from a costermonger's barrow painted like a fire engine and named 'The Gutter Hotel'.[13] The Aerated Bread Company shops, founded in about 1854, and the Lyons tea shops, founded in 1894, were on a slightly higher level and aimed at a clientele of clerks and white-collar workers rather than working men.

Secondly, the spread of cafés and coffee public houses forced publicans to widen their own range of services. As Charles Booth wrote in 1888, 'the licensed victuallers begin to see that they cannot live by drink alone. Look more closely at the signs in their windows. There is hardly a window that does not show the necessity felt to cater for other wants besides drink. All sell tobacco, not a few sell tea. "Bovril" (a well advertised novelty) is to be had everywhere. Hot luncheons are offered, or a mid-day joint; or "sausage and mustard" are suggested to the hungry passer-by; at all events there will be sandwiches, biscuits, and bread and cheese. Early coffee is frequently provided, and temperance drinks too have now a recognized place. Ginger beer is sold everywhere, and not infrequently kept on draught.'[14]

Victorian opinion cannot simply be divided into those for public houses and those against them. In between was a wide and variegated stratum of people who were neither teetotal nor prohibitionist but who deplored the flashiness and commercialism of what, in spite of the fact that gin was now drunk in them in comparatively small quantities, they continued to call gin palaces. Their attitude was to be found even within the trade. On 3 December 1897, for instance, the *Licensed Victuallers' Gazette* was regretting the passing of the old-fashioned Greyhound, Dulwich, to be replaced by 'one of the mahogany and plate-glass monstrosities yclept hotels'. Later on, in a similar vein, on 1 November 1899 the *Builders Journal and Architectural Record* published a lament for the passing of the suburban inn and an attack on the fashion for 'picturing the shame of it by decorating the halls of the gin-palaces that take their place with painted tile-pictures of what has disappeared to make room for all this glass and glitter . . . how superficial our sentiment and how ingrained our commercialism'.

Efforts to 'improve' public houses could be devoted to the facilities which they provided, the way they were run and organized, or the way they looked. They tended to be supported by a reforming upper- and upper middle-class group that shaded imperceptibly into the group supporting coffee public houses. Architecturally there is little if any difference in style or treatment between the coffee taverns designed by Ernest George and the drink-dispensing inns designed by Norman Shaw or his imitators. Both types were intended to evoke the village or small town inns of the eighteenth century and earlier, and were in the 'Queen Anne' or Old English styles which Shaw and his contemporaries had devised as a protest against contemporary commercial architecture. Swinging inn signs, horse troughs, generous roofs, tall chimney stacks, windows with small panes or leaded lights, rendered surfaces and half-timbering were at a premium; engraved plate glass, huge

lamps, abundant ornament and all the rest of the fun and games with which professional pub architects jazzed up 'Queen Anne' were noticeably absent. Food was always provided and there were large club or public rooms. The bar was usually one big room with a long counter and no subdivisions; this was a somewhat old-fashioned reversion to the plan of the mid-nineteenth-century gin palaces, but by now snugs had replaced long bars as the bogeys of contemporary reformers.

The first 'improved' public house of any importance in London was Norman Shaw's Tabard at Bedford Park, opened in 1880.[15] Bedford Park was exactly the right setting, for it was intended as a haven for artists and artistic people of modest means who wanted to get out (but not too far out) of the wicked city and enjoy something approaching village life. In the engraving of Shaw's original design in the *Building News* the inn is called 'ye hostelry' and what appears to be a figure in a smock is standing outside the door—an unlikely occurrence in Turnham Green, but symbolizing the spirit in which it was built (Plate 169). The inn adjoined the village stores and the two made up an extremely picturesque group. The interior has been a good deal altered, but tiles by De Morgan and Walter Crane still line the entrance porch and the original bar.

The Tabard was immediately followed by three splendid taverns built for the London and St Katharine Docks Company at the Royal Victoria and Albert Docks, to the design of the company architects, George Vigers and Thomas R. Wagstaffe. The first of these was the Ship by the Victoria Dock (*Building News*, 29 October 1880); then came the Galleons Hotel (*Building News*, 22 July 1881) and the Connaught Tavern (*Building News*, 1 August 1884) at either end of Albert Dock. All three are clever essays in the Shaw manner. The Ship is in his Old English style, with half-timbering, tile-hanging and an ingle-nook in the dining room. The Connaught and Galleons are 'Queen Anne'; the Galleons is clearly inspired by the Tabard, but goes one better all the way round. The lush external frieze of gambolling nymphs and cherubs was executed by M. E. Roscoe Mullins. The plan was skilfully arranged to give entrances at two levels, the upper one leading to a buffet and dining room for sea-captains and their passengers, the lower to a public bar and tap room for ratings and dock-workers. Both the Galleons (Plate 170) and Connaught (Plate 171) would have been entirely in place at Bedford Park, but become

169. The Tabard, Bath Road, Bedford Park (Norman Shaw, 1880)

170. The Galleons Hotel off Woolwich Manor Way, Royal Albert Dock, photographed on completion (Vigers and Wagstaff, 1881)

strange and romantic exotics in their unlikely setting between the mud flats and the docks.

Shaw's pupil and assistant Ernest Newton was responsible for a number of agreeable inns in the 'Queen Anne' style. His inn at Grove Park, Kent, was designed in 1881 for the Earl of Northbrook.[16] Local landowners quite often built and managed public houses of an 'improved' nature; in 1895 the Lords Wantage, Windsor and Spencer were all reported to be running 'model public-houses' with an

X. (top right) Glass screen of *c.* 1893 at the Elgin, Ladbroke Grove
XI. (right) Tiles by Simpson and Sons, mirrors by R. Morris and Son at the Princess Louise, Holborn (1891)
XII. (following page top) Window of *c.* 1900 at the Queens, Broadway Parade, Crouch End, probably by Cakebread, Robey and Company
XIII. (following page bottom left) Tiles and mirrors of *c.* 1893 at the Elgin, Ladbroke Grove
XIV. (following page bottom right) Lobby at the Bunch of Grapes, Brompton Road, Kensington (*c.* 1890), with mirror by William James of Kentish Town

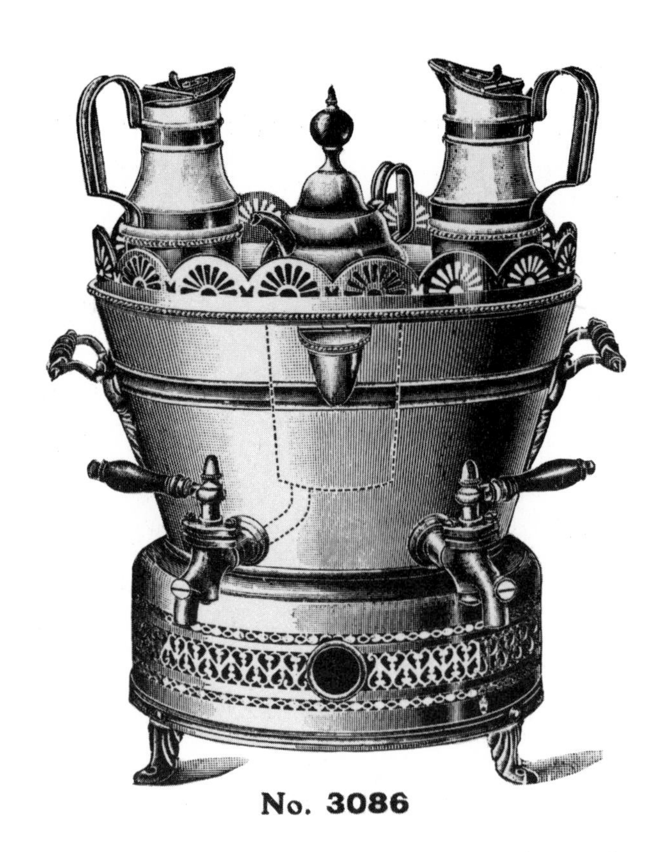

emphasis on non-alcoholic drinks.[17] In improving circles in the 1890s there was much discussion about the Swedish Gothenburg system, under which pubs were run by limited liability companies 'in the interest of temperance and morality' (though still providing alcohol), with all profits going to the local authority or some form of local benefit. In 1894 a co-operative pub at Scaynes Hill, Lindfield, Sussex, was being run on the Gothenburg system with 'a view to benefit the neighbourhood' and a clergyman as ground landlord. The experiment was a disaster: the managers took to drink, one committed suicide in the village pond, and the clergyman, who came from a brewery family, finally handed the pub over to the brewery.[18] The charming Fox and Pelican in Grayshott, designed by Reid and Macdonald and opened in 1899, was a Gothenburg pub managed more successfully by an association of local residents with Sir Frederick Pollock as president. It had a big tile-hung gable, a pillared verandah and an inn sign painted by Walter Crane, sure sign in the 1890s of a patron who was both artistic and progressive.[19]

But in spite of the weight of good intentions behind them, the 'improved' public houses of the eighties and nineties remained a minute group; there were scarcely more than a dozen of them. The 1,500 coffee houses of 1884 sound more impressive until one remembers the 100,000 licensed premises with which they had to compete. In spite of the blandishments of leaded lights, inn signs and ingle-nooks, by the end of the 1890s pubs unrepentantly splendid in engraved glass and overblown lamps were rising in more numbers than ever before.

171. (previous page) The Connaught Tavern, Connaught Road, Royal Albert Dock (Vigers and Wagstaff, 1884)
172. (above) Tea and Coffee muller, from a Gaskell and Chambers catalogue of *c.* 1900
173. (right) Bracket head of publican, King's Head, Upper Tooting Road, Walworth

Beneath all this investment of money there existed no doubt the prospect of a veritable golden egg of profit, but the bird that was to lay it has been priced too high and extravagantly decorated.

Booth, 'Life and Labour of the People in London', Final Vol. (London 1902), p. 98

9 Collapse

The 1896–9 boom was not confined to London. All over the country pubs were being rebuilt and breweries and speculators were bidding each other up. In September 1896, shortly after the Conservative victory, the *Leeds Mercury* reported: 'the word seems to have gone all along the line that now is the time to rebuild. I have never known so many public houses simultaneously in course of enlargement and improvement as now.' The alcohol graph, like the pub rebuilding graph, rose and fell with Tories. Beer and spirit consumption, which had been steadily declining since 1876, began to rise under the Conservative government of 1886–92, fell again under the Liberals in 1892–5, and started rising when the Tories came back at the end of 1895 to reach an even higher peak in 1899.

The figures in 1899 were not quite as high as in the record years of 1875–6, but they were a notable recovery from the decline of the eighties and were never to be equalled again. It was an impressive achievement, considering that the licensing authorities were still doggedly engaged in reducing the numbers of licensed premises and that the number of alternative attractions was growing yearly. But in spite of more museums, galleries, public libraries and public swimming baths, in spite of the arrival of the cinema and the opening of more and more halls that could be hired for public meetings, in spite of football matches to pull thousands out of the pubs on Saturday afternoons, and of increasing numbers of tramlines and underground railways to carry even more thousands past them on their way home from work in the evenings, drink consumption continued to rise.

With the Conservatives still securely at the helm, and drink consumption, brewery shares, property values and rebuilt pubs all rising together, the situation might have appeared a rosy one for the drink interest. It was not. In September 1896, when the boom was at its height, the *Sportsman* published a wry little note: 'It is an open secret that there are many holders of licences of large houses who are not paying, and never will be able to pay their way, under the heavy burden of interest which they have to labour. As a result such traders find difficulty in getting credit outside the brewer mortgagee.' Publicans in this position—and there were increasing numbers of them as prices soared to wildly inflated heights—made money, not from the income from their sales, but by selling their pubs every few years at a profit. If public house property ceased to rise in value, there was bound to be a crash.

The crash came in 1899. Almost all the pubs put up for sale at the beginning of that year failed to reach their reserve and were bought in. 'The present state of affairs', reported the *Licensed Victualler* guardedly on 29 March, 'cannot be called a slump; it is more of a deadlock.' Its analysis of the reasons suggested that there was little difference between the two. 'Men who bought at high prices hoping to sell again at a profit, cannot find customers, except at a loss.' The deadlock was broken by the middle of the year; the situation that it revealed was disastrous. In June a Southwark public house which had been sold at the end of 1897 for £33,000 was resold for £12,000.[1] The bankruptcies started at much the same time.

In November 1897 Henry Harris, 'late the popular proprietor of the Talbot, Engelfield Road, Kingsland', was handed the keys of the Freemason Arms, Long

Acre. 'The features of the evening', according to the *Licensed Victuallers' Gazette*, 'were much music, many dozens and perpetual good wishes.' The pub had been partly rebuilt in the previous year to the designs of Treacher and Fisher, and illustrated in the *Architect*; no doubt the seller made a good profit. In June 1899 Henry Harris went bankrupt; he had borrowed £7,500 from Bass and been unable to pay any interest.[2]

Harris was small beer. Much more alarming was the sudden disintegration of Grimes and Company, the whizz-kids of the public house world. Albert E. Mathams failed in May, with liabilities of £65,000. It was less than two years since he had been strumming classical melodies to the respectful correspondent of the *Licensed Victuallers' Gazette* in the 'richly upholstered lounges' of the Telegraph, Brixton Hill. In the same month one of the dimmer members of the group, E. J. Arpthorp of the Cock, Love Lane, and Earl Amherst, Hackney, was adjudicated bankrupt. On 26 May 1899 an extraordinary general meeting of the shareholders of Grimes Ltd voted to change the name of the company to the Gaiety Bars and Restaurant Company Ltd. The background to this is obscure; Grimes cannot be traced to the bankruptcy courts, but by 1900 he had completely disappeared from the Post Office Directory and he, Atherden and Mathams had ceased to be directors or shareholders of the company which had carried his name.[3]

Ironically, the bankruptcies of 1899 coincided with the opening of the last batch of splendid new pubs, started in the optimistic climate of the previous year. When the glittering Boston, Fortess Road, was launched in September the *Licensed Victualler* hopefully commented, 'The opening of such a palatial hotel is evidence against the statement that the public-house trade is doomed.'[4] But bankruptcies continued through 1900 and reached their peak in 1901. In that year the *Licensed Victualler* gave up its series on 'Up-to-date Public Houses' for another regular feature ominously headed 'The Gazette'.

The gravity of the situation was made clear in December 1900 when Richard Baker, managing director of Baker Brothers Ltd and Baker and Company, the biggest owners of licensed property in London, failed with liabilities of £650,000. He appeared in the bankruptcy court in March and explained the reasons for his failure. The Queen's Hotel, Hotel de l'Europe and Garrick Hotel had greatly exceeded the builders' estimates. There had been a depression in the trade since the Boer War began in 1899. In Leicester Square his aim had been to introduce an imitation of the French and German brasserie, and he had not anticipated an immediate profit; he 'had to invite largely, in order to attract the society clique'. By July his explanation was briefer and more to the point: 'Owing to lack of capital, his business was carried on with financial assistance from brewers and distillers, with the result that when the slump took place in the trade further assistance was refused.'[5]

Among the more notable bankruptcies of 1901 were those of Algernon Meekins of the Elephant and Castle, and James Kirk, the music-hall and public house dealer, late of the Oxford Music Hall, the Cock and Marquis of Granby, Shaftesbury Avenue, and many other pubs. Kirk was declared bankrupt in August 1901, although the initial receiving order had gone out in August 1899. At that time he had in hand public houses which had cost him £204,310. Meekins gave up possession of the Elephant and Castle in April 1901, four years after he had acquired the lease and less than two years after the new building had been opened. His debts were £81,484, of which £74,534 was said to be fully secured. The lease had cost him £30,000, of which £28,500 had been borrowed from the brewers; the newspaper reports do not make clear how he had raised the £39,800 and more required for rebuilding the pub and the shops adjoining it. He attributed his failure to 'bad trade and inability to let adjoining premises'.[6]

The roll of 1901 bankruptcies makes depressing reading. H. W. Maycock had started business as a licensed victualler in 1894. He bought and sold four pubs and ended up with the White Swan, Commercial Road, which he bought in October 1898 for £29,650, £28,600 of which was borrowed. He traded at a loss until October 1900, when the mortgagees foreclosed. Frederick Stanley had acquired the Windsor and the George, both in the Strand, in 1896 and 1897, and had had a heavy outlay on alterations at the George. He made £750 a year profit from the Windsor, and £1,400 a year loss on the George. His liabilities were £47,848, of which £33,848 was unsecured. In May 1897 W. J. Henderson had bought the Crown, Peckham High Street, for £22,000, of which £21,000 was borrowed. He traded at a loss and failed in July 1900. W. C. Guider had commenced business in 1875 with the Pemberton Arms, Bow. Thirty or forty pubs had passed through his hands. A receiving order was given in April 1901, when his liabilities were £127,762. Robert Ireland had started business in 1894 with £500 capital. He borrowed the money to buy the Horse Shoe, Charlotte Street, for £12,000 and sold it two years later for £19,000. In 1897 he bought the Lord Belgrave's Head, Spur Street, for £24,000 and the Apollo, Tottenham Court Road, for £2,800. He rebuilt the Apollo for £28,000. In 1898 he bought the Royal Fort, Bermondsey, for £22,100; the Warrior, Loughborough Junction, for £31,000; and the Prossers Rest, Chancery Lane, for £17,500. He suspended business in January 1901. His liabilities were £180,818, of which all but £18,757 was expected to be secured. His assets were £321. All his pubs were taken over by the mortgagees.[7]

The brewers were the main creditors of all these insolvent publicans. Before 1900 insolvent loans had rarely been more than 10 per cent of the total amount lent by Whitbread's; but as the publicans failed, they rose to 28·5 per cent in 1903, 38·25 per cent in 1907 and 40·5 per cent in 1912.[8] Of course in settlement of their debts, brewers collected large dollops of public house property, so that by 1915 they owned 95 per cent of all licences. But it was a crazy way of securing their markets; owing to the collapse in values, the pubs were now worth a great deal less than the loans which had been made to the publicans who bought them, and in addition the brewers had usually had no interest on those loans for several years. Moreover, in their own purchases of pubs, many of the breweries had been as wild as the publicans; the pubs owned by Whitbread's were bringing in 10 per cent profit in 1871–81, 4 per cent in 1882–8, and were running at a loss in 1890 and after; many of the other breweries must have found themselves in a similar

position. The large capital assets with which brewers' prospectuses tempted investors had mostly consisted of public house property valued at prices which had now collapsed.

The biggest of these flotations had been the result of Watney and Company, Combe and Company, and Reid's Brewery amalgamating in 1898 and floating £15,000,000 of public shares and debentures. In 1901 Watney, Combe and Reid passed their dividends. So did Ind Coope, while Allsopp's wrote down their capital. In 1905 (the year in which the Conservatives finally crumbled), Meux's were in bad financial trouble, Watney's wrote down £2,389,057 of their ordinary shares, Allsopp's wrote down another £1,430,000, and Hoare's £1,950,000. Bass wrote off £1,000,000 in 1908, and Ind Coope were in the hands of the receiver in 1909–10.[9]

Building of new pubs had virtually ceased in 1899 with the collapse of prices. The *Builder* tenders of over £1,000 for pubs were 84 in 1898, 30 in 1899 and 8 in 1900. They recovered a little in subsequent years, but until after the 1914–18 War they never anywhere approached the figures of the boom years. Once capital ceased to be pumped into redecorating and rebuilding pubs, alcohol consumption ceased to rise. After 1899 it began a steady decline from which, with minor fluctuations, it has never emerged.

The carnival was clearly over, but it had been fun while it lasted.

174. Bracket head of publican, King's Head, Upper Tooting Road, Walworth

From the sordidness of Victorian models to their clean, wholesome successors of today.

Basil Oliver, 'Renaissance of the English Public House', 1948

10

The Morning After

THE extent of the disasters of the early 1900s can be exaggerated. Not all publicans went bankrupt and not all breweries got into difficulties. Many provincial brewers, in particular, who had already owned a high proportion of the pubs in their territory, had not been forced to join in the brewers' war. Publicans who had kept out of speculation or bought their pubs before the inflation of the 1890s did not suffer. Anyone who still had money to invest in pubs after 1900 could buy them at much more realistic prices.

But by and large the situation in the drink trade was one of disarray and despondency. Although the breweries had an increasing monopoly of licensed premises, many did not have the funds to maintain or improve them. Those that did had increasing trouble with licensing justices and local authorities. Now that the drink trade was down, it was tempting to kick it in the face. Licensing authorities, whose powers were tightened up by the Licensing Act of 1902, were increasingly grudging in allowing improvements, let alone enlargements, in existing premises. When the new street of Kingsway was rebuilt in the early 1900s the LCC allowed no pubs in it at all.[1] This was in striking contrast to the many pubs that had studded the new Shaftesbury Avenue in the 1880s.

Rescue was at hand for the pub, but the knights (and indeed lords) who came to its aid tended to treat it less as a damsel in distress than as a fallen woman in need of redemption. In May 1901 Earl Grey founded a Public House Trust Company in his native Northumberland. Other county trusts with a similar upper-class or clerical backing soon followed and coalesced into a Central Public House Trust Association covering the whole country. The main principle of the association was that 'a public house as a social institution is a public necessity, and that consequently it is desirable to convert it as far as possible from a mere drinking bar into a well-conducted club'. It was, in short, yet another advocate for the 'improved' public house and quickly absorbed both the Bishop of Chester and his People's Refreshment House Association. But with the contemporary pub in disrepute the atmosphere was much more propitious than for the movement in the 1890s, and by 1903 the association had gained control of 114 houses, with another 200 on the way when their current leases expired. It continued to flourish until it had created the massive empire of the Trust Houses.[2]

The band wagon of the 'improved' public house proved so successful that more and more people jumped on to it. In 1909 the True Temperance Association was founded, with the blessings of Lords Salisbury and Balfour and other Tory grandees, including a former Tory Lord Chancellor, the Earl of Halsbury, as president. It regretted that 'the temper of a large number of our magistrates is opposed to reasonable improvements in our public houses' and hoped to make pubs more like continental cafés. In 1916 the government launched an experiment in improving pubs through state ownership. Five breweries and 321 licensed premises in the Carlisle district were acquired by compulsory purchase and 130 of the latter were closed. The survivors were cleaned up (one of the first steps was to get rid of all snugs), and after the war large numbers were rebuilt.[3]

175. Detail of the luncheon bar in the Black Friar, Queen Victoria Street (H. Fuller Clark, *c.* 1905)

Until the 1914–18 War the main impetus behind the 'improved' public house movement had come from outside the drink trade, but as the breweries gradually recovered from their financial difficulties they set about improving for all they were worth. The pioneers had been the Birmingham brewers, who had not suffered from the brewers' war and even in the 1890s had established excellent relationships with the local licensing magistrates. Mitchell and Butler's brewery was the most active local firm, and its first 'improved' pub, the Red Lion, Kingsheath (*c.* 1905), was later to be described as 'the pioneer of the public house of today'. During the 1920s and 1930s the breweries invested very large sums of capital in improving or rebuilding their houses all over the country.[4]

These 'improved' pubs laid emphasis on such things as serving meals, providing gardens, encouraging wives to come with their husbands, selling soft drinks as well as alcohol and generally being suitable places for a respectable family outing in the new family car. They were often very large, and were built with big car parks out of the town centres. They were over-illustrated and over-praised by the media at the time, and since the war there has been a corresponding over-reaction against them. They are about due for a reassessment.

The casualty of all this improving activity was the Victorian pub. The combination of its financial collapse in 1899 and inevitable reactions in taste put it in increasing disgrace. From 1900 the public house was looking for a new image but, in London, at any rate, it took some time to find it. The ten years after 1900 were largely years of neglect and decay in which the pubs of the 1890s gradually grew dingier and more squalid. There were exceptions but not enough to provide any immediately recognizable type of Edwardian pub.

One of the exceptions suggests the way London pubs might have developed if the slump of 1899 had not taken place. The Black Friar, by the railway bridge in Queen Victoria Street, was remodelled about 1905, apparently not for a brewery but for a publican of the name of Petit.[5] The architect was H. Fuller Clark, of whom little if anything is known, and the sculptor was Henry Poole, who was master of the Art Workers Guild in 1906. The theme of the remodelling was friars, the fat jolly friars invented by late nineteenth-century Academicians to titillate their Protestant buyers. Friars in bronze or marble carouse and gobble in a sumptuous setting of gold mosaic, striped marble, jokey texts and lush carving (Plate 175). In fact, the Black Friar bears the same kind of popular relationship to the Arts and Crafts movement as the pubs of the nineties did to its predecessor the Art movement. But although there are a few Arts and Crafts pubs scattered over the country, the style failed to catch on in the drink world; perhaps it was too close in spirit to the 1890s pubs to be what was needed once they were discredited.

A contemporary of the Black Friar, the Coal Hole (or New Strand Wine Lodge) in the Strand (Plates 176, 177) has more than a touch of Arts and Crafts in its elaborate wrought-iron sign and the frieze of willowy ladies running round the top of the bars. It was decorated in 1904[6] inside one of the buildings designed by Thomas Collcutt as part of the Savoy Hotel complex; but there is no evidence that Collcutt had anything to do with its fitting-up. More significant, perhaps, than its Arts and

Crafts trimmings were its leaded windows, black pseudo-oak beams, gallery and the slight feeling emanating from it of being a film set for a novel by Stanley J. Weyman.

This in fact was the way the pub was going to go—back to the semi-mythical golden age which had always been used as a stick with which to beat the gin palace, back to the days of 'mine hosts' and serving wenches, back to the Pickwickian tavern, the coaching house and the Elizabethan inn. A rash of publications of this date show how taste was flowing: *Among English Inns* (1904), *Old Inns of Old England* (1906), *Some Old English Inns* (1907), *London Taverns in History and London History in Taverns* (1908), *Inns and Taverns of Old London* (1909), *Inns, Ales, and Drinking Customs of Old England* (1909) and *Old Country Inns* (1910). In response to popular

176. The Coal Hole, Strand (1904)

177. (following page) Chimney-piece in the bar of the Coal Hole

BirdsNest
THE SIX BELLS
SIX BELLS PUB
ANTIQUES
FOOD

demand London pubs began to turn themselves back into taverns and, even if they were not old, to do their best to look it.

There were in fact two wings to this back-to-the-inn movement, one led by respectable architects and the other by architects perhaps rather less respectable. The former, who tended to design the 'improved' pubs, were in the line of Norman Shaw and his Old English style as developed by Voysey and Lutyens, and in fact carried straight on from the improved pubs of the nineties. Their exteriors favoured roughcast and low eaves; their interiors looked clean and bright with plenty of scrubbed oak and exposed brickwork, oak settles in the ingle-nook and Windsor chairs scattered across the tiled floors. The latter gloried in half-timbered gables, leaded lights, bottle glass, lanterns, wooden barrels, carved black oak, and artificially smoked ceilings between artificially warped beams. It is the style of Ye Olde Cock Tavern in Fleet Street and the George in the Strand, of Henekey's in Holborn, or Younger's houses like the Wheatsheaf in Rathbone Place and the Blue Anchor in Chancery Lane, and of dozens of suburban pubs.

An article on 'Mock Antique Taverns', published in the *Licensing World* of 14 March 1914, selected Crickmay's Six Bells, King's Road, Chelsea (Plate 178), of 1898, as the prototype of the style. It described with loving detail the interior, which, unlike the equally mock antique exterior, has long since been remodelled. 'Cosy nooks, high-backed chairs, oil paintings, and green plush curtains abound. Everything about the place carries one's mind back to days of yore. Even the electric light fittings consist of lanthorns and wrought-iron brackets.' Other recent examples chosen out of 'a very large number' were the former Elephant in Fenchurch Street, Hills Wine House in St Mary Axe, Yates's Wine Lodge and Henekey's Lyceum Tavern in the Strand and, rather surprisingly, the Black Friars. These pre-1914–18 'olde worlde' taverns were to have innumerable successors in the 1920s and 1930s. Their chronology is hard to establish, for the last date one is ever likely to find on them is the one in which they were built. But the vagaries of Ye Olde and Brewers' Tudor, and the doubtful pleasures of their successors or rivals, the jazz-modern cocktail bars, the streamlined roadhouses and the neo-Georgian lounge, have still to find a historian to chart their unexplored seas and draw what moral he can.

178. (previous page) The Six Bells, King's Road, Chelsea (G. R. Crickmay, 1898)

179. (right) Glass dome in the County, Commutation Road, Liverpool

Epilogue

A Tour Out of London

THIS book is essentially about the Victorian pub in London. To cover provincial city pubs in anything like the same depth would be a formidable, though very fascinating, task. The chapter that follows cannot pretend to offer more than the reactions of a London visitor taking a quick dip into a selection of cities, noticing differences and asking questions which he is usually unable to answer.

The differences certainly exist and make a provincial journey very intriguing for a Londoner. It is a journey into time as well as space. For while some of the differences are due to special local conditions, others are due to the fact that the plan of the provincial pub up till 1914 and even later was basically that of the London pub in the 1850s. Pubs of this type still exist in very large numbers, though remodelling by the brewers is gradually whittling them away. And a few pubs, in addition to their plan, retain equipment which one comes across with something of the emotions of an industrial archaeologist finding a beam engine still in position.

On the bar of Turner's Vaults in Underbank Street, Stockport, for instance, stand (no longer in use, but lovingly maintained) two fourteen-cock spirit fountains (Plate 180). In type they are similar to the ones illustrated by Loudon in his *Encyclopaedia* or by Cruikshank in *The Drunkard*, and they could well date from as early as 1840. Each set of cocks is supported on two columns; the case is of mahogany, delicately inlaid with brass and ivory and embellished with ivory finials. They are exactly the kind of bar fittings which Loudon commented on as setting new standards of luxury in London pubs of the 1830s. The spirit casks, as was not

180. One of the two spirit fountains of *c.* 1840 in Turner's Vaults, Underbank Street, Stockport

XV. (right) Interior of the Warrington Hotel, Warrington Crescent, Maida Vale

LOUNGE

unusual, were originally in a little room above the bar. Fourteen casks were connected to fourteen pipes, all of which ran down the hollow shaft of a Doric column standing between the bar counter and the ceiling. They then travelled under the counter and up the little mahogany column to their respective cocks.

Turner's Vaults occupies a long thin site running back from a narrow street frontage. The bar takes up only the front half of the site. Behind it is a compartment of little more than cupboard size, no longer used for drinking but possibly originally a snug. Behind this is a bigger (but still small) news room, with the racks on which the newspapers were hung still in position. Behind this, accessible from the news room but with independent access by a long corridor to the street, is a larger and rather superior back room. This is the smoke room. News room and smoke room are furnished with benches fixed to the wall. The accommodation is in fact similar to that in Cubitt's Albion, Bloomsbury, of 1820, or Loudon's suburban public house of 1833. Bar, news room and smoke room correspond to bar, tap room and parlour in London. The three rooms, with names varying from area to area, are still the standard accommodation in many northern and midland pubs. Their survival reflects the fact that the early Victorian combination of counter and waiter service, which in London was fast disappearing by the end of the nineteenth century, survived as the normal arrangement in provincial pubs up till at least the Second World War, for in the news and smoke rooms all drinks were brought to the customer. A standard fitting, still in position in many of these pubs although seldom in use, is a succession of electric bells set at intervals of a few feet into a wooden panel running continuously above the benches. This combination of benches and bells, with the substitution of electricity for cranked wires, is identical to that described in the inventory of the Clarendon Hotel, Clarendon Road, in 1847 (see Chapter II).

Even the name 'Turner's Vaults' is, by London standards, old-fashioned. In early Victorian London it was a commonplace for a licensed house to be called by the name of the publican, and to be described as a wine and spirit vaults. It is still common in the north, but very much less so in London, except for the houses of the big chains like Henekey's and Finch's. In many parts of the north, however, nomenclature has shifted from the whole to the part, in a way typical of pubs, and just the public bar is known as the vault. Similarly the news room is (or was) sometimes called the tap room and the smoke room called the best room, music room, snug, parlour or (a much later arrival) lounge. On the whole, it seems that women were allowed in the smoke room, but not in the news room or bar.

There are, of course, many variations in planning. Many pubs had a bar and smoke room but no news room. A development common in Liverpool and Manchester is on the way to the island bars of the south, with nothing but counter service: the serving-bar occupies an island or promontory site, but on one or two sides the counter is closed off by glazed partitions rising to the ceiling. On the customer side of this is a lobby or passage, and drink is obtainable through hatches in the partition; at the Griffin at Heaton Mersey, Manchester, the partition is made up of sash windows. Off the lobby are usually a news room and smoke room. There are numerous variants on the type: sometimes the lobby is little more than

XVI. The Barton Arms, Aston, Birmingham (1901)

a passage with a hatch in it; sometimes it is much more spacious and is decorated with some elaboration. For instance, at the Borough, Great Crosslands Street, Liverpool, which is dated 1900, a spacious lobby, with decorative tiles and the stairs coming down into it, is described as the news room on the glass of the door; beyond it, accessible either from the news room/lobby or direct from the street, is a smoke room. But more usually the news room remained a separate room off the lobby. News room and smoke room seem always to have been designed so that they could be reached without going through the bar, usually by a passage; the lobby appears to have been an enlargement of this passage into a drinking space and is probably a development of the 1890s. Its exact purpose and social status in the drinking hierarchy remain somewhat mysterious to a visitor.

The Victorian pubs of Manchester have suffered much from demolition or remodelling. Perhaps the best surviving exterior is the cheekily illiterate Oxford opposite Oxford Road Station; and the Crown and Kettle, Oldham Road, Gothic inside and out, is worth a visit for its crazy Gothic fan vaulting, which originally had gas lamps finishing off each pendant (Plate 181). Liverpool, by contrast, retains Victorian pubs in very large numbers, many of them little altered or restored (but for how long?) and some with fittings of great richness. It is a better place to get the feeling of Victorian pubs than London, where even in those pubs in which the brewers have conscientiously retained most of the original fittings, new bar furniture, removal of partitions, shifting round of the fittings and carpeting in the bars subtly erode the original atmosphere.

The Liverpool pubs are very much a world of their own, rather than a provincial version of London pubs, and deserve a separate book. Their planning is completely

181. (top left) Ceiling in the Crown and Kettle, Oldham Road, Manchester
182. (bottom left) A corner at the Goat's Head, Kirkdale Road, Liverpool
183. (bottom right) A head at the Albert, Seel Street, Liverpool
184. (above) Counter detail in the Vines, Lime Street, Liverpool

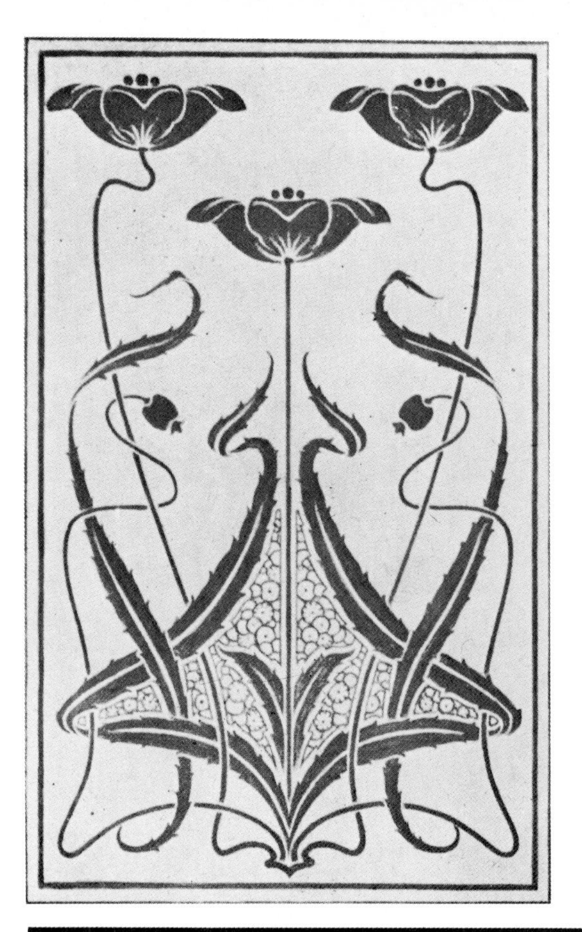

different, with lobbies, news rooms and smoke rooms prominent in addition to the bar. The fronts to the bar counters tend to be more splendid than in London, with elaborate carving, tiles or mosaics (Plate 184). Decorative tiles and glass are much in evidence everywhere, but their designs are different from London designs. The earlier embossed glass is rich in ebullient foliage, but there is a noticeable absence of the baskets of fruit and flowers and birds on twigs so beloved by the London firms. Surviving catalogues put out by Pilkington Bros. Ltd of St Helen's and Baxendale and Company of Manchester and Edinburgh reinforce the impression produced by the glass itself of the independence of Lancashire designers from London (Plates 185, 187). There is far more Art Nouveau glass in Liverpool than in London, along with dadoes of Art Nouveau lincrusta and Art Nouveau tiles, suggesting that the re-decoration of Liverpool pubs continued at the same rate in the early 1900s, when the London drinking world was in disorder.

It is impossible in the space available to mention more than a few examples. The Lion in Tithebarn Street is a good specimen of a medium-sized Liverpool pub with bar, lobby, news and smoke rooms; the news and smoke rooms have been opened into the lobby in recent years but retain their bells and benches. The

185. (top left) Glass design from catalogue of 1902 issued by Baxendale's of Manchester and Edinburgh
186. (top right) Window in the Vulcan, Bolton, Lancashire
187. (left) Glass design from an 1898 catalogue issued by Pilkington and Company of St Helen's, Lancashire
188. (above) Lobby screen at the Lion, Tithebarn Street, Liverpool

lobby screen is an especially elaborate one, glazed with embossed and brilliant cut glass and tiled up to counter level with resplendent Art Nouveau tiles (Plate 188). There are equally splendid tiles in the Central, Ranelagh Street. The latter had a plum site opposite the Central Station and is one of the biggest and most elaborately decorated of Liverpool pubs. The large island bar in the front is divided by ceiling-high partitions into what were originally a bar and buffet, and at the back are large smoke and news rooms. Both of these are lined with embossed and brillant cut mirrors, but the news room is much more elaborately furnished. A low partition divides it into two portions each lined with benches, and the bench ends and partitions are embellished with leaded glass set with coloured roundels, flowers and views of Windsor Castle.

Most splendid of all is the famous Philharmonic in Hope Street, built in 1898–1900.[1] Its fame is justified, but it is not a typical Liverpool pub. Its architect was Walter Thomas, who had worked in the early 1880s on a pub on St Domingo

189. The main bar space in the Philharmonic, Hope Street, Liverpool (Walter Thomas, 1898–1900)

Road, Everton, and the Shaftesbury Hotel, Mount Pleasant,[2] and is described as 'a jovial man of large proportions, who was always immaculately dressed and wore spats'. He married one of the Lewis family, who owned a big store in Liverpool, part of which he designed. One would like to know more about the background history of the Philharmonic. It was and is one of the most select areas of Liverpool; it was built by Robert Cain, whose newly founded brewery was the most enterprising and aggressive in the city, and he must have intended it as a prestige job aimed to attract a clientele extending further up the social range than was usual in late Victorian pubs. To give the building class Cain called in the personnel of the University Schools of Art and Architecture across the road and let them loose with, to judge from the results, almost unlimited funds at their disposal.

The plan is a nice compromise between London and Liverpool planning. A very large island bar counter serves a large public bar, a small private bar and a much grander than usual lobby. The bar counter in the lobby has no partition, although one wonders if it may originally have had snob-screens, as in the Barton Arms, Birmingham. Off the lobby are two rooms, corresponding to news and smoke rooms but smaller than one might have expected in a pub of this size. A passage between them leads to an enormous room, originally a billiard room (the bar in this is a later alteration).

Billiard room, passage and serving-bar are on the same axis, giving an agreeable sense of direction to this huge, crowded and animated pub. And everything is

190. Wrought-iron gate at the Philharmonic

encrusted with Arts and Crafts trimmings of the greatest richness (Plate 189). The billiard room has huge caryatids and a naked boy emerging out of a shell above panelling inlaid with panels of beaten copper. There is embossed glass in the public bar and a wealth of stained glass of Art Nouveau or neo-Renaissance design everywhere else. The bar counters are faced with mosaic and the counter tops covered with copper sheeting. Off the lobby is a large ingle-nook with stained glass windows of Kitchener and Lord Roberts to underline its date. Even the gents is heavy with marble and mosaic. Paul Neil and Arthur Stratton, from the School of Architecture, collaborated with Thomas on the interior design. The caryatids were modelled by Charles Adams, other plasterwork was by Pat Honan, and the stone carving was by Frank Norbury. H. Blomfield Barr was responsible for the copper panels and for the resplendent wrought-iron gate (Plate 190) which proudly carries the motto and arms of the brewery across the main entrance porch.

The exterior of the Philharmonic is, roughly speaking, 'Queen Anne' turning into free classic. Walter Thomas's other great Liverpool pub, the Vines, Lime Street, of 1907, is free classic turning into Edwardian baroque (Plate 191). Its plan has the same elements and the same semi-palatial scale of the Philharmonic, but the long lobby is more conventionally typical of Liverpool, with hatched partitions closing off the bar. The decoration is almost as sumptuous, but the flavouring is baroque rather than Arts and Crafts (Plate 192).

Birmingham must once have been nearly as rich in Victorian pubs as Liverpool, but they have suffered more, partly from wholesale demolition in recent years, partly from remodelling between the wars, when Ansell, and Mitchell and Butler, the two leading breweries, were vigorous protagonists of the 'improved' pub. A good selection still remains, however.[3] The typical Birmingham pub plan is recognizably similar to the Lancashire one, but the lobby is much less common and the bar is frequently accompanied by only one room. This, as in the north, was called a smoke or smoking room and was identically fitted up with bells and benches round the wall. The second room, if there was one, seems also to have been called a smoke room, rather than a news room, but was for men only; in fact the difference between it and the northern news room or southern tap room seems to have been only one of name.

The Gothic Stores, a Mitchell and Butler pub in Great Hampton Street of about 1880 (to judge from the architecture), has a bar and one smoking room only; as its name suggests, it is a gaily polychromatic Gothic design with a slender tower and spire, and a nice Gothic back fitting in the bar. Down the road is another slice of Gothic polychromy, the Hen and Chickens on Constitution Hill; here the bar was originally subdivided into large and small sections, the large described on the door as 'Bar. Gentlemen only' and the small just as 'Bar'. Presumably women were allowed in the small bar, and this may have been the usual Birmingham practice. Brooks' Vaults in Jamaica Row, near Smithfield Market, has a big bar with a smoking room behind it and beyond that a Vaults with its own bar and separate access to Market Street at the back. The nearby St Martin's in St Martin's Lane has a Liverpool-type plan with lobby and counter screen.

The Woodman, Albert Street, across the road from Philip Hardwick's abandoned Curzon Street railway terminus, is a typical example of a medium-sized Birmingham pub of the 1890s, with a smoking room tucked behind the big *L*-shaped bar (where in London in the 1860s one would have expected a bar parlour) and separate access to it from the street by a tiled corridor. To judge from the doors, the bar was originally divided into at least two sections. It still has a good back fitting and plenty of embossed glass. But it nowhere near approaches the elaboration of the other Woodman, in Easy Row, alas demolished in the 1960s.[4] The plan of the Easy Row Woodman (which looks as though it dated from the late nineties) was of the simplest, and indeed similar to its namesake in Albert Street: an *L*-shaped bar divided by a partition into a small private bar (with snob-screens) and a large public bar, and a smoke room at the back, approached by a corridor running along the side of the private bar from the street. The difference was in

191. The Vines, Lime Street, Liverpool (Walter Thomas, 1907)

192. Inside the Vines

the scale and the richness of the fittings. The street front, with elaborate glazing set back behind columns and two oriel-shaped show cases, must have been inspired by London examples. The bars were lined with tiles incorporating pictures of old Birmingham, and the ceilings were tiled as well. But the glory of the pub was the immensely long smoke room, bench-lined, subdivided by screens, lit by a bronze lady brandishing a light on a pedestal halfway down the room, and encircled by two amazing ingle-nooks, each like a little room, subdivided from the main space by arcaded screens of bulbous joinery with the choice of a 'Queen Anne' or a baronial hooded chimney-piece for customers to warm themselves by (Plate 193).

In its latter days the Woodman smoking room had a small bar at one end. Was this an original feature? If so, it was by no means typical, and in effect, though not name, turned the smoking room into the equivalent of a London saloon bar. Smoking room bars are in fact illustrated in a handsome Birmingham publication of 1896, *New Designs of Cabinet Bar Fittings*. The designs were by George A. Cox and the catalogue was put out by James Yates, 'high class barfitter' of 39–42 Coleshill Street, Birmingham (established 1826; telegraphs 'Pewter'). Yates also provided beer engines, spirit fittings, etc., and announced, 'I shall be pleased to make Special Drawings and Estimates to suit any individual case free of charge.' His fittings (Plates 85, 194) are very similar to what was being made in London at the same date but with a Birmingham inflection; there are no wagons and apart from his smoking

193. The Woodman, Easy Row, Birmingham (demolished)

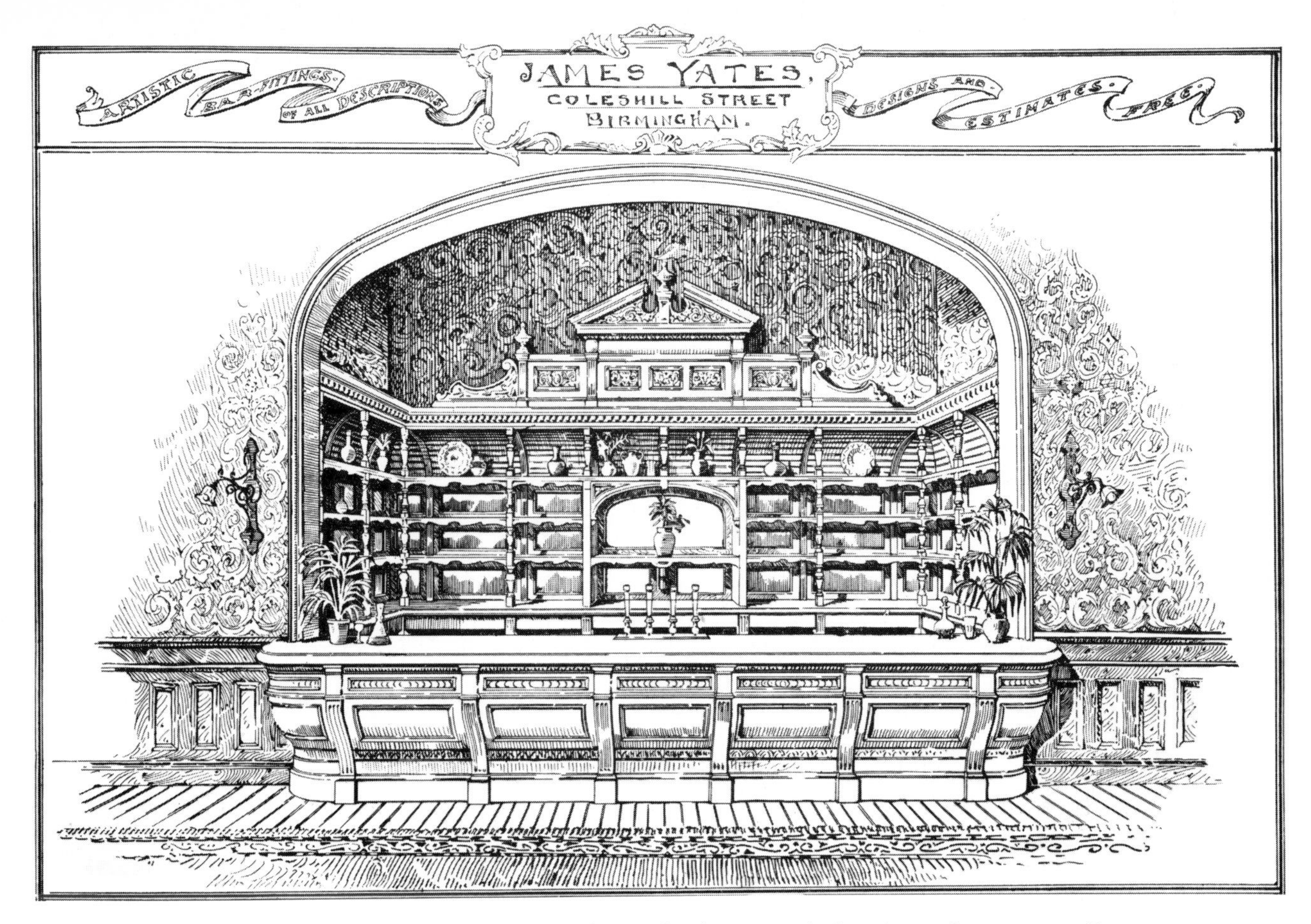

room bars his saloon bar, although no doubt intended to introduce a new London fashion to Birmingham, is a large private bar rather than a saloon bar in the London sense.

A so-called saloon bar of exactly the same type is one of the less prominent features of the gorgeous Barton Arms, Aston, Birmingham's rival to the Philharmonic. This, as the stained glass window on the staircase proudly announces, was erected in 1901, by Mitchell and Butler, whose name or initials figure prominently in all the windows. The architect (Mr Brassington of James and Lister Lea, a local firm specializing in pubs) had clearly seen Aston Hall, the great Jacobean mansion a mile away from the pub, and thought he could do as well or better. The exterior is Jacobean with a clock tower and from the distance looks more like a small town hall than a pub. Inside there is a series of radiating bars at one end (including the small and un-saloonish saloon bar) and large and small smoking rooms off a very spacious lobby at the other. The lobby is served from a recessed bar counter lined with snob-screens, in effect one end of the central serving space pushing through the wall that divides bars from lobby. The scale is very generous, space flows freely into space, walls and ceilings are lined with tiles by Minton Hollins and Company of Stoke-on-Trent, the smoking rooms and lobby are rich in stained glass, elaborate chimney-pieces and bronze light brackets and the bars in embossed glass. Richest of all is the staircase which leads off the lobby up to more large rooms on the first floor: a curving and richly painted wrought-iron balustrade, a huge

194. Bar fittings designed by G. A. Cox for James Yates, Birmingham, 1896

stained glass window at the top, a massive iron light standard at the bottom, a tile picture of a pink-coated hunt across one wall and the panels of the lobby snob-screen glittering through an archway (Colour Plate XVI).

The Barton Arms was an expression of the good relations between brewers and licensing magistrates that had developed in Birmingham in the 1890s.[4] With the approval of both parties many small pubs in the centre were closed and the licences transferred to a few big pubs strategically placed at main road junctions in the suburbs. Initially these suburban pubs continued the gin palace tradition, but about 1905, starting with the Red Lion at Kingsheath, Mitchell and Butler went over to the 'improved' pub styling that was to produce the huge Tudor, half-timbered or neo-Georgian Birmingham pubs of the next twenty-five years. The Waterloo, in Waterloo Road, Smethwick, was probably Mitchell and Butler's last kick in the old manner, and a very good kick it is, too. It is dated 1907, a cheerful Edwardian baroque eruption of brick and terracotta on a prominent corner site, with good tiles and embossed glass in the bars, two big smoking rooms and (foretaste of the 'improved' pubs) a big grill room in the basement richly tiled with an Art Nouveau frieze of sailing ships.

It would be interesting to know to what extent the multi-compartmented pub plan found in London in the late eighties was also found in the provinces. The evidence of the Peel Commission quoted in Chapter III shows that they were a feature of Hull, and a row of 'boxes' appear in the plan of the bar at the Central Hotel, Portsmouth, published in the *Building News* of 19 October 1888. I have come across no trace of them in Manchester, Liverpool or Birmingham, which is by no means to say that they did not exist.

In Dublin the tendency to compartmentation seems to have been even slighter than in the British industrial cities. The typical Victorian pub in Dublin contains

195. A panel from the Irish House

196. The Irish House, South Quays, Dublin (demolished)

two elements, a bar and a snug, and some contain just a bar. The Dublin snug is usually very similar to an English smoking room: a smallish bench-lined room with bells above the benches, approachable by a corridor from the street without going through the bar. In Dublin bars the counter-to-wall partitions that subdivided English bars into different compartments are usually replaced by partitions that run across the counter and only a few feet into the bar, giving a degree of privacy without complete separation. On the whole Dublin bars do not, or did not, have the feeling of social segregation so strongly apparent in London and, to a lesser degree, in English provincial pubs; the distinction between bar and snug is one of type or sex (the snugs are much frequented by women) rather than class. The socially superior Dublin 'lounges' are post-Victorian. Many Dublin pubs sell (or sold) tea or sugar, kept in drawers behind the bar, a variant of the grocery or general stores with a bar at the back which are still a feature of Irish towns and villages.

One can mention in passing Lynch's in Aungier Street and the Long Hall in South Great George Street, shed a passing tear for the crazy interior of the Irish House on the South Quays (Plates 195, 196), demolished in the early 1970s, and

linger a little longer at the Stag's Head in Dame Court and Ryan's across the river from Huston (Kingsbridge) Station in Parkgate Street. The Stag's Head was built in 1894–5 to the designs of J. M. M'Gloughlin for G. W. Tyson, an immigrant from Westmorland who also started up a fashionable haberdashers in Grafton Street. The English influence is apparent only in its name (most Irish pubs are called after a present or past publican) and perhaps its 'Queen Anne' exterior. Inside, a typical long Dublin bar divided into stalls by shallow partitions led to a top-lit smoking room, now a luncheon bar; the pub had electric lights from the start (Plate 197).[6] Rich stained glass, heavy brass lamps and handsome joinery abound, so that the atmosphere is almost an ecclesiastical one. Generally speaking, a dedicated not to say religious attitude to drinking is typical of Dublin pubs, and the fittings tend to accentuate it. It seems apposite that Dublin barmen are usually called 'curates'. The bar divisions at Lynch's in Aungier Street look like miniature confessionals; at Ryan's in Parkgate Street the massive polished brass lamp standards on the counter are equally ecclesiastical and the Gothic centre fitting could without difficulty be adapted as a reredos (Plate 198).

197. The Stag's Head, Dame Court, Dublin (J. M. M'Gloughlin, 1894-5)

The plan of Ryan's came closer to the London 1890s types than any out-of-London pub I know. The bar is basically one big room with a three-sided promontory serving-bar round a central wagon. There is no separate room used as a snug; instead there are four box-type snugs attached to the counter, with doors that can be opened only when the barman pulls a cord from behind the counter. The joinery of the snugs, incidentally, looks later than that of the rest of the bar.

But the Crown Liquor Saloon, opposite the Great Northern Station in Great Victoria Street, Belfast, is indisputably the crown of Victorian pubs in Ireland, and many would say in the British Isles. For how long? Most of the windows have already been blown in by an explosion across the street, and the survival chances of the rest cannot be high. The Crown was built by a publican called Patrick Flanagan, reputedly in about 1885.[7] Its plan is like that of the London Equestrian turned inside out: instead of a central serving-bar with boxes attached and an outer circulation space, there is a central circulation space with the bar to one side and a row of box snugs, fitted with swing doors, benches and tables, to the other. Bell pushes on the boxes used to set bells jangling up on the wall where the bar men could

198. Ryan's, Parkgate Street, Dublin

see them. A burst of polychromatic tiles on the outside prepares one for the splendours within (Plate 199). Its heraldic beasts, columns scaled like fir cones, painted boxes, patterned tiles, heraldic glass, barrels poking out of arches, marble-topped bar counter and red-and-gold ceiling are accepted with sublime unconsciousness by the totally untrendy clientele who frequent it.

A tour round city pubs in Great Britain inevitably suggests certain questions. How big did a town have to be before it generated what, for lack of a better phrase, one is reduced to calling gin palaces, of the later Victorian variety—large pubs rich in tiles, decorated glass, elaborate joinery and other expensive fittings? It certainly is not the case that, for instance, a town of 100,000 inhabitants had ten of them and a town of 10,000 had one; they are very much a city phenomenon. Why was it that waiter service survived in the provincial cities while it disappeared in London? What were the individual circumstances special to particular cities and

199. The Crown Liquor Saloon, Great Victoria Street, Belfast

how did they affect the pubs? How did Liverpool and Birmingham manage to produce pubs as grand as or grander than anything in London?

The following suggestions are only very tentative. There seem to have been two requisite fertilizers to produce the soil in which gin palaces could flourish: a constant daily (rather than just on market days) stream of people in the streets to maintain sales, and enough customers drinking spirits rather than beer to boost profits—which in Victorian terms meant a sizable lower middle-class population between the working men who went to pubs but could not afford spirits and the better-off classes who could afford spirits but considered it beneath their dignity to go into a pub. Very approximately I would suggest a population of about 100,000 as the threshold at which full-blown gin palaces normally start to appear, though they are also to be found in smaller towns with a quick turnover of money-spending customers, such as ports and seaside resorts. And yet why is it that Leeds, with a population of 402,450 in 1898 (admittedly reached only by including in the city an area nearly double that of Liverpool's and containing outlying country and townships), appears to have had so few gin palaces? Its only visible one today (though there has been much destruction) is the Jubilee, an ebullient pub hotel opposite the town hall with a few splendid Art Nouveau windows surviving from a holocaust of redecoration—and the Jubilee is as late as 1904. The much and rightly loved Whitelock's in an alley off Briggate is not really a gin palace, but a much older low-ceilinged tavern converted into a luncheon bar with tiled counter and Art Nouveau stained glass in the early 1900s, and with other embellishments added later.

The fact that waiter service vanished in London and survived in the provincial cities can hesitantly be ascribed to three causes. First, the enormously greater size of London may be surmised to have produced an, on average, greater weight of pedestrian traffic in its main thoroughfares; and the quick-drinking passer-by was the main generator of the bar. Second, for reasons which deserve further research, there were more people to each licensed premise in London than in the provinces, so that the pressure to provide quick, efficient service must have been greater. Finally, if, as seems probable, running costs in the form of rates, interest on the purchase price and wages were higher in London, this would be another stimulus to get the maximum out of each site.

Finally, a few local peculiarities can be listed and, in some cases, their influence tentatively assessed. In Liverpool, Manchester, Birmingham and Leeds the breweries owned far more pubs than they did in London: about 75 per cent in Manchester in 1896, for instance, and 63 per cent in Liverpool in 1892.[8] This meant that the great brewers' war of 1896–9 affected them only to a minor degree, and there was no corresponding collapse in the early 1900s; as a result elaborate new pubs or pub interiors of this period appear to be much more common.

But there were variations within this pattern of brewery ownership. In Leeds (as in London) almost all the brewery-owned pubs were let to tenants;[9] in Manchester, Birmingham and Liverpool the manager system predominated. In Liverpool in 1892 out of 1,275 brewery-owned pubs 1,057 were run by managers.[10] The

breweries do not appear to have been willing to spend large sums of money on their tenanted houses; in London it was common for the brewery to provide only the main structure and to leave the fitting out of the bar to the tenant. But brewery-managed pubs were a much more direct form of advertisement for the brewery, and when they wanted to produce a prestige building they had at their disposal funds in excess of anything that publicans (except perhaps for a tiny group of big-time operators in London) could hope for. Hence the magnificence of the Philharmonic and the Barton Arms.

Manchester with 168 people to a licensed premise in 1898 appears at first sight to have been much better equipped than Liverpool with 279, but the figures are deceptive. Manchester had many more beerhouses and off licences but only 513 fully-licensed houses as opposed to Liverpool's 1,895.[11] The Liverpool situation was the result of a brief but disastrous experiment in free licensing in 1862–5, during which spirit licences were as easy to obtain as beer ones and most beerhouses became fully licensed.[12] Liverpool in the 1890s was considered 'notoriously a much more drunken place than Manchester'. In both towns the pubs appear to have been much more frequented by prostitutes than they were in London.[13]

In Dublin the organization of the drink trade was quite different. In 1896 there were only two brewery-owned pubs, largely as a result of the Guinness policy of not acquiring pubs. Publicans borrowed money, not from the brewers or distillers, but direct from the banks. This was because, owing to the 'Clitheroe Case' of 1878 (which found the exact opposite to Sharp v. Wakefield in England), a licence was considered almost as secure a piece of property as a house. Dublin, as a result, was (and indeed still is) a city of small independent pubs, and huge prestige brewery pubs are conspicuously absent.[14]

200. Glass decorations from a pre-1914 catalogue issued by Reed, Millican and Company, Newcastle-upon-Tyne

NOTES ON SOURCES

(*Abbreviations used in the notes are given in the left-hand margin*)

Principal Nineteenth-Century Sources

1. ARCHITECTURAL PERIODICALS

a. The many pubs included in the weekly list of 'Tenders' published on the last pages of the *Builder* (tenders published in other periodicals seem to be derived from the same source and for the most part to duplicate the *Builder* material)

b. Illustrations, plans and descriptions of pubs published in the main pages of the *Builder*, *Building News*, *British Architect* and *Architect*

2. LICENSED VICTUALLERS' AND ALLIED PERIODICALS

LVG *The Licensed Victuallers' Gazette*
LW *The Licensing World*
LVCTJ *The Licensed Victualler and Catering Trade Journal*

These weekly periodicals became much glossier and more informative in the later 1890s. *The Licensed Victualler*, although it started publication only at the end of 1898, is especially valuable during the short relevant period which it covers.

The Morning Advertiser. The daily paper of the licensed victualling trade. Essentially a general newspaper but the advertisement columns and the occasional news item sometimes provide relevant information.

The Brewers Journal. A monthly periodical published for brewers rather than licensed victuallers, but with useful information on property prices, bankruptcies and the economic background of the trade.

3. ARCHITECTS' DESIGNS

Camberwell
South Central Licensing Division, Camberwell Magistrates' Court. The South Central (which covers the old Newington, Southwark and Camberwell licensing district) appears to be the only London licensing division which has retained large numbers of architects' drawings of late Victorian pubs, originally submitted along with petitions to alter or rebuild. None of these dates from before 1880; they often show the plan (and sometimes the elevation) of the pub before as well as after alteration. The pre-1914 plans are now on loan to the RIBA Drawings Collection, Portman Square, London.

GLC M & D
Greater London Council Records Department. Music and Dancing plans. From 1878 the Metropolitan Board of Works and its successor the London County Council increasingly became the issuing authority for Music and Dancing Licences. Numerous plans (and less often elevations and sections) of pubs or of music-halls incorporating pubs, submitted along with applications, are preserved.

GLC Valuers
Greater London Council Records Department. Metropolitan Board of Works and LCC Valuers Department deposited plans. Architects' plans and elevations of new pubs built as a result of road improvements by the LCC and its predecessor the MBW. The earliest surviving date from about 1875.

4. BREWERY ARCHIVES

Although their relevance is limited by the fact that the majority of London pubs in the period covered were built by publicans rather than breweries, I have done less work on these than I would have liked. Examination of plans belonging to Ind Coope and Watney Mann suggest that in the case of Ind Coope very few, and in the case of Watney's relatively few, original Victorian architects' designs are preserved. All breweries retain many nineteenth-century leases and deeds for their individual houses, which often include plans, but these are seldom detailed enough to be of much use. My own work on the Cannon Brewery archives (see Chapter IV, note 14) and D. M. Knox's on the Whitbread archives (Chapter IV, note 7) suggest that the most useful information to be derived from brewery archives may relate to the economic background of Victorian pubs rather than their architecture.

5. PARLIAMENTARY PAPERS

The most important are the following reports. References in the notes are to the numbered questions and answers except where otherwise indicated.

Buckingham
Select Committee of the House of Commons on Drunkenness, 1834 (Chairman, James Silk Buckingham). *Parl. Papers* 1834 VIII.

Villiers
Select Committee of the House of Commons on Public Houses, 1852–4 (Chairman, C. P. Villiers). *Parl. Papers* 1852–3 XXVI, 1854 XIV.

Westminster
Select Committee of the House of Lords on Intemperance, 1877–8 (Chairman Duke of Westminster). *Parl. Papers* 1877 XI, 1878 XIV, 1878–9 X.

Peel
Royal Commission on the Liquor Licensing Laws. 1896–8 (Chairman, Viscount Peel). *Parl. Papers* 1897 XXXIV, XXXV, 1898 XXXVI, XXXVII, XXXVIII, 1899 XXXIV, XXXV.

6. GUILDHALL LIBRARY, CITY OF LONDON

Norman, Noble
The Norman and Noble collections contain many prints, cuttings and other material relevant to Victorian pubs although the cuttings are often, infuriatingly, filed with no reference to their source. The Norman collection covers London hotels and inns only. The Noble collection covers London buildings of all types; pubs are filed alphabetically in volumes under the heading C.23.1, with miscellaneous material at the beginning of the first volume.

7. POST OFFICE DIRECTORIES

POD
Invaluable for plotting the movements of publicans and of the architects and firms involved on the design and decoration of pubs. Full runs for central (but not suburban) London are easily accessible in the Reference Section of the Westminster Public Library, Buckingham Palace Road, and in the GLC Library, County Hall.

Modern Sources

There are innumerable general books on pubs, but only a few contain any worthwhile treatment of the architectural, visual or social aspects of the Victorian pub. *Inside the Pub* by Maurice Gorham and H. McG. Dunnett (London 1950) is an excellent analytical study of the qualities of a good pub and has been highly influential. It contains an account of the development of the pub plan which as a pioneering work could scarcely be improved on. *The Victorian Public House* by Brian Spiller (London 1972), although short and without plans, is lively and sympathetic and has first-class illustrations. *Bricks and Beer: English Pub Architecture, 1830–1939* by Robert Elwall (London 1983) was published to accompany the admirable exhibition of the same title held at the RIBA Heinz Gallery in 1983. *The Traditional English Pub: A Way of Drinking* by Ben Davis (London 1981), although not a historical work, is worth mentioning as an analysis of the pub by an architect who has restored or converted many Victorian pubs with sensitivity.

For individual towns, *Birmingham Pubs, 1890–1939* by Alan Crawford and Robert Thorne (Birmingham 1975) is an illuminating and enjoyable study, and there is an excellent short account of *Nottingham Pubs* by Robert Tressider (Nottingham Civic Society 1980).

George B. Wilson *Alcohol and the Nation* (London 1940) contains a comprehensive collection of statistical and other information concerning alcohol. Brian Harrison *Drink and the Victorians* (London 1971) is an exhaustive account of the Temperance question in England, 1815–72, and the same author deals directly with the pub in his essay 'Pubs' in H. J. Dyos and Michael Wolff (eds.) *The Victorian City* (London 1973).

NOTES TO THE TEXT

Notes to the Introduction

1. Peel appendix, *Parl. Papers* 1898 XXXVII et seq.
2. George B. Wilson *Alcohol and the Nation* (London 1940) pp. 24–5.
3. Henry Blyth *The Pocket Venus* (1966) p. 73; Peel 6324, 6325.
4. LW 26 September 1896. LVG 3 August 1888, p. 75; 31 October 1890.
5. For illustrated articles on these pubs, see LW 13 November 1897, p. 323 on the Blue Last: *Daily Graphic* 10 September 1891, on the Daniel Lambert (filed in Norman); article of 1890 in Norman on Ship and Turtle.
6. Mark Longaker *Ernest Dowson* (Philadelphia, 3rd ed. 1967) pp. 66, 142, 170, 245, etc.; Edgar Jepson *Memories of a Victorian* (London 1933) pp. 218, 248; *Times* 9 October 1902.
7. Jepson (*op. cit.* note 6) pp. 212–65; Grant Richards *Memories of a Misspent Youth* (London 1932) pp. 337 ff.; William Rothenstein *Men and Memories* Vol. I (London 1931) p. 238.
8. For boxing at this period, see early chapters of Guy Deghy *Noble and Manly: The History of the National Sporting Club* (London 1956).
9. For Highbury Barn, see Noble, especially an anonymous article 'The Northern Cremorne'. For pleasure-gardens in Victorian London in general, see article in LVCTJ 31 May 1899.
10. Hermione Hobhouse *Thomas Cubitt, Master Builder* (London 1971) p. 167; H. J. Dyos *Victorian Suburb* (1961) p. 155.
11. Peel 33867, etc.; *Daily Graphic* 4 October 1895 (filed in Norman).
12. Plans of Cock and Horns, GLC M&D 3509, 163; description of Crown, *The Post, Kilburn, Willesden, Paddington and Hampstead Echo* 25 February 1899; description of Albion, Norman.
13. For a description of the rites and ceremonies of the Oddfellows and Buffaloes as existing in 1938, see 'Mass-Observation' (Tom Harrisson) *The Pub and the People* (London 1943) pp. 275–80. The licensed victuallers' periodicals of the eighties and nineties had regular accounts of their meetings.
14. LVCTJ 26 July 1899, pp. 804–6; LVG 27 July 1896; LW 12 February 1898; LW 3 January 1896, p. 245.
15. *Builder* 25 February 1854, p. 96; Peel 35597–8; John Hollinshead 'Evolution of the Tavern' LVCTJ 15 February 1899.
16. E. Hepple Hall *Coffee Taverns, Cocoa Houses and Coffee Palaces* (London 1878) p. 89; LW 6 August 1898, p. 89.
17. E.g. Duke of Fife, Upton Park; Elgin Arms, Ladbroke Grove.
18. LW 26 March 1898 (Crocker); LVG 21 February 1896 (Duke of Kent); LW 25 September 1897, p. 203, Norman III p. 5 (Edinburgh Castle); and especially C. E. Laurence 'Public House Museums' *The Ludgate* 1895 (filed Noble miscellaneous), with numerous illustrations.
19. Charles Chaplin *My Autobiography* (London 1964) p. 57.
20. *Ibid.* pp. 31–2.
21. Advertisement LVG 5 November 1897 (Monopol); LVCTJ 3 April 1901, p. 319 (automatic games).
22. E.g. see Norman I p. 139 for anonymous article of 5 February 1898, 'The Barmaids Lot' by 'One who pities them'; Joint Committee on the Employment of Barmaids, *The Barmaid Problem* (London 1904).
23. See Norman, under Norfolk Arms.
24. LVG 16 August 1889, re W. Torrington of the Coach and Horses, Piccadilly.
25. LVG 3 March 1899 (Standbrook); LVG 30 September 1898 (Pease); LVG 10 February 1899 (Bennett); LVG 2 September 1898 (Haynes and Wheeler).
26. *The Barmaid* 14 January 1892, pp. 36–7; POD; information from his descendants.
27. LVCTJ 21 August 1901; LVG 20 January 1899; LW 9 March 1894; LVG 17 January 1896.
28. For the plan of the Oxford, see *Building News* 20 January 1895. For the Hammersmith and Rosemary Branch, see GLC M&D 137 and 031; for the Washington and Royal Standard, see plan in Ind Coope archives.
29. *Builder* tenders 21 April 1883 (Swan, High Street, Islington); 14 April 1888 (Rose and Crown, Grooms Hill, Greenwich).
30. LVG 30 September 1898, p. 708.
31. LVG 14 October 1898, p. 744.
32. Chaplin (*op. cit.* note 19) p. 1.
33. *Ibid.* pp. 7–8, 54–5.
34. Peel, Whittaker Memorandum, *Parl. Papers* 1899 XXXV p. 357; Wilson (*op. cit.* note 2) pp. 428–9.
35. Wilson (*op. cit.* note 2) pp. 331–4; *Report of Departmental Committee on Liquor Licensing* (HMSO 1972).

NOTES TO CHAPTER 1

1. For a detailed discussion of the gin scare and the subsequent Beer Act, see Chapter 3 of Brian Harrison's *Drink and the Victorians* (London 1971).
2. *Times* 1 December 1829.
3. Edward Gibbon Wakefield *England and America* (London 1833); George Cruikshank *Sunday in London* (London 1833).
4. George B. Wilson *Alcohol and the Nation* (London 1940) p. 101.
5. E.g. R. E. Broughton, Buckingham 121.
6. J. C. Loudon *Encyclopaedia of Cottage, Farm, and Villa Architecture and Furniture* (London 1833) sec. 1444.
7. Buckingham 3190.
8. Henry Bradshaw Fearon *Suggestions and Correspondence Relative to Magistrates Licences* (London 1830) p. 41, quoting from a resolution passed by the Retail Spirit Dealers.
9. Maurice Gorham and H. McG. Dunnett *Inside the Pub* (London 1950) p. 70.
10. Henry Vizetelly *Glances Back through Seventy Years* Vol. I (London 1893) p. 122.
11. H. M. Colvin *Biographical Dictionary of English Architects* (London 1951) under Papworth. Papworth's elevation of Thompson and Fearon's is in the RIBA Drawings Collection.
12. Fearon (*op. cit.* note 8) p. 31.
13. For a good account of the earlier development of the pub, see Gorham and Dunnett (*op. cit.* note 9).
14. Loudon (*op. cit.* note 6) sec. 1415.
15. *Ibid.* secs 1442–4.
16. Colvin (*op. cit.* note 11) under Laxton.
17. Archives, Bedford Settled Estates, Bloomsbury. The elevation is reproduced in Hermione Hobhouse *Thomas Cubitt, Master Builder* (London 1971).
18. Dickens *Sketches by Boz* (1836) ch. XXII.
19. Fearon (*op. cit.* note 8) p. 31.
20. Local History Collection, Newington Branch, Southwark Public Library, where there is a good collection of bills, broadsheets, price lists, etc., including many issued by pubs.
21. Noble.
22. Fearon (*op. cit.* note 8) p. 31, and prices given on broadsheets and circulars at Newington and Guildhall.
23. For coffee shops, see Harrison (*op. cit.* note 1) pp. 38–9.
24. Buckingham 121.
25. Lady Holland *Memoir of Revd. Sydney Smith* Vol. II (London 1855) p. 310.

NOTES TO CHAPTER 2

1. Newington Library Collection (see Chapter 1, note 20).
2. For the Eagle, see the large cuttings collection in the Finsbury Public Library (Borough of Islington) and Frances Fleetwood *Conquest: The Story of a Theatre Family* (London 1953). The date of the rebuilding is given by Fleetwood (p. 67), who does not quote the source.
3. Hermione Hobhouse *Thomas Cubitt, Master Builder* (London 1971); *Survey of London* XXXVII Northern Kensington (London 1973).
4. *Survey of London* N. Kensington p. 293 (Prince of Wales); p. 273 (Pembridge Castle); p. 81 (Campden Arms); p. 220 (Phillips); *Builder* tender 6 November 1852 (Walmer Castle).
5. *Survey of London* N. Kensington pp. 214–15.
6. *Ibid.* pp. 220–5, 247; *Building News* 20 January 1860, p. 43.
7. Hobhouse (*op. cit.* note 3) p. 214.
8. Original lease, Ind Coope archives.
9. *Survey of London* N. Kensington p. 293.
10. Hobhouse (*op. cit.* note 3) pp. 154–5, 213, 226, 293; POD.
11. *Survey of London* N. Kensington p. 117.
12. *Ibid.* p. 220.
13. Plan of 1875 showing existing arrangement and proposed alterations, Corporation of London Records Office, C3/E.
14. Plan in Corporation of London Records Office, 47.B.25.
15. Kensington Public Library, MS 4883.
16. Now the property of the Kennel Club.
17. Select Committee of House of Commons on Wine Duties, *Parl. Papers* 1852 XVII 3817.
18. The classic account of the beginnings of the music-halls is in Charles Douglas Stuart and A. J. Park *The Variety Stage* (London 1895).
19. There is an incomplete list of the works of the firm in E. L. Paraire's *Builder* obituary 1882 (2) p. 225, which can be supplemented from the *Builder* tender lists, other references and illustrations in the building magazines, lists of designs exhibited by them at the Royal Academy, and Valuers Department drawings at the GLC.
20. *Builder* tenders 10 January 1852, 13 May 1854. *Survey of London* XXXVI St Paul's, Covent Garden (London 1970) pp. 168–9, 178.
21. For a list of illustrations of these, see the alphabetical entries in Diana Howard *London Theatres and Music Halls, 1850–1950* (London 1970).
22. *Building News* 12 November 1858, p. 1123.
23. *Builder* tenders 18 June 1859 (King's Arms) ; 1861, p. 452 (Rising Sun); Howard (*op. cit.* note 21); article on T. B. Turnham, LW 19 March 1898. Both pubs were rebuilt in the late nineteenth century.
24. *Builder* tenders 20 January 1855 (Museum Tavern); 1860, p. 304 (Hat and Feathers).
25. Warehouse illustrated *Building News* 1866, p. 832. Royal Oak is in the list of the firm's work given in Paraire's obituary (see note 19) and was probably built in the early 1860s when John Hancock was the publican (see note 27).
26. John Summerson *The Architectural Association, 1847–1947* (London 1947) p. 17.
27. Paraire was certainly working for Hancock at the Admiral Keppel and Duke of York (Metropolitan Board of Works Records, GLC). Hill and Paraire are known to have designed the Royal Oak at an unspecified date (see note 25) and Hancock is in the POD as publican in the early 1860s. The Alfred's Head can be attributed to Paraire on stylistic grounds; John Hancock was the publican in 1862–3 and 'Hancock and Co.' in 1870–2.
28. *Builder* 15 May 1875; *Building News* 7 May 1875; *Builder* tender 1865, p. 684.
29. *Building News* 17 December 1858, p. 1242, 4 March 1859, p. 218 (Mitre); *Building News* 2 January 1857, p. 21 (Rising Sun); *Builder* 1 April 1871, p. 244 (King Lud).
30. Letter to *Pall Mall Gazette* 16 March 1872.
31. *Building News* 29 August 1879; GLC Valuers 237.
32. GLC Valuers 241.
33. For the years preceding the 1872 Aberdare Act, see Brian Harrison *Drink and the Victorians* (London 1971) pp. 247–78.

NOTES TO CHAPTER 3

1. Peel 1008.
2. Peel 35503.
3. Peel 1779, 11765.
4. List of owners of two or more on-licences in London district, *Parl. Papers* 1890–1 LXVIII. Lady Henry Somerset was a prominent witness in the Temperance interest at the Peel Commission.
5. See my 'Note on the Sources', 1b, 3 and 4, for the plans used in my analysis of the development of the London pub plan between 1870 and 1899. These, with a few miscellaneous extras, gave me plans of about 130 pubs to work from, with many more of the 1880s and 1890s than the 1870s.
6. For the ten-minute stop at Swindon, see L. T. C. Rolt *Isambard Kingdom Brunel* (London, Pelican edition, 1970) p. 186. Brunel's sketchbooks are now in the library of Bristol University. For the Crystal Palace Hotel, see *Civil Engineer and Architects' Journal* July 1853, p. 241. All these examples were brought to my notice by Christopher Monkhouse, who kindly supplied me with photographs.
7. GLC Valuers 148.
8. Westminster 9124–5.
9. Camberwell S114 (Noah's Ark); Maurice Gorham and H.

McG. Dunnett *Inside the Pub* (London 1950) p. 73; *Builder* tender 24 September 1887 (Dun Cow); *Builder* 22 September 1888 (Equestrian); Camberwell (Green Man); Lady H. Somerset, Peel 31481–502.
10 Camberwell S45 (Duke of York); Camberwell S178 (Thomas à Becket).
11. Peel 34962.
12. Peel 34921.
13. James Greenwood *The Seven Curses of London* (London 1869) p. 319.
14. Peel 36875 (Maitland). For magistrates and snugs, see e.g. Peel 35600, 13308, 11576, 8687, etc.
15. Peel 8322.
16. Peel 8317–20, 8389–94, 8550, etc. (Hull); 17590–4 (Plymouth).
17. *Times* 22 April 1896, p. 4; LVG 17 April, 17 July 1896.
18. Peel 8389–92.
19. Peel 31506–14.
20. Peel 32067.
21. GLC Valuers 276 (Britannia); GLC Valuers 260 (Stirling Castle); GLC Valuers 203 (George); *Builder* 22 September 1888 (Equestrian).
22. *Building News* 21 February 1890.
23. Graham Hill 'Bar and Saloon London) (from *Living London* 1906), Noble miscellaneous.
24. Peel 31506; Westminster 9135.
25. Peel 1006.

Notes to Chapter 4

1. Brian Harrison's exhaustive *Drink and the Victorians* (London 1971) unfortunately stops at 1872. Useful sources for the political history of the licensing issue in the later Victorian period are Lord Askwith *British Taverns: Their History and Laws* (London 1928) pp. 107–31 and George B. Wilson *Alcohol and the Nation* (London 1940) pp. 107–9.
2. In the opinion of D. H. Robertson *A Study of Industrial Fluctuations* (1915) p. 197, the consumption of alcohol varies more with constructional than with other forms of consumptive activity. 'The inference is that the consumption of alcohol is more subject than that of other things to the psychological influence of hope and excitement, and is a better index of mental temperature than (as Mr. Beveridge, for instance, is inclined to treat it) of genuine prosperity.'
3. E.g. *Leeds Mercury* 23 September 1896; *Daily Mail* 5 May 1899.
4. List of owners of two or more on-licences, 1890–1 (see Chapter III, note 4).
5. Peel 34973, etc., together with a good general account of the London custom.
6. F. W. Thornton *How to Purchase and Succeed in a Public House* (London 1885) gives specimen figures for raising £6,100 to buy a public house (£5,500 lease and goodwill, £600 valuation and expenses): £4,200 is borrowed from brewers, £700 from distillers and £1,200 is the purchaser's own capital.
7. I have drawn exclusively for the next few paragraphs on D. M. Knox's excellent article 'The Development of the Tied House System in London' *Oxford Economic Papers* N.S. 10 (1958) pp. 66–83. See also John Vaizey *The Brewing Industry, 1886–1951* (London 1960) pp. 8–12 and Wilson (*op. cit.* note 1) pp. 85–7.
8. *Coffee Public House News* 1 June 1882, 1 January and 1 August 1883.
9. It advertised regularly in the licensed victuallers' periodicals of the 1890s.
10. E.g. Charrington in 1872 and Mann Crossman Paulin in about 1874. Hurford Janes *Albion Brewery, 1808–1958* (London 1959) pp. 55–60.
11. LW 26 November 1898, p. 388.
12. LVCTJ 17 May 1899, p. 388.
13. LVCTJ 12 July 1898, 27 February 1901.
14. All my information about Cannon Brewery purchases came from its 'Freehold and Leasehold Book' recording all its houses, the date of their purchase, their cost and type of tenure. This is now in the archives of Ind Coope at Allied House, St John Street, Clerkenwell.
15. LVCTJ 17 July 1901.
16. *Brewers Journal* November 1896 (Victoria); Peel 1168, 1762, 22129–33, *Builder* 25 March 1882, p. 369 (Chippenham); *Brewers Journal* July 1896 (Volunteer); Peel 22129–33 (Railway Tavern); LVG 18 June 1897 (Royal Oak).
17. E.g. *Builder* 25 March 1882 for a list of prices paid in 1880–1 (maximum £18,000) or the £8,000 quoted as a top price for a pub in the *Builder* of 26 February 1854.
18. Elgin leases, Ind Coope archives.
19. LW 25 April 1896 (Davies); LVCTJ 6 November 1901 (Guider); LVG 25 August 1898, p. 555 (Goddard).
20. The principal sources of information about Baker Brothers Ltd are the Limited Liability Company papers of Baker Brothers Ltd (1889) Public Record Office BT31/4571/29932 and Baker Brothers Ltd (1896) PRO/BT31/15705/50460 which provide lists of directors and shareholders with their addresses and holdings, properties owned, mortgages, etc. LVCTJ 20 March 1901, p. 280 has a useful synopsis of Richard Baker's activities inside and outside the limited liability companies, with further details on 12 December 1900, and 3 January and 30 January 1901. This family's complex history as pub owners and builders can be approximately charted through the *Builder* tenders and the POD. Further family details were kindly supplied by Professor Richard Wollheim, the grandson of Henry Baker. Valuable unpublished work on the Bakers has since been done by Jean Tsushima.
21. *Brewers Journal* November 1896.
22. Norman II p. 51 (anonymous press cutting of 3 March 1888).
23. LW 24 November 1893.
24. For Saville and Martin's work for the Bakers, see *Builder* tenders 15 May 1886 (Victoria); 10 September 1887 (Cock); 2 March 1889 (Load of Hay); 25 January 1890 (Duke of York); 18 June 1892 (Garrick); 9 July 1892 (Tottenham); 13 August 1892, 13 May 1893 (Horse Shoe); LVCTJ 3 May 1899, p. 416 (Queen's); Nikolaus Pevsner *Buildings of England: London I* (Hotel de l'Europe).
25. LVG 29 September 1899, p. 732.
26. *Builder* tender 13 September 1890 (originally Horse and Dolphin).
27. LW 17 October 1896; *Builder* tender 1 June 1889 (Royal Vauxhall).
28. Charles Douglas Stuart and A. J. Park *The Variety Stage* (London 1895) pp. 72, 234; *Builder* tenders 1 June 1889, 12 April 1890.
29. For Grimes, see LVG 21 October 1898 with illustrations, and the Limited Liability Company papers of Grimes Ltd, PRO/BT31/7719/55168.
30. Stuart and Park (*op. cit.* note 28) p. 75.
31. For Mathams, see LVG 22 July 1898, p. 512 with illustrations.
32. For Atherden, see LVG 27 January 1899 with illustrations.
33. Stuart and Park (*op. cit.* note 28) p. 162.
34. For Brutton and Burney, see LVG 30 December 1898, p. 971; for Grimes Ltd papers, see note 29; POD.
35. *Builder* tenders 20 February 1892 (Prince William Henry, Blackfriars Road, for W. H. Burney); 16 October 1897 (King and Queen, Newington Butts, for W. H. Burney); 16 October 1897 (Cannon, Cannon Street, giving J. H. Cross as client; but POD for 1897 gives R. H. Brutton as occupant).
36. *Builder* tenders 23 May 1891 (Old Friends); 2 July 1892 (New Crown and Cushion); 14 September 1895 (Red Lion); 11 July 1896 (Telegraph); 16 October 1897 (Earl Russell); 6 November 1897 (Union Arms); 6 November 1897 (Swan and Horseshoe); 11 July 1896 (King's Head); 16 October 1897 (Fitzroy); 30 April 1898 (Princess Victoria); 17 July 1899 (Loughborough); design for 'proposed theatre' New Cross Road exhibited R.A. 1894; LVCTJ 12 April 1899, p. 295 with illustrations; GLC M&D (Hammersmith New Theatre of Varieties); Diana Howard *London Theatres and Music Halls, 1850–1950* (London 1970) under Alhambra. The New Crown and Cushion was illustrated in the *Building News* 20 January 1893.
37. Camberwell L211.
38. LVG 22 July 1898, p. 512.
39. *Builder* tender 11 July 1896.

Notes to Chapter 5

1. For High Victorian eclecticism and the Architectural Association, see John Summerson *The Architectural Association, 1847–1947* (London 1947) pp. 7–9. There is no full account of the style.
2. See Mark Girouard *Sweetness and Light: The 'Queen Anne' Movement, 1860–1900* (Oxford 1977). For a short account, setting it in its place as the architectural expression of a decorative revival, see Elizabeth Aslin *The Aesthetic Movement* (London 1969) Ch. II.

Notes to Chapter 6

1. M. H. Port 'An Architect's Progress in the 1850s and 60s' *East London Papers* Vol. II No. 1 (Summer 1968) pp. 20–39 describes the manuscripts and gives numerous extracts, including Fletcher's full list of his works. The autobiography takes his life up to 1887 and is then continued in diary form. Checking with the *Builder* tenders shows that in some, and possibly most, cases Fletcher did only minor alterations at the pubs given in his list. Much of my account of Fletcher is derived from parts of the manuscripts not quoted by Port.
2. E.g. T. H. Smith's remodelling of the Warwick Arms, Gillingham Street, Pimlico, 1898 (plans, Watney Mann Estates Department, Elliot House, Allington Street, SW1); Shoebridge and Rising's Crown, Cricklewood, 1899 (plans, Ind Coope Architects Department, Allied House, Clerkenwell); F. A. Powell's Skinner's Arms, Camberwell New Road, 1897 (Camberwell L189).
3. His plans are stamped with his name incorporated in the Watney stamp.
4. *Builder* tender 1867, p. 518 (Britannia); Camberwell (Father Red Cap); *Builder* tender 30 July 1892 (Cow and Calf).
5. GLC Valuers 237.
6. *Builder* tender 17 June 1871 (Red Lion); 19 April 1879 (Opera Tavern); Camberwell L188 (Sir Sidney Smith); *Architect* 25 September 1896 with illustrations (Freemason Arms).
7. *Builder* tenders 21 September 1878 (Artichoke); 26 March 1881 (Adam and Eve); 11 February 1889 (George and Dragon).
8. *Builder* tender 29 May 1886. The pub was leased by Watney's to Wheeler and Sons, who paid for the fittings.
9. *Builder* tender 4 May 1889 (Brighton); *Notes and Queries* 10 October 1896, LVG 6 October 1899, p. 752 (Assembly House); LVCTJ 4 October 1899, pp. 257 and 260, and inscribed foundation stone by entrance (Boston).
10. Public swimming baths at Forest Hill, 1884, Lewisham, 1885 and Kentish Town. Gates illustrated and described in *Builder* 26 July 1879.
11. *Builder* 18 June 1904, p. 665.
12. *Builder* tender 27 October 1877 and *Architect* 30 November 1878 with illustrations (Yorkshire Grey); *Architect* 25 September 1896 (Half Moon); *Builder* obituary (Spanish Patriot).
13. *Architect* 18 June 1897 Supplement, p. 21. The design was exhibited at the Academy in 1896. For his office practice, see *Builder* 5 October 1934, p. 570.
14. *Builder* tender 3 September 1887, *Builder* 19 January 1889 (Goat in Boots); *Builder* tender 31 March 1888, *Builder* 22 September 1888 (Equestrian); *Builder* tender 8 June 1889, *Building News* 21 February 1890 (Fox and Hounds); *Builder* tender 30 August 1890 (George and Dragon).
15. *Builder* obituary 1907 (2) pp. 532, 591. *The Architectural Notebook of Thomas Hardy*, ed. C. J. P. Beatty (Dorchester, 1966) pp. 3–4, 6.
16. *Builder* obituary, GLC M&D 163 (Horns); *Builder* tender 12 December 1896 (White Swan).
17. Design for No. 2 exhibited RA, 1884. The adjacent No. 1 is clearly by the same architect.
18. E.g. The Green Man, Old Kent Road, 1891 (Camberwell and *Builder* tender 30 April 1892).
19. E.g. the Jolly Gardeners, Lambeth, the Black Lion, Kilburn, the Black Lion, Bayswater, and the Wheatsheaf, Goldhawk Road.
20. For the Cantons, see LVG 28 July 1899 and LVCTJ 21 June 1899, p. 643.
21. Camberwell S52, *Builder* tender 18 August 1888 (Flying Horse); *Builder* tenders 3 May 1890 (Noah's Ark) and 24 October 1891 (Old Leather Bottle).
22. Camberwell S35 (Dover Castle); Camberwell (Larkhall Tavern); *Builder* tender 29 September 1888 (Railway Hotel); Camberwell L112 (Loughborough Park Tavern); Nikolaus Pevsner *Buildings of England: London II* (Angel).
23. Pevsner (*op. cit.* note 22).
24. Obituary of H. J. Treadwell, *Builder* 5 November 1910, p. 559; *Builder* tenders 12 May 1894 (Leicester); 24 February 1894 (Old Dover Castle); 5 November 1898 (Old Shades). LW 31 January 1896 has an account of the opening banquet at the Old Dover Castle, with a list of guests, including many representations of the firms involved. There is an illustration of the Buchanan building in Noble, filed under 'Black Swan'.
25. *RIBA Journal* 6 February 1937.
26. *Builder* tenders 1 May 1897 (King William IV); 11 March 1899 (Boleyn); original designs Ind Coope Architects Department, Allied House (Crown). The Cannon Brewery houses are all listed, often with the date of the rebuilding, in its 'Freehold and Leasehold Book' (see Chapter IV, note 14).
27. LW 30 April 1898, p. 285.
28. *Builder* tenders 7 February 1885, 13 June 1891 (Duke of Edinburgh); 21 March 1896 (Two Brewers); 16 July 1898 (Britannia); 24 July 1897 (White Hart). The Duke of Fife can be confidently attributed to Ashton, both on stylistic grounds and because of the fact that Langman was the publican.
29. *Times* 19 June 1901; Camberwell; *Builder* tender 1 January 1898; LW 3 December 1898.
30. LVCTJ 26 July 1899, pp. 804–6 (Salisbury); March 1899, p. 55 (proposals for Queens Hotel).
31. For Hill, see *British Clayworker* June 1898, January 1899, April 1905, March and April 1915; *Hampstead and Highgate Express* 10 April 1915, p. 7.

Notes to Chapter 7

1. *Sketches by Boz* (1836) Ch. XXII.
2. GLC Valuers C2/86, C2/135A.
3. POD; advertisements LVCTJ 15 February and 13 September 1899, p. 186; descriptive note LVCTJ 3 November 1899. p. 99.
4. LVCTJ 25 October 1899, p. 357; 3 November 1899, pp. 396, 402.
5. LVCTJ 25 October 1899, pp. 355, 382; LVG 16 March 1888.
6. Elgin leases, Ind Coope.
7. LW 8 December 1893; LW 10 February 1900, p. 109.
8. Noble, filed under 'Lion'. For Jones and Willis, see also POD and advertisements in *Building News* 23 July 1897, etc. The firm's ecclesiastical catalogues are in Birmingham Central Library.
9. LVG 6 October 1899, p. 752.
10. For Simpson's, see Elizabeth Aslin *The Aesthetic Movement* (London 1969) p. 131. *Builder* tenders 12 November 1887 (Old Cock); 15 August 1891 (Princess Louise); *Builder* advertisement 30 June 1888, p. XX (mosaic work).
11. LVG 1 August 1885.
12. An album of photographs of work by the firm now belongs to the Ironbridge Gorge Museum Trust, and includes an illustration of the Warrington.
13. W. G. Sutherland *The Sign Writer and Glass Embosser* (Manchester 1898) p. 15.
14. James Callingham *Sign Writing and Glass Embossing* (1871) and price list in the Cakebread, Robey catalogue (see note 30).
15. J. M. East *'Neath the Mask* (London 1967), p. 40.
16. *Building News* 7 May 1875; *Builder* 15 May 1875.
17. *Builder* tender 29 November 1873.
18. POD; *Building News* 27 July 1860, p. 593.
19. The techniques of glass painting are described by Sutherland (*op. cit.* note 13), where enamelling is not mentioned.
20. Quoted as by 'a late writer in the *Daily News*' in E. H. Hall *Coffee Taverns, Cocoa Houses and Coffee Palaces* (London 1878) p. 18.
21. *Builder* tender 14 April 1888.
22. *Descriptive Account of South London, Illustrated* published by W. T. Pike and Company, Grand Parade, Brighton, not dated;

but a publication in the same format, *Descriptive Account of Peckham and Camberwell* published by Robinson, Son and Pike, Duke Street, Brighton, can be dated 1892 on internal evidence.
23. *Pottery Gazette* 1 February 1887, p. 145.
24. See note 22.
25. Sutherland (*op. cit.* note 13) p. 19.
26. Peel 35595, 35600, 36847–850; LVCTJ 22 February and 15 March 1899; LVG 3 April 1896.
27. See note 22.
28. Advertisements *Building News* 30 January 1857 and 25 May 1860.
29. LVG 16 October 1899, p. 752.
30. The catalogue is undated but contains a tariff for polished plate glass dated 13 February 1899, and another for extra large polished plates revised 1 September 1900. Cakebread, Robey now have their offices in Enfield.
31. POD; LW 5 November 1898 Supplement, p. iii.
32. *Architect* 30 November 1878.
33. LVG 30 September 1898, p. 708 (Callcott at the Greyhound); *Builder* tender 2 April 1898 (Lewock and Callcott); *Builder* 13 September 1890, 16 November 1889 (Lewcock at Jolly Gardeners and Black Lion). The fact that Lewcock had worked for the father of Sydney Pease, publican at the Greyhound, in 1894 (*Builder* tender 17 February 1894), suggests the probability that he also designed the Greyhound.
34. *Builder* 22 September 1888 (Equestrian); 19 January 1889 (Goat in Boots); *Builder* 25 September 1897 (Holmwood).
35. POD; LVG 6 October 1899, p. 752.
36. POD; LVCTJ 12 April 1899; Diana Howard *London Theatres and Music Halls, 1850–1950* (London 1970) under Hackney Empire.
37. Quoted in East (*op. cit.* note 15) p. 51.
38. LVCTJ 16 August 1899 (Prince of Wales); LVG 6 October 1899, p. 753 (Crown).
39. *Builder* tenders 2 October 1886, 25 July 1891.
40. POD; LVCTJ 3 November 1899, p. 400.
41. For Lascelles, see POD; Aslin (*op. cit.* note 11) p. 68; *Builder* 24 March 1877, p. 295. *Builder* tenders 19 May 1877 (Victory); 29 May 1886 (Archway).
42. LVCTJ 26 July 1899, p. 801.
43. Advertisements *Licensed Trade News* 9 May 1896, etc. (Coaney); LW 14 November 1896, 5 November 1898, p. 309 (Turner); LVG 31 October 1885, etc. (Paine).
44. LVCTJ 15 February 1899; 21 March 1900, p. 290; 13 March 1901, p. 245.
45. Advertisement LVG 3 January 1896.
46. LVG 28 October 1898, p. 774; LW 31 January 1896.
47. LVCTJ 21 June 1899; LW 19 February 1898; advertisements LVG 5 November, 10 December 1897, etc.

Notes to Chapter 8

1. *Notes and Queries* 15 April 1871, p. 320.
2. E. Hepple Hall *Coffee Taverns, Cocoa Houses and Coffee Palaces: Their Rise, Progress and Prospects* (London 1878) p. 15. Much of the material in this chapter derives from Hall.
3. *Coffee Public House News* (cited subsequently as CPHN) 1 October 1884, 1 January 1883, etc.
4. *The Post, Kilburn, Willesden, Paddington and Hampstead Echo* 9 July 1898.
5. Charles Booth *Life and Labour of the People in London* Vol. I (1889) p. 8.
6. Advertisements CPHN 1 December 1883, 1 January 1885, 16 March 1886.
7. CPHN 1 June 1882; Baylis and Hamilton *Lilian Baylis in the Old Vic* (London 1926).
8. CPHN 1 September 1883, p. 102.
9. CPHN 2 December 1878, 1 September 1879, 1 December 1882.
10. CPHN 1 November 1878.
11. *The Porcupine* (Liverpool) 1 November 1879, p. 487.
12. Hall (*op. cit.* note 2).
13. Peel 33647, etc.
14. Booth (*op. cit.* note 5) pp. 114–15.
15. *Building News* 2 January 1880. The original designs are in the RIBA drawings collection.
16. *Building News* 17 February 1882. A number of designs by Newton for public houses are at the RIBA.
17. *Daily Mail* 7 September 1895.
18. J. Martin Skinner *The Reformed Public House* (London 1901).
19. Norman III p. 7; Joseph Rowntree and A. Sherwell *British Gothenburg Experiments and Public House Trusts* (London 1901) pp. 15–42; Skinner (*op. cit.* note 18); Maurice B. Adams *Modern Cottage Architecture* (London, 2nd ed. 1912) Plate LXVII (Fox and Pelican).

Notes to Chapter 9

1. Norman I p. 163.
2. LVG 5 November 1897; LVCTJ 21 June 1899.
3. *Times* 3 May 1899 and 24 February 1900 (Mathams); *Times* 6 May 1899 (Arpthorp); Grimes Ltd papers PRO/BT31/7719/55168.
4. LVCTJ 4 October 1899, pp. 257, 260.
5. LVCTJ 12 December 1900; 2 January, 20 March, 24 July 1901.
6. *Times* and LVCTJ, June 1901 (Meekins; LVCTJ 14 August 1901 (Kirk).
7. LVCTJ 30 January 1901 (Maycock); 6 February 1901 (Stanley); 12 June 1901 (Henderson); 6 and 13 November 1901 (Guider); 24 July 1901 (Ireland).
8. D. M. Knox 'The Development of the Tied House System in London' *Oxford Economic Papers* N.S. 10 (1958) pp. 66–83.
9. *Ibid.*; John Vaizey *The Brewery Industry, 1886–1951* (London 1960) pp. 13–17.

Notes to Chapter 10

1. LVCTJ 29 December 1900.
2. For the early days of the Trust Houses, see letter from Earl Grey to *The Times* 30 November 1905.
3. For the Central Public House Trust Association, see its various reports, etc., catalogued in the British Museum under 'Societies: London'. For the Carlisle experiment, see Basil Oliver *The Renaissance of the English Public House* (London 1947).
4. Oliver (*op. cit.* note 3).
5. For the Black Friar, see Nicholas Taylor 'Black Friar' *Architectural Review* November 1964, pp. 373–6.
6. Ind Coope leases, Allied House.

Notes to the Epilogue

1. For the Philharmonic and Vines, see James Quentin Hughes *Seaport: Architecture and Townscape in Liverpool* (London 1964).
2. *Builder* tender 6 August 1881.
3. See notes on Sources for the excellent monograph on Birmingham pubs by Crawford and Thorne.
4. There is a full set of photographs in the Local Studies Department of Birmingham Central Library.
5. Basil Oliver *The Renaissance of the English Public House* (London 1947).
6. Information from G. W. Tyson's descendants and *Irish Builder* 15 October 1895, p. 245 (I owe this reference to Jeanne Sheehy).
7. C. E. B. Brett *Buildings of Belfast, 1700–1914* (London 1967) pp. vi, 49. The Crown Liquor Saloon has been acquired and restored by Northern Irish National Trust.
8. Peel 24186 (Manchester); Peel appendices, *Parl. Papers* 1898 XXXVI p. 552 (Liverpool).
9. Peel 15305–9.
10. Peel 24191, 26337.
11. Peel 41238.
12. Peel 26268, etc.
13. Peel 41239, 26644, 19900–20001.
14. Peel 56152, 64398, 64410.

INDEX

INDEX

INDEX

INDEX

INDEX

PHOTOGRAPHIC SOURCES

Allied Breweries Ltd—97; Architectural Press—14, 37 (Michael F. Reid), 41, 42, 43, 48, 52, 71, 77, 78, 129, 130, 131, 132, 133, 135, 141, 147, 149, 150, 151, 152, 153, 155, 156, 157, 160, 162, 172, 175; Aslin, Elizabeth, *The Aesthetic Movement*, 1969—76, 79 (personal collection); Batley, H. W., *Studies for Domestic Furniture and Decoration*, 1883—86; *Barmaid*—55 (14 January 1892); *Building News*—3 (28 October 1887), 63 (20 January 1893), 65 (20 January 1893), 168 (4 July 1879), 169 (2 January 1880); *Builder*—34 (15 May 1875), 38 (1 April 1871), 81 (1866, p. 877), 89 (2 August 1873), 101 (22 September 1888), Fig. 4 (22 September 1888), Fig. 18; *The Builders' Practical Directory*—24, Fig. 3; Cakebread, Robey and Company Ltd, Enfield (catalogue)—137, 138; *Coffee Public House News*—164 (1 January 1885); Corporation of London, Guildhall Library—4, 10, 123; Corporation of London Records—Fig. 2; Cruickshank, Dan—1, 21, 22, 31, 36, 58, 59, 63, 64, 65, 66, 67, 69, 72, 80, 82, 87, 90, 92, 93, 96, 98, 99, 100, 102, 103, 104, 107, 110, 111, 113, 119, 124, 143, 144, 145, 146, 154, 167, 173, 174, 176; Cruickshank, George, *Sunday in London*, 1833—8; Ferriday, Aileen—180; Girouard, Dorothy—88, 171; Girouard, Mark—Col. Pl. II; Gorham, M. and H. McG. Dunnet, *Inside the Pub*, 1950—Fig. 20; Greater London Council Photograph Library—2, 9, 125, 126, 127; Greater London Council Record Office—19, 33, 40, 49, 68, 94, 95, Col. Pl. III; Arthur Guinness and Company Ltd—195, 196; Hall, E. H., *Coffee Taverns, Cocoa Houses and Coffee Palaces*, 1878—165, 166; *Illustrated London News*—28 (26 January 1856); The Kennel Club—Col. Pl. I; Lambton, Lucy—Col. Pl. XV; *Licenced Victualler*—5 (13 January 1899), 6 (17 February 1899), 51 (28 July 1899), 61 (21 October 1898), 62 (27 January 1899), 114 (26 July 1899), 117 (15 February 1899), 118 (25 October 1899), 158 (15 February 1899), 159 (15 February 1899), 161 (15 February 1899); London Borough of Islington Public Libraries—20; London Borough of Southwark Public Libraries—15, 16, 17, 18, 32; Loudon, J. C., *Encyclopaedia of Cottage, Farm and Villa Architecture*, 1833—12, 13, Fig. 1; Mander and Mitchenson—29; Mitchell, B.R. and P. Deane, *Abstract of British Historical Statistics*, 1962—Fig. 15; National Monuments Record—35, 39, 105, 106; New Scotland Yard—84; *Observer*—73; Pilkington Brothers Ltd, Group Archives—128, 187; Public Works Department, Birmingham—193; *Punch*—44 (11 October 1879); Reed, Millican and Company Ltd—200; RIBA Drawings, South Central Licensing District Loan—54a, 74, 112, Col. Pl. IV; Rossmore, Patrick—30, 45, 46, 56, 70, 91, 108, 109, 115, 116, 121, 122, 134, 140, 142, 148, 163, 177, 178, 197, 198, 199, Col. Pls. V, VII, VIII, IX, X, XI, XII, XIII, XIV; Sala, G. H., *Twice Round the Clock*, 1859—25, 26; Savigear, N. W.—7; South Central Licensing Authority Loan—54b; South Central Licensing District Plan—Figs. 14, 21; Spender, Humphrey—47, 53, 120, 136, 139; Starkey, Alex—Col. Pl. VI; Victoria and Albert Museum—170; Whybrow, John—Col. Pl. XVI; Wilson, G. B., *Alcohol and the Nation*, 1940—Figs. 5, 6, 16, 17; Wollheim, Richard—60; *Working Man's Friend*—27 (N.S. I, 1852, p. 56); Wrightson, Dan—179, 182, 183, 184, 188, 189, 190, 191, 192; Yates, James, *New Designs of Cabinet Bar Fittings*, 1896—85, 194.